TRUE BLUE

A TRIBUTE TO
MIKE
KRZYZEWSKI'S
CAREER AT DUKE

COMPILED BY DICK WEISS

FOREWORD BY JIM BOEHEIM
AFTERWORD BY AL FEATHERSTON

www.SportsPublishingLLC.com

ISBN: 1-59670-105-6

Publishers: Peter L. Bannon and Joseph J. Bannon Sr.
Senior managing editor: Susan M. Moyer
Acquisitions editor: John Humenik
Developmental editor: Regina D. Sabbia
Photo editor: Erin Linden-Levy
Art director: K. Jeffrey Higgerson
Dust jacket design: Heidi Norsen
Interior layout design: Kathryn R. Holleman
Copy editor: Elisa Bock Laird
Imaging: Dustin Hubbart, Kathryn R. Holleman, and Heidi Norsen
Media and promotions managers: Andi Hake (regional),
  Randy Fouts (national), Maurey Williamson (print)

Printed in the United States of America

Sports Publishing L.L.C.
804 North Neil Street
Champaign, IL 61820

Phone: 1-877-424-2665
Fax: 217-363-2073
www.SportsPublishingLLC.com

This book is dedicated to The V Foundation for Cancer Research
and the work they do, funding research to find a cure for that dreaded
disease. My father died of lung cancer in 1998.
Hopefully, The V Foundation can help others.

—D. W.

CONTENTS

FOREWORD

When I think of the great coaches I've seen since I've been at Syracuse, I always have to start with John Wooden of UCLA because of his 10 national championships.

But if you're building a Mount Rushmore of great coaches in the modern era, you'd also have to include Bob Knight of Indiana, former North Carolina coach Dean Smith, and, of course, Mike Krzyzewski of Duke. I don't think anybody can argue with those people.

Mike has won 621 games and three national championships, and taken his team to 10 Final Fours. He's also won 10 ACC regular-season titles and eight ACC Tournaments.

What he's done in this era is as close as you can come to what Coach Wooden accomplished. Obviously, I don't think anybody can duplicate that, but I don't think he's very far behind.

Look at the numbers.

It's very difficult today to get to the Final Four in a 64-team bracket. You have to win four games in a row. In Coach Wooden's day, you had to win four games to win the national championship.

In today's world of parity, to be that dominant, to win the league, to win the league tournament, and then do well in the NCAA Tournament is a hard trifecta.

Not many can do that.

When we won the national championship at Syracuse in 2003, we didn't win the Big East. The same thing when we went to the Final Four in 1996.

I guess, in a way, it's fortunate for everybody else guys leave early—because Duke probably has been hurt the most by that trend. Otherwise, they might have a couple more banners hanging in Cameron.

I became the head coach at Syracuse in 1976. Mike was at Army at the same time. I didn't know much about him back then. But I've since come to realize Tom Butters, the A.D. who hired him at Duke in 1980, was a very smart guy. He made a smart move and he stuck with it. I know at the beginning Jimmy Valvano was getting all of the credit at N.C. State. He hit the scene right away. Mike didn't get off to that kind of start.

What's interesting about Duke is it took the North Carolina model and became North Carolina. Mike started signing the kind of players—Johnny

Craig Jones / Getty Images

Dawkins, Danny Ferry, Christian Laettner—that North Carolina used to get, and he built a national power.

That's not to say North Carolina hasn't been good, too—because they have—but Duke has become a perennial national contender.

Mike is a lot tougher coach than a lot of people on the outside would know. He's a guy who's going to fight you. He puts tough demands on his players. I think he learned that from Knight.

We played Duke twice since I've been at Syracuse. We beat them once in Greensboro in the 1989 ACC-Big East Shootout when we had Derrick Coleman and Billy Owens and Christian Laettner and Bobby Hurley were underclassmen. We lost to them in the 1998 NCAA Southeast Regional semi-finals.

I don't like to schedule guys I'm close to. We won't schedule him.

Mike and I got to know each other in 1990 when he asked me to be his assistant in the World University Games and the World Championships. The whole thing was set up by a mutual friend, P.J. Carlesimo, who was coaching at Seton Hall at the time.

We just hit it off from the beginning. We really intertwined through the years. We go to the Michael Jordan Fantasy Camp in Vegas, and the three of us and our wives spend a lot of time together on the Nike trip every summer.

I usually go to Duke every year for the Jimmy V Golf Classic and the Duke Children's Hospital Classic.

I haven't been able to convince Mike to take up golf, yet.

He's too smart for that.

He's one of the smartest people in our profession. He embodies the best qualities of coaching. He's a leader on the court, a leader in the National Association of Basketball Coaches and is always willing to push issues that are good for the game, even if they might not be in the best interest of Duke.

Take recruiting, for instance. He knows we as coaches need more access to players. At Duke, they don't need access. The fewer times you can go out and see kids is better for them. But he's always for rules like more phone calls, a longer observation period.

Most coaches don't think that way.

Mike is constantly in demand—from USA Basketball, the NABC, charities, clinics, fund-raising. Ever since his back problems in 1995 when he missed most of the season, he's cut back and is focusing most of his energy on Duke and The V Foundation for Cancer Research.

But he's still willing to step up for a good cause. Just last winter, he and I were asked to serve on the board of the Basketball Partnership to open a dialogue with NCAA executive director Myles Brand. Mike was instrumental in getting the 5/8 rule—which used to limit the amount of players you could bring in in any one-to-three-year period—repealed so coaches have a shot at rebuilding if they lose an unusual amount of underclassmen to the NBA. And he helped change a rule that allows coaches to work out more than one position at a time in the gym.

When Mike speaks, other coaches listen. So do people like Myles Brand. Mike is very good at finding common ground and articulating his position.

He's become the face of our sport. I think that's why some people cringed last summer when he was offered all that money to go to the Los Angeles Lakers. I think he could have gone, too, if Shaquille O'Neal and Kobe Bryant were still there and still getting along.

I don't think money was an issue, although $8 million is a lot of money. But there's also the idea of the challenge: could I do that?

I would say his interest in the pros is over now, although I don't buy into the theory college coaches can make the jump to the NBA. Most college coaches who've gone to the NBA have gotten horrible teams to coach.

That's why jobs open. You don't see college coaches getting a job like the Bulls when a Michael Jordan is there. I think if Mike was coaching in the NBA, he would do well. But he's done very well in college.

We've already discovered how hard it is to recruit against Duke. They play in a great league, have a great school, and are fortunate enough to have good weather. And they have Mike, who was inducted into the Hall of Fame in 2001.

Mike is 58 now. If his back holds up, I can see him coaching at least until he's 65, maybe longer. Duke is always going to win. The program is now at a point where, at worst, they will do what they did in 2005—get to the Sweet 16. And if they ever put in a 20-year-old age restriction for players entering the NBA, that's going to help Duke big time, big time.

Most coaches should be against that rule. The way it is right now, there's at least some parity. If players must go to school for two years or even three, no one will ever beat Duke. They'll be in the Final Four every year.

—JIM BOEHEIM
Head Coach, Syracuse University
Naismith Hall of Fame Inductee, 2005

ACKNOWLEDGMENTS

There are two people who deserve enormous credit for their help in this book: my wife, Joan Williamson, who is by far the best writer/editor I've worked with at any level and who spent countless hours on the manuscript; and Al Featherston, who, in my mind, is one of the leading authorities ever on the ACC, corrected my mistakes and offered his knowledge and invaluable perspective to this project.

I'd also like to thanks publishers Peter L. Bannon and Joseph J. Bannon Sr., senior editor Susan M. Moyer, and acquisitions editor John Humenik for promoting this idea and developmental editor Gina Sabbia, photo editor Erin Linden-Levy, art director Jeff Higgerson, interior layout designer Kathryn Holleman, dust jacket designer Heidi Norsen, copy editor Elisa Bock Laird, Dustin Hubbart for imaging, and media and promotions managers Jonathan Patterson, Randy Fouts, and Maurey Williamson for carrying it out.

This book would not have been possible without longtime friends and colleagues Dick Vitale and John Feinstein and 23 others—Johnny Dawkins, Jay Bilas, Mark Alarie, David Henderson, Tommy Amaker, Danny Ferry, Billy King, Christian Laettner, Grant Hill, Bobby Hurley, Chris Collins, Steve Wojciechowski, Elton Brand, Shane Battier, Jason Williams, J.J. Redick, Bob Harris, Tom Butters, Dave Gavitt, Pam Valvano Strasser, Mike Brey, Bobby Cremins, and Howard Garfinkel—who were gracious enough to share memories of their experiences at Duke and a man and his family they deeply respect.

In addition, I'd like to mention Mike Cragg, Jon Jackson, Bill Brill, Frank Dascenzo, Brian Morrison, Barb Dery, David Teel, Amy Yokola, Lennox Rawlings, Bill Cole, Ron Morris, Rob Daniels, Steve Kirschner, Caulton Tudor, Mike Sobb, Johnny Moore, John Roth, Luci Chavis, A.J. Carr, Bryan Strickland, Matt Pligza, Eddie Landreth, Steve Phillips, Dan Collins, Barry Svrluga, Ken Tysiac, Brett Friedlander, Bob Sutton, Neil Amato, Ron Green, Sr. and Jr., Larry Keech, Ed Hardin, Taylor Zarzour, Art Chansky, Dave Droschak, Dean Buchan, Annabelle Vaughan, Tim Peeler, Chip Alexander, and Barry Jacobs—members of the media and university staffs on Tobacco Road whose work reflects their genuine passion for Atlantic Coast Conference basketball; Leon Carter, Adam Berkowitz, Jim Rich, Teri Thompson, Delores Thompson, Roger Rubin, Bill Price, Mike O'Keefe, Will Pakuta, Kristie Ackert, Julian Garcia and Wayne Coffey of the New York *Daily News*; and friends like Bob Ryan, Brian McIntyre, Mike Flynn, Pat Plunkett, Tom Knochalski, Ronnie Norpel, Mark Blaudschun, Steve Richardson, Malcom Moran, Chris Dufresne, Joe Mitch, Tony Barnhardt, Tom Liucci, Joe Mitch, Ronnie Naclerio, Steve Wieberg, Lesley Visser, Mike Sheridan, Dan Wetzel, John Akers, Mark Whicker, Robyn and Phillip Norwood, Vahe Gregorian, Jim O'Connell, Marty Cohen, Clark Francis, Sam Albano, Gene Whelan, Allen Rubin, Pat Forde, Joe Biddle, Rick Bozich, Andy Katz, Joe Timony, Joe Cassidy, Nick Blatchford, Chris Matesic and Saul Rafel-Frankel of New Heights, Jerry McLaughlin, Rick Troncelliti, Frank Morgan, Frank and Alma Bonini, Bill Jackson, Mark and Nancy Radomile and their children Alexis, Danielle, and James, Steve and Anthony Radomile, David M. Razor, M.D., Nanci Donald, Don Hazelton, Scott Mason, Dr. Joseph Lamb, Eric, Theresa, Abigail, and Chloe Menear, Liz and Joe Capra and Scott, and Suzanne, Hayden, Madison, Delaney, and Griffen Schenker.

— DICK WEISS

TO COACH MIKE KRZYZEWSKI

THE A.D.

TOM BUTTERS

Duke 1976-1998

In the alternative history of Duke basketball, it would be Bobby Knight who's celebrating a quarter-century as head coach.

In 1980, Duke University was heading back to the NCAA Tournament. Under coach Bill Foster, the school had been to the 1978 NCAA championship game, losing to Jackie Givens and Kentucky. Foster had just won the ACC Tournament against Maryland and was one of four ACC teams going to the Big Dance.

That was the good news.

The bad news was that, at the same time, Bill Foster announced he was going to South Carolina.

And Duke needed a replacement.

Tom Butters, the athletic director, knew about coaches. He was a former pitcher for the Pittsburgh Pirates who came to Duke in 1968 as the school's baseball coach before moving into administration.

Butters called Bobby Knight and asked him if he would be interested in the job.

Knight had already refused an offer to coach Maryland, but Butters was a man who always aimed high. A former baseball coach, he had been athletic director since 1977. Later, he would go after Bill Walsh to replace Steve Spurrier as Duke's football coach.

Walsh, too, declined.

Butters had been friends with Knight for years and thought the Indiana coach was as bright as any man he knew. Also, Butters remembers, he wanted

a great defensive coach. Knight's response was, "Tom," he said before and he named three or four Durham sports writers, "I'd be throwing them out the second-story window within a week, and I don't think you need that."

Agreed. On to Plan B.

So Butters and Steve Vacendak, who had played basketball at Duke and was about to become the associate athletic director there, discussed the situation.

"Well," said Butters, "I have to hire a basketball coach."

Then he mentioned a few names he had been considering.

Vacendak replied, "I know you well enough to know that you think everything is won on defense."

"I do."

"Let me throw a name out to you," and he gave Butters Krzyzewski's name.

"We talked a little about him," Butters recalled. "Then I called Bobby Knight about him. Bobby was very interested in some of his protégés, and he had mentioned Dave Bliss and Bob Weltlich to me as possible candidates for the job.

"I asked him, 'Well, what about a guy by the name of Krzyzewski?'

"Knight's comment was, 'If you like me as a basketball coach, there's a man who has all my good qualities and none of my bad ones.'

"'Hmm, that's kind of interesting,' I thought."

Butters called Krzyzewski and interviewed him.

Butters's first impressions of Krzyzewski were, "He was about 33 years old or thereabouts; he was 9-17; and Army basketball was not the ACC. And I knew that.

"So I sent him home.

"But I couldn't get him out of my mind."

Meanwhile, Krzyzewski had turned down the Iowa State job on the advice of Colonel Tom Rogers, and against the advice of Bobby Knight, who thought that the Midwestern school would be a good fit for the Chicago native.

Krzyzewski had played under Knight at the United States Military Academy and served five years in the military after graduation, achieving the rank of captain. For the last three years of his military service, he had coached at the U.S. Military Academy Prep at Fort Belvoir, Virginia. He then had joined Knight's staff at Indiana as an assistant. He had returned to West Point as head basketball coach and stayed there for five years.

Although he had guided Army to an appearance at the NIT in 1978, the program was drifting. He was ready for a change and was willing to take a chance on Duke.

But was Butters willing to take a chance on him?

Duke was playing in the Mideastern Regionals against Kentucky in Lexington. The Blue Devils had won that ball game, and then Purdue beat them 68-60 in the regional finals.

Prior to flying out there, Butters called Krzyzewski again, and asked him, "Can you get to Lexington? I want to talk to you again."

"He kind of chuckled," said Butters, and told me, 'Look, we've just had 13 inches of snow; but I'll try to get there.'

"So he came to Lexington and I interviewed him that week for, gosh, five or six hours.

"And I sent him home."

Again.

Butters just could not pull the trigger.

At this time, besides Mike Krzyzewski, the other candidates on Duke's short list were Bob Weltlich of Mississippi (another former assistant of Knight's); Paul Webb of Old Dominion; and Bob Wenzel (who had been an assistant under Bill Foster).

The following week, Butters called Krzyzewski again, and said, "Look, I'm bringing in four guys, and I'm going to bring you in last. And I want you to bring Mickie, because I don't think you hire a man; I think you hire a family."

He was interested in meeting her as well as in interviewing him.

The interview committee was composed of Tom Butters, chancellor Ken Pye, and vice president Chuck Huestis. They interviewed all four coaches in Durham. As he had been told, Krzyzewski was the last to meet with them. At the conclusion of that interview, the committee told Butters, "These are four good quality coaches. You name any one of them, and he has our support."

After going over the qualifications of all of the candidates, Butters turned to Vacendak and said, "I know you're not on the payroll yet, but get to the airport. Don't let him go."

"I'll do that. Who is it?"

"Krzyzewski."

"My God, you're not going to interview him again?"

"No, I'm going to hire him."

Butters said, "When Mike came back with Steve, he was kind of bewildered, and I told him, 'I've come to the conclusion that you're the right man at the right time for this university. Will you accept this job?'"

And with that invitation, Krzyzewski said yes.

Then Butters added, "Well, wait a minute; we haven't talked about salary."

And Krzyzewski replied, "You'll be fair."

He asked if Duke could wait before it announced his hiring so he could get back to West Point, speak to his players, and talk to the administration.

On May 4, 1980, Duke held a press conference to introduce its new basketball coach at the Duke News Bureau Building. According to Butters, "Of course, nobody knew. The morning paper had said there was going to be a press conference at 6 p.m. and that the new coach's name begins with W because I'd interviewed Paul Webb of Old Dominion—a great coach who already had 600 wins but was a little old at the time—and Bobby Weltlich and Bob Wenzel."

Three coaches whose last names began with W.

"So we walked in to the press conference," Butters continued. "Mike walked out and I said, 'I'd like to introduce the new basketball coach at Duke University—Mike Krzyzewski.'"

Krzyzewski walked out and joked, "The papers said the name of the new coach would start with a 'W' . . . so maybe you should call me, 'Coach Who.'"

"And the media went nuts. They couldn't pronounce his name. They had never heard of him. They were all lined up, packed in there; and everybody was dumbfounded.

"I remember Mike tried to help them out: 'That's Krzyzewski—K-r-z-y-z-e-w-s-k-i. And if you think that's bad, you should have heard it before I changed it. For those of you who can't pronounce it, you can just call me Coach K.'"

And that was the beginning.

Krzyzewski inherited a program whose cupboard wasn't completely bare. Kenny Dennard, Gene Banks, and Vince Taylor were coming back from the NCAA Tournament team. His first year as coach, Duke won 17 games and played in the NIT. Duke opened with a victory over North Carolina A&T in the first round, but Banks broke his wrist and did not play the rest of the tournament. The Blue Devils upset Alabama in the second round but lost to Purdue in the third round 81-69.

The following two seasons were thin. His overall record was 21-34, and Duke went 7-21 in the ACC.

According to Butters, "The first year, Mike didn't really have a chance to do any recruiting for Duke, though he did get Doug McNeely out of Texas."

It seems he was always coming in second with every kid he wanted. But he wasn't coaching the horseshoes team, so that didn't count.

Then, for the 1982-1983 season, he recruited a class with Johnny Dawkins, Jay Bilas, Mark Alarie, and David Henderson; and, for Butters, at least—and at last—"the handwriting was kind of on the wall."

But it was written in invisible ink that first year when Duke had an 11-17 season. In 1984, things started to percolate.

As Butters recalls it, "We got off to a fairly quick start. We started with eight straight wins and 14 of the first 15; then we lost four straight league games."

Then people started howling; the wolves were out.

But Butters had a plan: "I always met with my coaches in my office because 1) I thought they were more comfortable there; and 2) I could control the length of the meetings.

"Carolina beat us at home. Five days later, on January 26, I called his office shortly after 8 a.m. His secretary answered, and I asked if Mike was in yet.

"She said he hadn't arrived yet.

"So I said, 'When he does, send him over to my office.'

"A half-hour later, there was this knock on the door. He came in and sat down. I told him, 'We've got a public who doesn't know how good you are. We've got press who are too stupid to tell them how good you are. And the biggest problem right now is I'm not sure you know how good you are.'

"With that, I opened up my desk and tossed a new five-year contract to him.

"He sat there, and he had tears in his eyes. This was a constant flow—one tear after the next—for several seconds. Then I recall him saying, 'Tom, you don't need to do this.'

"I said, 'Mike, on the contrary, I not only have to do it. I need to do it right now. You make the announcement today. I'm not making it. You tell them you've been extended five more years and let's let the people know.'

"And I don't know if it's worth publicizing, but I got a couple of death threats afterwards.

"And that's not customary."

Duke lost to N.C. State that night 79-76 at Cameron.

But the Blue Devils went on to win 24 games that season. Then they lost to Maryland in the ACC Tournament finals and to the University of Washington 80-70 in the second round of the NCAA Tournament at Pullman, Washington, after receiving a first-round bye as a No. 3 seed.

But the handwriting was on the wall.

Two years later, Duke won 17 in a row, losing back to back to Carolina and Georgia Tech. Then they won 20 more and got to the NCAA Tournament finals.

Butters noted, "It's interesting. I don't know how many letters I got during Mike's first three or four years, but I got an equal number after that 1986 season and, interestingly, they were from the same people.

"But the contents of the letters were different."

Butters stepped up again in 1990 when the Boston Celtics came calling, trying to lure Krzyzewski to the NBA.

"I told Mike a lot of things. First of all, I admitted to him that I was worried. And I was worried because Boston, at that time, was not just the NBA; it was a step above the NBA. And we also had a mutual friend who was the president—Dave Gavitt. He's one of my dearest friends and I believe one of the brightest people in my business that I ever had the pleasure of working with.

"He is a brilliant man.He has the ability not only to tell you something; but he also has that inimitable ability to listen to what you have to say. Well, Mike knew him and thought highly of him as well. So when Dave called me before he called Mike—which was not necessary but was certainly proper—I was worried.

"I really believed that Mike—for the reasons I mentioned—would seriously consider it. And it was going to be extremely lucrative.

"I recall saying to him something to the effect—and I'm paraphrasing myself here—'You know, Mike, if you want to deal with 27-, 28-, 29-year-old guys who are making a lot of money, then I'll drive you to Boston. But if you want to do what you do and touch the lives of 17-, 18-, 20-year-old men, then my suggestion is you get back to work.'

"And he called later that night and said, 'Coach, I'm back to work.'"

And what work he's done.

Two national championships, back to back, in 1991 and 1992; and a third in 2001.

And suddenly everybody could spell d-y-n-a-s-t-y.

But success has a price, and Coach K—as the media had long ago started to refer to him—was paying for his with his health.

In the summer of 1994, Krzyzewski suffered what he thought was a pulled hamstring. For three months, he put up with the pain. Finally, his wife, Mickie, persuaded him to go to his doctor because pulled hamstrings usually don't last that long.

He was diagnosed with a spinal disc problem. However, he didn't slow down his pace. But while on a recruiting trip to Kansas City, the disc ruptured.

The pain was obvious. At his annual October 15 press conference, he couldn't sit in a chair and had to lean on a stool while he spoke to the media.

Several days later, he underwent surgery to repair a severely herniated disc.

Within 10 days, he was back at practice. Even though his doctors had recommended that he come back on a limited basis and use a special chair, it was business as usual for Coach K.

But the problem didn't go away. In fact, it was exacerbated by a trip to Hawaii for the Rainbow Classic. Krzyzewski was in such pain that he spent much of the long flight back lying in the aisle.

A crisis was looming.

Krzyzewski coached two more games that season. Duke defeated South Carolina State and lost to Clemson at home.

The date was January 4, 1995—a day that would live in infamy with Duke fans. That was the last game he coached that season. Two days later, Duke was scheduled to travel to Atlanta for a game with Georgia Tech.

Krzyzewski was insistent on going. But a higher power prevailed. Wife Mickie put down her foot, threatening to leave him if Krzyzewski didn't see a doctor. She scheduled an appointment with Dr. John Feagin at Duke Sports Medicine for 2:30 p.m., the day they were to leave. It was the time Duke normally starts practice. She enlisted Butters as an ally.

Dr. Feagin told Krzyzewski he had to be admitted to the hospital for a series of tests. Butters remembered that time: "I visited him in the hospital. I think he was scared. He had just lost a close friend, Jimmy Valvano, to cancer. And Jimmy's problems had started with a backache. I know Mickie was concerned."

Krzyzewski underwent two days of tests. The doctors ruled out cancer, but said he was trying to do too much, too soon. He was just being Coach K. They issued him a mandatory leave for the rest of the season.

Krzyzewski was concerned about Duke.

He went to see Butters and told him he was willing to resign if Butters thought that would be best for the program.

Finally, here was an offer Butters could refuse.

Butters said that he wouldn't hear of it. "You're my coach," he told him.

Duke was 9-3 when Krzyzewski left. He missed 19 games. Duke was 4-15 during his absence. He finally came back in April and hasn't slowed down in the decade since his return.

Butters retired in 1998. He summed up his feelings for the man in whom he had such faith and trust and who has been so loyal to the school over the past 25 years: "I think he's done so much more than just coach. He's an educator, a teacher who believes in people. He wants people to believe in themselves as he's learned to believe in himself.

"I think that his legacy will be substantially greater than the fact that he won 721 games. He touches the lives of so many people at Duke—players, colleagues, faculty, doctors, the community. There isn't any facet of our university that he hasn't had a substantial impact upon.

"His legacy for me is how many people he touched so positively.

"He will never be as good a basketball coach as he is a human being, and I think he's as good a coach as anyone I've ever known."

And about that hire he made a quarter-century ago?

"I couldn't be more pleased for his success. I'd love to take credit for that, but all I did was tell Steve to stop him from getting on the plane. And I remember years when there were a lot of people around here who didn't agree with that decision. But, you know, I thought it was going to work out. It didn't take courage; it took ability to see in a man something that perhaps he didn't even see in himself."

On November 14, 2001, Mike Krzyzewski signed a lifetime contract with Duke University.

After all, loyalty is a two-way street: true blue in both directions.

2

THE WRITER

JOHN FEINSTEIN

Duke Class of 1977

D anny Feinstein, who is 10 years old, has become a basketball fan in the last few years.

Not too surprising, considering his age and the fact that his father, John, is the author of *A Season on the Brink* and *A March to Madness*, two bestsellers on college hoops.

According to Feinstein, "Danny has watched Duke on TV, and I take him to a lot of games. He kept saying, 'I want to go to a game at Duke,' so I took him down last year. We went down, we went to the game, and Danny loved it—Cameron and all that.

"After the game, we went into the press room. I took Danny over to the side of the room to keep him out of the way of the guys who were working.

"Mike came in, looked around the room, saw me, and said, 'Hey, Danny, how are you doing?'

"Danny looked at me and said, 'Dad, Dad, that's Coach K.'

"'Yeah, yeah, Danny.'

"'But Dad, that's Coach K.'

"When the press conference was over, we went into the back, to Mike's office. Danny was still so excited—he kept saying, 'Coach K. You're Coach K.'—because he'd seen him on television so many times.

"And Mike said to him, 'Danny, do you want to know why I'm important?'

"Danny said, 'Yeah. You're important because you're Coach K.'

"Mike said, 'No. I'm important because your dad and I have been friends for a long, long time. That's what makes me important.'

Duke Photography

"That's a cool thing to say to a kid, trying to teach him a lesson in the same moment.

"Then he said to me, 'John, I can see you all the time. Give me a few minutes with Danny.' He knew I wanted to say hi to people. So he and Danny chatted by themselves for about 15 minutes, just talking hoops.

"And when I came back, Mike asked, 'How did you get such a smart kid?'"

(Note to reader: John's wife, Mary, can take some credit for that.)

"A few days later," Feinstein recalled, "when Danny and I were talking about it, his exact line to me was, 'Dad, I don't think I'm ever going to get this smile off my face.'

"About two days later—now, remember this was in the middle of the season—we got a letter at home, hand-addressed to Danny Feinstein. We opened it up and it's a handwritten note from Mike—not something he dictated to Gerry Brown, Mike's administrative assistant—a handwritten note from Mike.

"It read: 'Dear Danny, Thanks so much for coming down to the game. It was great having you here. I really enjoyed talking hoops with you. Come back any time, even if you have to bring your dad with you.'"

That's why Feinstein's answer to the perennial, "What's Mike Krzyzewski really like?" is "He's a better person than he is a basketball coach."

"Obviously, that says a hell of a lot. If he has a weakness as a coach, it's that, as a person, he can't say no to people. He doesn't ever want to let anybody down. He's like the clearinghouse for every coach who gets fired. He's always the guy they call: '"Can you make a call? Can you do this? Can you do that?"'"

He can and he will, according to Feinstein.

"The other night, when I was down there, Calvin Hill was there. And Mike was standing there, kind of going through Grant's progression this [2005] season, from week to week: how last week he started doing this, and he's doing that; and in the last 10 days his game has gotten to a new level. I'm thinking, 'Where does he find the time?'"

John Feinstein, who grew up in New York City, graduated from Duke University in 1977. He worked at *The Washington Post* as a political writer before he became a sportswriter for the same paper.

He remembers when he first saw Krzyzewski.

"I first met Mike in New York when I was a senior in college. Duke was playing in Madison Square Garden against Connecticut. The day before the game, I flew up with Tate Armstrong and Bill Foster to attend the old New York Basketball Writers lunch at Mama Leone's. The featured speakers were Bill Foster, Lou Carnesecca, Dee Rowe, and Jim Valvano.

"And I was sitting at a table with Foster, Valvano, and Tom Penders—who had straight hair and was coaching at Columbia—and this coach from Army, Mike Krzyzewski. I remembered seeing him play in the NIT because I grew up there. And I remembered the game his senior year when he shut John Roche down—held him to six points. Army beat South Carolina in the quarterfinals.

"So I was talking about that game, and he looked at me and said, 'How can you possibly remember that game? My mom doesn't remember that game.'

"I said I'd seen all the NIT games. So we sort of hit it off.

"The other thing I remember about that lunch was that Foster made me do my Dean Smith imitation. And he and Penders both thought that I was pretty cool."

But was Krzyzewski cool enough to be the new Duke coach?

Feinstein remembered, "That was the first time I met him. So, when he got the Duke job, I was disappointed. I'll be honest. I wanted Bob Wenzel to get it, because Wenzel is my friend. And I loved Foster and I wanted what Foster built to continue.

"But when they named Krzyzewski, I was like, 'Yeah. I know that guy. He's a good guy.'

"And I was telling people, 'That guy is a good guy.'

"And they were saying, 'He's the ***** coach at Army. He went 9-17.'

"'Yeah, but he's a good guy.'

"So when we met again, he remembered the lunch and everything, so we got it right from the start."

They hit it off so well that Feinstein started calling Krzyzewski by a nickname, "The Captain."

"Keith Drum, who was working for the *Durham Herald* at the time before he went to work as a scout for the Sacramento Kings, and I just started calling him that because we were kind of perturbed by the fact that all the TV guys called Knight 'The General.' Of course, in real life, Knight was a private in the Army. But Mike really was a captain in the Army. So we said, 'Well, we ought to call Mike "The Captain."' And we just started calling him by his rank."

On one memorable occasion, Drum and Feinstein found themselves in the unlikely role of the cavalry, riding to the rescue.

"I've written about the famous Denny's night—after the 109-66 loss to Virginia in Atlanta," Feinstein said. "It was actually Bobby Dwyer who came back to the arena to get Keith Drum and me. Duke had played the 7 p.m. game, and Maryland played Georgia Tech in the last game.

"Bobby came back and said, 'You guys have got to come back to the hotel.'

"We're like, 'Yeah, sure. What's up?'

"'Well, Mickie's in the room, crying, saying that they're going to get fired. Mike has to have somebody to talk to. He's climbing the walls.'

"So Keith and I drove out there; they were staying somewhere out in the 'burbs. I remember it was a horrible, rainy night. We grabbed Mike and said, 'Come on. Let's get something to eat.' Bobby and his fiancée, now wife, Patty, went with us. Tommy Mickle, the former Duke sports information director who was the associate commissioner of the ACC and Johnny Moore, the Duke assistant SID, went too.

"We went to Denny's and sat down. It was late. It was one, two in the morning. They served us water. Johnny Moore holds up his glass and says, 'Here's to forgetting tonight.'

"And Mike just holds up his glass, and he says, 'Here's to never ***** forgetting tonight.'

"I will never forget that.

"What I also remember is when they won in 2001 in Minneapolis when they beat Arizona, I was out on the floor afterward. I congratulated him, and he put his arm around me and whispered in my ear, 'We've come a long way from the ***** Denny's; haven't we?'"

They had.

Feinstein's career was about to take off, too.

"Mike played a big role in the start of my book-writing career, but it's not as big a role as Knight and others would have you believe, because what happened was when I came up with the idea for *Season on the Brink*, I was invited by Knight to go to this dinner that he used to put together at the Final Four every year with his coaches and staff.

"So that night, after the dinner, I said to Knight, 'Hey, have you got a few minutes to talk?'

"And he said, 'Sure. Come on back to my room.'

"This was in Lexington, in 1985. He and Mike were driving back to Bloomington for a clinic the next day, so Mike needed to come back to talk to him, too. So Mike and I and Knight and Pete Newell went back to Knight's room because he and Newell were rooming together.

"I told Knight what I wanted to do, and he said, 'Yeah. Sure. Fine. If you can get a publisher, great, go on ahead.'"

The longest journey begins with a single step.

Feinstein remembers that, "Mike and I walked out a couple of minutes later. As we got into the hall, he looked at me and said, 'Are you out of your ***** mind?'

"'Why?' I asked.

"'You're volunteering to spend a year with him? What, are you crazy?'

"'Why? You spent four years with him.'

"'I didn't have any choice.'

"'Ah, you know,' I said, 'it can't be that bad.'

"And he said, 'No, no. It CAN be that bad.'

"And I remember I called Mike later—after one of Knight's really bad tirades—and said, 'Okay, now I know what you were talking about.'"

All that was still in the future.

But what happened the next day, according to Feinstein, was, "When they were driving from Lexington to Bloomington, Knight said to Mike, 'Hey, you trust John; don't you?' And Mike said, 'Yes, I trust John implicitly.'

"And so that confirmed for Knight, I guess, in his mind that it was okay.

"But the way Knight has turned the story around is that Mike somehow intervened on my behalf and said, 'This guy is a good guy, and you ought to give him access.'

"But that's not how it happened. I had a relationship with Knight that led to my being invited to that dinner. And that caused me to come up with the idea for the book. And I never asked Mike for help with that.

"When Knight asked the next day in the car, 'What do you think?' Mike said, 'Yeah, I trust John absolutely.'

"So, of course, when the book came out, Knight called Krzyzewski and cursed him out and acted like it was Mike's fault because he, Knight, had ultimately made the decision to give me the access."

While Coach Knight has never been known for his even temper or his patience, Feinstein credits Krzyzewski's success at Duke, in part, to that virtue as exhibited by Duke's former A.D., Tom Butters.

"I felt Mike would make it if Tom Butters had the patience that Tom Butters did have. I disagree with Tom Butters on 10 or 20 million things, but he deserves credit A) for hiring Mike when he was a coach with a 9-17 record and was at Army, and B) for giving him a contract extension to get on track.

"But I believe Mike had what it took to be a great coach because he was smart. Add to that his work ethic and his ability with people, which you can see right away.

"Like any coach, he needed to get the right breaks. And that first year of recruiting, when he lost all of those kids, had to be so discouraging for him. But again, as I've written, I've never met anybody who learned from his failures better than Mike Krzyzewski.

"It goes back to West Point. Mike said that at West Point, they set you up to fail, because if you can't deal with failure on a battlefield, then people die. So they want to find out before you're on a battlefield how you deal with failure. They want you to find out why people are dying. That's why they have the beast barracks. That's why they harass you constantly. That's why they put you in situations that are virtually impossible to get out of.

"The story that Mike always tells about it is that when you're a plebe at West Point and an upperclassman addresses you, you have three answers: 'Yes, sir.' 'No, sir,' and 'No excuse, sir.'

"As a plebe, he was walking to class one morning with a buddy. They step off a curb, and the guy splashes mud onto Mike's boots. They go about five more steps and, sure enough, they encounter an upperclassman, who starts screaming at him for having mud on his boots.

"And the only answer he was allowed was, 'No excuse, sir.'

"He couldn't say, 'I shined my boots. My buddy splashed mud. It just happened. I'm late for class.'

"And Mike said, 'The point is there was no excuse. I either should have been more alert about the mud as we stepped off the curb so I didn't get splattered or the minute I got splattered, I should have turned around and sprinted back to the barracks and gotten a new pair of shoes or something. But there was no excuse. And you learn in life that ultimately your failures are your failures.'"

A creed he follows to this day.

"You've been around him," Feinstein said to another member of the media. "Have you ever heard him make an excuse after a loss? No. He just doesn't do it. He gives credit to the other team. He'll take blame for himself. He doesn't put down his own players. You've never heard him say, 'It was a good play. We just didn't execute.' And he never will."

While excuses are not acceptable, humor is.

Take the story about Mark Acres, a six-foot-10 kid from Oklahoma, who was one of the top prospects in the country in 1981.

"When Mike made the home visit," Feinstein related, "he noticed the mother hadn't said a word.

"'Mrs. Acres,' Mike said, 'is there anything at all you'd like to know about Duke, about our program, about why I think our school would be a great place for your son?'

"And the mother says, 'No. I don't really need to ask you anything. The only thing that's important is that Mark goes some place where he can be close to God.'

"Mike knew at that point the kid wasn't coming. So he tried to inject some humor; 'Mrs. Acres, you know if Mark comes to Duke, God will be coaching eight miles down the road in Chapel Hill, so you might want to give us some serious thought.'"

Acres went to Oral Roberts.

"There are times when you just have to laugh," Feinstein concluded. "Acres was a hell of a player and he really could have helped them.

"We were on the phone after the visit and I asked him how it went with Acres.

"He said, 'We're definitely not getting him.'

"'Why not?'

"And then he told me the story.

"'If there was any chance at all, it went out the window when I said that.'"

Krzyzewski was frustrated when he was losing recruits, especially in the early days.

"Why don't they understand that Duke is a better place for them; I'm a better coach for them?" he would ask.

Maybe it didn't look that way to the outside world.

"They'd had that terrible year when they lost to Maryland. I still remember this. It was 1982 and they played Maryland at home on a Saturday night.

"It was the same day that Carolina played Virginia in one of their classic Ralph Sampson versus James Worthy games in Chapel Hill, and Carolina came from way behind to win.

"Then, at night, I had to cover Maryland at Duke. Maryland won the game 40-36. Duke got 12 points from Vince Taylor and Tom Emma and 10 from Chip Engelland.

"That was it. Three guys scored. I still remember Mike looking directly across at me and just shaking his head. 'Can you believe this shit?'"

But things were about to get better for the program.

That year, Duke ended up getting Johnny Dawkins, Mark Alarie, David Henderson, Jay Bilas, and Weldon Williams, who was supposed to be a big deal.

Feinstein was pleased about at least one member of this class: "Johnny was huge because they had to beat Notre Dame and Digger for Johnny.

"I remember, that was back in the days where there was no limit on how many times you could see a kid. They must have seen him play every game from his sophomore year."

Feinstein was no slouch in that department, either.

As he remembers that time, "Bobby Dwyer saw every game. I would go, too, even though I was out of sports. I was covering politics then. But I'd go with Bobby—because I had no social life, of course—to watch Dawkins play a little bit.

"So one night, I walked into wherever they were playing, and I saw Lefty Driesell from Maryland in the lobby. And he's got Dawkins's dad backed up against the wall; and he's talking and waving his arms. Clear as can be: illegal contact.

"So I walk over to where he can see me and I'm like, 'Lefty, what are you doing?'

"And he comes over to me and says, 'What's up, Feinstein? You got a scoop?'

"So, I go, 'Lefty, that's an illegal contact. You were talking to Mr. Dawkins.'

"And he said, 'I didn't know that. I figured he was just a fan. We were just talking about what a great player Johnny is.'"

And so he proved to be.

The class of 1986 is credited with laying the foundation for Duke's success, but other teams contributed to the growth of the program.

And early on.

Feinstein thinks, "The 1987 season was as important—if not more so—than the 1986 season. 1986 was a senior year. Amaker was the only starter back in 1987.

"Everybody thought, 'Okay, Duke had that big run. They had that one big class. They finished 37-3, came up just short in the championship game. And now they're sliding.'

"Mike kept it together the next year with Amaker, with Ferry starting to come on. Billy King was a junior, although he was starting for just the first time. He had Phil Henderson flunk out of school after the first semester.

"And he kept it together, won 24 games, and had a chance to beat Indiana in the Sweet 16. It was a two-point game with a minute and a half to go. I think Steve Alford made a couple of big-time plays and won the game for them.

"But that team kept it going. And since there was no slippage, there was no going back to the NIT or being mediocre. They finished third in the conference; and I think that was just huge for them.

"Then the next year, they started their Final Four run, where they went to five in a row. That was amazing, especially in this day and age."

For Duke, the fourth time was a charm.

In 1991, Duke won its first national championship. The Blue Devils defeated UNLV 79-77 in the semifinals. They then beat Kansas 72-65 in the championship game.

It was a victory won on lessons learned in defeat.

In 1986, Duke had beaten Kansas in the semifinals but had gone on to lose to Louisville in the championship game.

"It was just a draining game—physically, emotionally, mentally. Alarie and Henderson were getting fluids put into them after the game. And they never got their legs back.

"Mike learned from what had happened in the Louisville game, where his team was just worn out," Feinstein said. "And he found enough ways to help them. I can't tell you how key that was to their winning the Kansas game in 1991, because it was the same kind of draining game.

"That was a helluva game, and Kansas was a helluva team."

The semifinal game had been no walk in the park, either.

"The national championship game against Kansas in 1991 was the same way. Laettner was exhausted after getting pounded on by those Vegas guys the entire game in the national semifinals. Mike realized that. That's why if you go back and look at the tape, every time they got within 30 seconds of a TV timeout, Christian was out of the game. He kept his legs just long enough to get them through the game. And Thomas Hill, too.

"That's why Mike started McCaffrey in the second half against Kansas. And McCaffrey hit all those big shots, 16 points."

The next year, Duke did it again, beating Michigan 71-51, thus winning back-to-back national championships.

In nine seasons, Krzyzewski's Blue Devils had gone to seven Final Fours. Then came 1995.

And with it, the first chink in the armor.

Feinstein remembers the reactions to Krzyzewski's health problems.

"I think everybody was concerned. He was concerned. Mickie was concerned. Everybody in the school was concerned. Mike being Mike—and this is probably his greatest strength—he never blames anybody else, so he blamed himself.

"He said he'd come back too soon after the back surgery, which he did, because he knew he had a young team and he didn't think he could afford to miss practice time. And for the military guy in him, it's mind over matter: you can't accept the fact your body can't do something if you have to get something done.

"So, he wouldn't cut back on his hours. He was staying up all night looking at tapes. I think they lost a game in Hawaii and they stayed up all night looking at tape. And by the time they flew home, he couldn't sit down the whole plane trip back.

"He pushed himself, not only to the wall, but through the wall.

"And finally, everything just broke down.

"He offered to resign because he felt he'd let the team down and let the school down.

"And Butters said, 'Mike, go home. Get better. And when you come back, we'll talk. There's no one else I want coaching the team. You know that.'

"I think the beginning of his getting better was when he accepted the fact he couldn't coach again that season. He kept saying, 'I'll be back next week.' Finally Mickie made him go to the hospital and had the doctors basically say, 'Mike, you're killing yourself.'

"Mickie was key there. Butters was key there. I was talking to him, 'God damn it, you can't do this to yourself.'

"So finally, he accepted not coaching the rest of the year. That's when he started to get better.

"And, typically Mike, he re-evaluated himself."

And made some much-needed changes.

According to Feinstein, "The year he won the first national championship, I described him at a high school game and how it turned into an autograph show. He literally couldn't watch the game because people were coming up and asking him to sign autographs. Fans wanted to take pictures with him. Other coaches wanted to talk with him. And he realized he had to find a way to cut down on this because he had to coach his team.

"There were a bunch of us who were on him about that, long before 1995 came around. Unfortunately, he's hardheaded.

"Mike knew he needed younger guys. And, in many ways, that was unfair to Pete Gaudet, because Pete had been such an important part of the program. But Mike felt like, 'I need younger guys A) for recruiting and B) to energize me.'

"That's when Quin came back, and Tommy came back, and David. And now, it's his guys. Steve and Chris are like the sons he never had.

"But it can be dangerous to hire your ex-players. They can be yes men. They can be intimidated by you. And Mike can really be intimidating at this point in his life. I kid with him a lot, 'You need me around more. If there's anybody who can tell you that you're full of shit, it's me. You're Mike to me. You're Coach K to everybody else.'

"But these guys have really done a great job in recruiting for him. They've gotten better as they've gotten more experience. I think, right now, he'd tell you he's got a helluva staff."

And a great family.

Feinstein remembers meeting them "almost right away when he got to Duke. I was covering Maryland then and the ACC, so I probably covered them in Durham, I don't know, maybe four or five times that year. I know I went down and wrote a big Gene Banks feature, so I was down there a fair bit. That was also the year I did my huge, two-part take-out on Dean, so I was down there a lot.

"I was actually dating a woman from there, so I found every excuse I could to go down. I would go back to the house after games a lot, and that was when I first got to know Mickie and the girls.

"Jamie wasn't born yet. Jamie was conceived the night Gene Banks hit the shot. That's a fact.

"In fact, I think I talked to Mike on the phone about an hour before Jamie was conceived.

"It was Carolina. It was Gene Banks's last home game. It was the Carolina team that ended up losing the championship game to Indiana. Banks hit a 25-

footer at the buzzer over Sam Perkins to send it into overtime. And they won it in overtime.

"I was actually covering Maryland and Virginia that night. That was when Bill Brill made the statement: 'All the great Duke players win their last home game.'

"I called that night. Mike was just flying high. Mickie told me later that Jamie was conceived that night.

"I got to know both Jamie and Lindy when they were both little girls."

It's 25 years later, and their father's legacy is being discussed.

Feinstein's opinion: "I'm not sure that his legacy will be everything it should be. Obviously, people will acknowledge all the wins. He'll be the winningest coach ever before he steps down. And he'll be recognized for the championships and the Final Fours and everything."

But Feinstein thinks there should be more than just Ws and Ls involved.

"What about what he's done adapting to changes in college basketball—whether they are rules changes, or the reality of losing kids early, or the way recruiting has changed, the way the game has changed—while doing it the right way?

"There are so many people who resent him for his colossal success.

"I've always contended that Gary Williams's autobiography is going to be titled *Duke Gets All the Calls*.

"And I've had people come up and say to me, 'Well, Coach K uses bad language all the time.' That's the only bad thing they can find to say bad about him.

"As his success has grown, there are actually people who resent him. Look at this year's team. Is there any way they should have won 27 games? He's an unbelievable coach. His kids believe in him so totally."

Krzyzewski has his own legacy from West Point.

"Army is all about leadership," Feinstein said. "And one of the things they teach you is that leadership is convincing people they can do something they really can't.

"And that's what great coaches do. And that's what Mike does."

Krzyzewski is also great at friendship, according to Feinstein.

"When my mother died, he called me and basically he said, 'What do you need me to do? Do you want me to come up there? Do you want to come here? Do you want to use my beach house so you can get away?'

"He remembered what it was like when his dad died.

"And it was, 'What do you need?'

"You don't forget something like that.

"When he was back before he was coaching again, he wrote me a letter. It was about our friendship: how there are certain people in your life you can count on. And that the conversations I'd had with Mickie during that period had really meant a lot in his life.

"Again, he didn't have to do that. He knows we're friends.

"It is harder to develop a relationship with a coach now. We have less access now. I hear people talk all the time about how inaccessible Krzyzewski is. And I believe them. But I call him. I either call him at home or on his direct line; and if I don't get him, he calls me right back.

"But we've been friends for, like, 25 years. I think it takes the right kind of person on both sides. It's a matter of trust."

3

THE
COMMUNICATOR

JAY BILAS

Duke Class of 1986

G rowing up in Rolling Hills, near Los Angeles, Jay Bilas was used to star sightings.

As he recalled, "I went to high school with tennis player Tracy Austin. Seeing how she handled the pressure and the recognition she got really helped me out. Nobody knew me on the street. They were too busy looking for Marcus Allen or Christie Brinkley."

It was a good thing that he learned about coping with recognition at an early age.

He would need it later on.

Bilas loved the West Coast. He would have enrolled at UCLA, but Larry Farmer showed no interest.

There was someone who did show interest in him, though: Mike Krzyzewski.

According to Bilas, "Coach K would fly out on a Friday, fly back on Saturday morning, play a game, and then fly out to see me play in a tournament Sunday."

In the beginning, the recognition was not mutual.

"When he first called me, I'd never heard of him," Bilas remembered. "I grew up in Los Angeles and never heard of him. Duke? All I knew about Duke was from the 1978 championship game. I knew Spanarkel, Gminski. Honestly, I wasn't sure if Bill Foster was still the coach or not.

"For me, it was coaches. I'd love to sit here and say Duke was a great school and that's what attracted me, but it was the coach. It was Jim Boeheim, Lute Olson, and Coach K—those three guys. They all have over 700 wins now.

Duke Photography

"Coach K had the least stable program at the time. I just trusted him. He put in a lot of work on all of us. I know he used to fly out cross country—just to watch me play in a pick-up game. Then he'd jump on a red eye and get back to practice.

"There were times we couldn't get in the high school gym before practice would start in October so we'd have to play outdoors. I remember him sitting on the front steps of those portable classrooms they had at Rolling Hills High School and just watching us play. He was all by himself.

"Nobody knew who he was.

"Now, if you sit there, everybody knows, but it was different then.

"He had missed with all those kids—Chris Mullin, Jimmy Miller, Mark Acres.

"That was an issue for me. A couple of assistants had tried to turn up the heat on me. I remember Chuck Swenson had called me. John Feinstein was doing an article for *Inside Sports* magazine on Coach K, and all the players he had missed out on the year before. Chuck was saying, 'Boy, it would be great if you could commit. And that would sort of be the postscript to the article.'

"I said, 'I'm not making the commitment based on the deadline of some article. That's not real smart.'

"It felt like he was pressuring me. He said something to the effect that I had told them I was leaning that way but now I wasn't willing to commit. What was that saying? What kind of message was I trying to send?

"I hung up on him. I was really mad.

"Afterwards, Coach K talked to my mom and me and totally smoothed things over. He knew everything about my situation.

"I had a really bad high school coach. I'd had three high school coaches in four years. The last one was not qualified for the position. But he had been there for years. He had coached my brother. Initially, he was a freshman coach who had inherited a team. It was a bad situation for everybody. Coach K knew that. He really knew every detail—things that most people would not bother with. I just think it's in his makeup to know that stuff.

"So I was willing to trust him with the most important thing to me other than my family—and that was playing."

The day Bilas committed, Krzyzewski had just watched him play and called his father, asking for recommendations where he and Swenson could go for dinner.

Bilas called back and suggested he drive by the house and the directions would be in the mailbox. They were, along with a note written by Jay.

"By the way," the note said, "If it matters, I'm coming to Duke."

Bilas wasn't the only one who trusted Krzyzewski.

He remembered the others Coach K signed that year:

"The first guy was Weldon Williams, from Chicago. He had an unbelievably good reputation and wound up not really doing anything.

"Bill Jackman, from Nebraska, was my roommate. He wound up transferring to Nebraska because he had a tough time after his father passed away. Then it was me, then Mark Alarie, then Johnny Dawkins. And David Henderson was the last one.

"Johnny was the big one. But every one of us was top 50, so we had a good class of guys. None of us knew one another. This was pre-Internet, pre-AAU tournaments, pre-Nike camp, pre-adidas.

"I actually met Johnny before school started.

"My family had never been to the East Coast, except for me—and I had visited Syracuse and saw Durham on my visit to Duke.

"I'd never been to Washington, D.C. My parents thought that when they dropped me off at school, we would fly to D.C. and drive from there to Durham. They wanted to drive down to show my sister the University of Virginia. My parents didn't go to college. This was new for them, too. We didn't grow up in a house with college memorabilia. We didn't have a rooting interest in bowl games. I was the first in my family who graduated from college.

"When we got to D.C., I told Coach K what I was doing, 'My parents are going to drive me down to school, make a little vacation of it.'

"He said, 'Well, while you're in D.C., you ought to go see Johnny and maybe you guys can go play pick-up ball.'

"So I called Johnny, and he told me how to get to his house. I drove over there and knocked on the door. Johnny answered the door. I didn't know it was him. I said, 'Hi, I'm looking for Johnny Dawkins.'

"Johnny was so slight, that when he answered the door, I asked to speak to his older brother," Bilas recalled.

"I figured that couldn't be him.

"He looked like a stiff wind would blow him over. He lived in Rockville, Maryland. He wanted you to think he was like, inner city, but he was really from the suburbs.

"He said, 'I'm Johnny.'

"And I said, 'We're screwed.'

"He's the savior? He's the No. 1 player?"

But Bilas's first impression of Dawkins changed. And quickly.

"We went to a playground, and I was the only white player," Bilas recalled. I thought I played really well, but he was awesome. Oh, my God. Not only was he greater than this team of guys we had—we had won eight- or 10-straight games, then we lost one—but Johnny, some way, somehow, was able to argue with this group of asskickers that, 'No, that basket didn't count. Here's why.'

"I was just standing off to the side.

"So we ended up replaying it. And we won that one, too.

"If we had lost, we were gone for the rest of the day."

Bilas thought Dawkins "had street smarts. I had never seen anybody play like him.

"Johnny was obviously the star."

But he was a star in a bright constellation.

"Mark was the most competitive," Bilas said. "He had sort of an anger. We always used to call him 'Ray Guy.' When we had shooting drills, he would make 10 in a row. If he missed the 11th, he would just punt the ball. But he was really quiet. He never said a word in meetings. He was never the guy to give a big speech. But he was a great player.

"David was the toughest of all of us, by far. He didn't take any crap from anybody. My freshman year, we played Carolina and lost. Bill Jackman was from this small town in Nebraska, and he had never seen anything like this. We were on the bus back. Carolina had kicked our ass; and Jackman was talking about how good Jordan was.

"I thought David was going to kill him, he was so mad at him. We had gone there to beat Carolina, not to talk about how great they were.

"David would challenge everybody."

Some freshmen fared better than others.

Bilas recalled: "Williams pledged a national fraternity our freshman year, and it was just all-encompassing. He wasn't allowed to speak outside of the fraternity except during practice—so he wouldn't shut up then. He was my roommate on the road, so he was always yapping in the room, too, because he wasn't supposed to speak at other times. Because of the fraternity and all the things he had to do, his basketball suffered."

Their inaugural season was not that easy for the class of 1986.

"Freshman year, the losing was really hard—especially the Virginia game," Bilas remembered. "That didn't go away, either. The first day of practice the next year, Coach K put it up on the scoreboard. It wasn't like, 'Forget it.' It was like, 'Let's overcome it.'"

Another bonding experience was an exhibition tour to France the team took during the summer before their sophomore year.

Of that trip, Bilas said, "We knew Johnny was on a different level than the rest of us. A guy named Bill Sweek who played with UCLA and adidas set the trip up.

"We won some, but we got screwed everywhere we played. The last game we played, they gave us gifts—hats and a bottle of champagne. We gave them Duke T-shirts.

"That last game, we got cheated, start to finish. One time they inbounded the ball while we were still in the huddle.

"I'm drinking water—and we're all listening to Coach K—and all of a sudden, Johnny's tearing from the huddle and steals the inbounds pass. We wound up losing. Afterward, Coach K tore into their officials. They couldn't understand English, or it would have been all over.

"We gave the gifts back.

"He wouldn't let us settle for less. It wasn't like we were on a fun trip over there. It was no lace 'em-up jaunt. We were going to play to win. And we weren't going to let anybody jerk us around."

They provided their own fun, as Bilas remembered.

"David had gotten Johnny pretty good with some joke. So Johnny had gotten up early, about two in the morning, packed up all his stuff, got dressed, and switched all the clocks in the room. He put his stuff somewhere else in the hotel.

"Then he came back into the room and said, 'David, what are you doing? I woke you up. What are you doing? We're ready to go.'

"David got up, got his stuff together, and tore out of there without brushing his teeth, taking a shower, or anything.

"It was pitch dark outside.

"David was so mad, he sat out there until the bus came, until we were ready to leave. He was livid.

"We did stuff like that the whole trip."

The team started to turn around sophomore year when Tommy Amaker got there and handled the ball and Dawkins could concentrate on his shooting.

That was the good news.

The bad news was the pressure on Coach K to resign.

Bilas recalled that time: "We heard a lot of hard things going on when we were there, including the fans who were vociferous about wanting to get rid of our coach.

"Now if you go to Duke, the program is already established, and you're carrying on the tradition. Our thing was building it, so we had to listen to the negative side as well. While Duke supporters are wonderful, they're human beings, too.

"That was freshman, beginning of sophomore, year. Mark and I both talked about it: 'If they fire him, we'll leave with him. I'll come back and pack my stuff.' You know that rag, *The Poop Sheet*, well, Coach K's picture is on the front of it, with a caption, something like, 'How much longer?'

"You see that when you're 19 years old, that's hard.

"It wasn't something you heard every day, but it was an undercurrent for a year and a half. It was a hard time. Through a girl he was dating, Mark and I knew one of the Iron Dukes. And he was talking about a petition that was being circulated to fire Coach Krzyzewski. A guy tells that to a couple of 19-year-old kids: it was awful.

"But it was the way it was back then. We just had to deal with it. Sometimes we dealt with it well. Sometimes we didn't

"There was no question that there was a level of frustration when things would go wrong. We felt like things were crumbling, but Coach K never let on. He never spoke about it, not once. But we would talk about it. It wasn't anything like, 'We've got to play well so Coach doesn't get fired.' But there was a heaviness in the air on certain days.

"It was always a sort of criticism. One day, I think it was Mark and I who went with him to the local country club, where the Blue Devil Club met at a once-a-month luncheon deal. Coach K would take a couple of players. He would speak, then we would say something, and then there would be a q-and-a session.

"That day, we got asked some pretty hard questions: 'Did we think we should be playing zone?'

"And Coach K is standing right there.

"I just hated that stuff. At the time, I hated being questioned by people who didn't know what they were talking about. It bothered me. And it bothered me when we would be somewhere, and people would say everything was great when everything wasn't. That really pissed me off.

"You learned quickly that you're by yourself. Those fair-weather fans we had back then bothered me. It was funny: we didn't see them at our practice after we lost to N.C. State. We were pretty much by ourselves then.

"We enjoyed it when it got really good. We enjoyed the attention, everybody rallying around the team and the school. But we didn't forget who hadn't been there before.

"Coach K handled it great. He's combative about certain things, like the double standard he felt was in place with Carolina. The players liked that. He wasn't going to let us settle. We were not second-class citizens."

At the time, Carolina was stepping on everybody's neck.

They were acting like young bucks.

"Coach K is a very competitive guy. And he will get in your grille when he's not happy. You see him doing American Express commercials and writing his books—and he's always very positive. But if you don't do what you're supposed to do, it isn't positive.

"There were times, especially when we were younger, when he stood up and challenged us to fight. Now we knew he was not serious; but at the same time, he was. His thing was, 'I'll fight you. You may beat me up, but you'll have to kill me.'

"That's what he wanted to inject in us: 'Step out there. Step on the floor. If they beat us, fine. But they're going to have to kill us.'"

The team stepped out—and stepped up in the final games of the 1984 season, Bilas's sophomore year—and overcame Carolina.

Like his teammates, Bilas has his memories of that contest: "The last regular-season game we played was against Carolina. We lost. We just gave it away. Guys were really upset in the locker room. Nobody said much. Coach K didn't say much in the locker room, either. He just came in, looked at the guys, and said, 'The next time we play them, we're going to beat them.'

"We played them a week later. It wasn't like we snuck up on them. We beat them. Coach had told me before the tournament game, 'We're going to win this game. And after we do, just walk off the floor like we expected to win.'

"The buzzer went off—we won—and he's in the middle of the floor, hugging Johnny. I see Johnny trying to get away from him. We got a big laugh out of that one.

"It was an important win: just to prove to ourselves that we were as good as anybody else. It was another step."

But it took its toll.

Bilas said, "We were spent after that game. It was a semifinal. We lost to Maryland in the finals. Len Bias had 26 on us. We just ran out of gas. You could almost see it grind to a halt.

"But I'll never forget: after we beat Carolina—after Coach K got finished hugging Johnny—we were walking off the floor. Now remember that the next teams were waiting to warm up. Maryland was just as excited as we were. Their thing was, 'We can beat these guys.'

"I don't know if they thought they could beat Carolina. When you played Carolina then, not every team expected to win. Maybe it's like playing Duke today—not every team expects to win.

"But the way Coach K taught us to win was like, 'We're No. 1, and we want to be No. 1. If they're giving it out, we're taking it.'

"We embraced it."

So did other schools in the ACC.

Of Duke's rivalry with Georgia Tech, Bilas said, "They were sort of the mirror image of us. We started four freshmen; so did they. They had young coaches, too. It was Dawkins-Price; Alarie-Salley. They had a lineup full of pros; we had a good lineup. We were both very competitive from the beginning. That's where rivalries develop. Carolina was just eight miles away. But with Tech, that rivalry developed because we were both fighting to stay out of the cellar.

"Our senior year, I thought we were better. In 1985, we were ranked No. 2. We did better in the regular season. In the postseason they beat us in the semifinals of the ACC Tournament in Atlanta when Mark was hurt. Then they had a run before they lost to Georgetown in the regional finals.

"The following year, they were the team standing in our way. We had won the regular season. We were 12-2.

"I remember Mark saying after we'd won the ACC championship by one, 'If we didn't win that game, that would have ruined our whole season.'

"That's all we had."

Not quite. There was still the Final Four.

Bilas remembered, "We got criticized after the regional final for not having enough fun. We beat Navy by 20, we cut the nets down, but we didn't jump around. I don't want to say it was matter of fact, because we were really thrilled. But we hadn't had any illusions that we were going to lose. And Coach K had done something extraordinary that year.

"The tournament had always seemed so big for us. It had blown up to 64 teams my junior and senior years. We'd actually had a bye the year before, played in the second round—so that was our first game.

"My senior year before the tournament, he talked about the bracket. He looked at the other side of the bracket and said, 'Who cares who's coming out of there? Only one team is coming out of there.'

"He broke the tournament down the first weekend. He said, 'This is a four-team tournament.'

"'We play in Greensboro—the Greensboro Invitational. The next week, it's the Meadowlands. Then we get to the Final Four.'

"'It's a four-team tournament.'

"It was just so simple, easier to manage in your head. The unmanageable became manageable. I don't know whether he came up with it or it just happened. But I'd never heard of it before.

"It was certainly not easy, but we had a grasp on it."

So did Louisville.

Bilas thinks that the championship game against Louisville "validated everything we'd done. It still hurts that we didn't win. We were better.

"We were tired, in a way. That was our 40th game. We'd won 37 and played only seven guys who had been through a number of different games in the tournament. We didn't shoot it well as a team. We had the lead late in the game and went into a motion delay. In the past, if we were up six with two minutes to go, we'd usually salt it away. But this time, we sort of lost momentum. And it was brutal.

"We felt we had the best team. But you know how championship-oriented this society is. I understand how hard it was to get to the Final Four—all well and good. That was something we were really proud of.

"Before the championship game, there were articles in the Dallas newspapers asking, 'Where does this team rank among the greatest teams ever to play?'

"If we had won, we would have easily been one of the top 10 teams of all time—38-2. And our two losses would have come against North Carolina and Georgia Tech—the No. 1 and No. 3 teams in the country—on the road.

"A couple of the articles did a position-by-position breakdown against the great UCLA teams. It was like UCLA 1967: Dawkins is better than Lucious Allen and Tommy Amaker is better than Mike Warren. But then it got down to me against Alcindor and Bill Walton or Patrick Ewing. And I never had a chance—Goddamn it. Why couldn't I play power forward, be matched up against Lynn Shackleford? He might win it, but at least it would have been a fair fight."

Of Krzyzewski's status as a great coach, Bilas said, "It doesn't shock me. It's kind of like Jordan. You knew he was great in college. But, at the time, were you saying he was going to be the best ever?

"Coach K—you knew he was great. But could you have predicted he'd be in the Final Four all those years?

"No.

"I'm not shocked at his success. But at the same time, I'm in awe. When I'm with him, I do have to check myself and not call him 'sir.' I did know him when. And that's nice. I'm glad.

"Everything I know about a work ethic, I learned from two people—my dad and Coach K.

"He's the only guy who comes within shouting distance of my dad. My father never went to college. Before I was born, he was a commercial fisherman. He went to technical school for a couple of years and he built a nice business for himself in television service and repair. Then he began buying real estate and manages storefront properties now.

"I learned about competing from Coach K—and accountability. He used to talk all the time about taking responsibility for your actions. And that doesn't mean if you rob a bank, you're going to jail.

"His thing was that everything you do has repercussions, and you have a responsibility to your teammates. You are responsible for being in the right place, for getting your rest, for taking care of yourself so you're ready to play. And you're responsible for being prepared to play."

After graduation from Duke, Bilas played in Europe: two years in Italy and in Spain for a year.

Then, as Bilas remembered, "Both of my parents were intent on my going to law school. My dad wanted me to make a living sitting down. He felt that law school was the way to go. You don't have to be a lawyer; it's a versatile degree. They always figured, 'What if you get hurt? What if this happens? Get accepted somewhere and then defer. Then when you're done playing, if you quit in the middle of the season, you can just go to school.'

"I took all the law school exams overseas. I applied to Duke, hoping I wouldn't get in, so I could keep playing. But I got in. When I got accepted, Coach K called and said, 'All of a sudden, I've got an opening on my staff. Are you interested?'

"So I was going to do both. I'd be an assistant and go to law school.

"The law school balked at it. But Coach K went to the mat for me."

And it worked out.

"It was one of the best experiences of my life. Not just law school, but coaching. I'd always thought I'd get into that, but getting married changed an awful lot of things."

Being a coach taught Bilas a few good lessons.

Lessons he uses today as a basketball analyst for ESPN.

"When I was an assistant there, we won in 1991 when we probably shouldn't have. Then the next year, one of first things he told the team collectively was, 'We're not defending anything. That's done. We're pursuing the next one.'

"In 1992, we almost lost to Clemson. The starters had fallen behind by 16 points. Coach K cleared the bench, with 14 minutes to play. And he put all the subs in. It wasn't a white-flag thing. Laettner, Hill, Hurley, Thomas Hill, and the subs made a comeback and cut the lead to eight. Clemson folded, and we wound up winning 98-97.

"Afterward, it was hailed as this genius move—and maybe it was. At the time, I remember thinking, 'I'm not going to watch this.' A part of the reason it turned out great was because he coached the game with the guys who were going to play it.

"He said one time, 'There is no such thing as garbage time. If we're playing, we're going to play the right way. Even if we're playing the worst team on our schedule, it is the most important game, because we're playing it.'

"It's a great approach. I use it today.

"When I did my first game for ESPN, it was Hampton vs. The Citadel. And I treated it like it was the NCAA championship game. I got that from him: it was important because I was doing it. I took the tack that maybe very few people are watching it, but the ones who are watching it really care.

"The other thing I remember thinking was, 'You know what? This may be the only time these guys are on TV. Make it important.'

"Another thing I learned from Coach K—but you would never hear it from him: a win is a win. Without the belief that you're going to do it, you're never going to do it.

"His ability to get us to believe in him and what we're doing collectively: I can't imagine it's better anywhere else. I didn't play for Dean or Knight. I can't believe they'd be better, but they might have done it as well."

Thinking back on that recruitment summer long ago, Bilas reflected:

"If I'd gone to school at UCLA, I might have been an All-PAC-10 player. But then I wouldn't have played on those Duke teams."

The road not taken.

"We just had good guys," Bilas said. "That was a great group of guys. We were really lucky. We all had a good appreciation for our similarities and our differences. We all got along great.

"It wasn't like we all hung out 24 hours a day. But even now, 20 some years later, I talk to Johnny all the time; I talk to Mark Alarie. We get together in the summertime."

Bilas remembers one particular get-together: "Back when Coach K was doing his thing with the Lakers, we were all in Washington, D.C., playing golf together. The foursome was Johnny, Mark, David Henderson, and me.

"While we were playing, I got a call from ESPN and the producer says, 'We just heard a rumor that Coach K has accepted the job.'

"I said, 'That's not true.'

"'Well, how do you know that?'

"'Well, I'm standing right next to the associate head coach. It's not true. There, you know. I'm busy now.'"

There's only one fly in the Duke ointment for Bilas: "The only problem I ever had with Duke is the way they retire numbers.

"On one hand, Duke will say, 'We know what it takes to win a championship. You have to subvert the individual for the good of the whole. But when it comes to hanging banners or inducting people into the Hall of Fame, we go by the judgments of others.'

"So you've got to be the National Player of the Year.

"But what if Grant Hill had played in the same year as Tim Duncan? And if he'd finished second, you're not going to hang the jersey up?

"It's absurd. Look at Mark Alarie. He's been good about it, but I know it hurts him that his jersey wasn't retired. It hurts him to this day. And he left there the third all-time leading scorer with over 2,000 points.

"I still think he should have had his number retired. I think it was an error in judgment by the school. But they're not going to go back and fix it now, because Laettner's number was the same. They screwed up.

"Nobody had any idea there'd be another team like that at Duke—let alone four of them. For Mark to be passed over like that kind of sucks.

"I'm beside myself that David Henderson is not in the Duke Hall of Fame, too.

"I wrote a letter to Joe Alleva, making a case for him. David doesn't know; he has no idea I did this."

Once a team player, always a team player.

And speaking of teams: "Every one of us has the same team picture in our homes. I have that picture in my living room. Those guys have been my best friends for years. In school we won a lot of games. Laettner's class, Battier's class won more, but nobody had the richness of experience we had.

"I would not trade those four years for Laettner's four or Battier's four."

4

THE SAVIOR

JOHNNY DAWKINS

Duke Class of 1986

Johnny Dawkins doesn't need a team picture to remind him of his playing days at Duke University.

The facts speak for themselves.

He is the all-time leading scorer at the school with 2,556 points.

The class of 1986 has been credited with laying the foundation for the modern basketball marvel that is Duke. It was the nucleus of the first Mike Krzyzewski team to get to the NCAA Final Four. In addition to Dawkins, the roster included seniors David Henderson, Mark Alarie, Jay Bilas, and Weldon Williams; juniors Tommy Amaker and Martin Nessley; sophomores Billy King and Kevin Strickland; and freshmen Quin Snyder, John Smith, Danny Ferry, and George Burgin.

Their team picture hangs prominently in Dawkins's office on the third floor of Krzyzewski towers.

Dawkins is the Blue Devils' associate head coach in charge of player development these days. But, back then, he was the prize recruit of that class, hailed as a savior by his teammates.

"I'm sure you can grab team pictures of Shane Battier's group or Grant Hill's group and see the same kind of success stories that don't necessarily have anything to do with what they're doing on the court," Dawkins said. "You get enough balance here so that you realize there's life after this. And you're also preparing yourself for that. You don't come to a university like this and not take advantage of what it has to offer."

Dawkins used his opportunity to change the destiny of Duke basketball.

Duke Photography

The skinny, left-handed six-foot-two guard was a two-time consensus All-American and the National Player of the Year his senior year.

In many ways, he may have been the most important player ever to wear a Duke uniform.

Dawkins was the National High School Player of the Year in 1983 when he played for Mackin High School in Washington, D.C. The school has since closed its doors and merged with Archbishop Carroll.

And Duke was desperate for a big-name recruit.

Krzyzewski was coming off a 10-17 season. He and his staff had tried—and struck out—the previous year with Chris Mullin, Bill Wennington, Uwe Blab, Rodney Williams, and Jim Miller from Parkersburg, West Virginia.

Jim Miller's high school coach had told Krzyzewski that his star player was ready to commit, so Krzyzewski dispatched assistant coach Bob Dwyer to West Virginia with letter of intent in hand. He checked into a motel for the night. At 8:30 the next morning, he was awakened by a phone call from an embarrassed high school coach who told him Miller had signed with Virginia.

West Virginia was not "almost heaven" to Krzyzewski that day.

Krzyzewski not only lost Miller, but Duke had to play against him for four years. In 1983, Miller came off the bench, had 12 points and four rebounds against the Blue Devils in a horrific 46-point loss in the first round of the tournament in Atlanta.

At the time, Krzyzewski was taking heat from boosters who questioned his ability to attract enough blue-chippers to compete with rivals North Carolina and N.C. State. He definitely did not want to miss on Dawkins, who was also being recruited by Georgetown, Notre Dame, and Maryland—three already established powers.

Dawkins came from a middle-class neighborhood in northwest Washington, D.C. His parents were a social worker and a bus driver. During his summer vacations, he'd play on outdoor courts from 9 a.m. until 9 p.m.

Dawkins was the best young player in the city.

But Dawkins knew if he wanted to be recruited at the highest level, he'd have to pay attention to his grades. His marks started improving—much to the delight of the Duke coaching staff, who were earning frequent-flyer points to see him play.

"There was no limit on how many times you could see a kid play back then, so you can imagine how many games they were at," Dawkins said. "Mike was at several games, and Coach Dwyer was at every game since I was in 10th grade.

"So I'm sitting there and I'm going, 'Wow.' You could see they were so committed. During my visit, I got a chance to spend some time with Coach and really got to know him even more as a person."

Dawkins liked what he saw.

"I was excited. You always choose the university. Even as a young kid, I was going to try to choose a university first and foremost. But I was also picking a coach. Out of everyone, I felt most comfortable with Coach."

The rest of the city wasn't so sure.

"There was a lot of pressure to stay home, but I had a lot of support," Dawkins said. "My father, my coach, and the people in my camp were strong. They figured if I was happy with my decision and felt good about it, then they weren't going to let anybody get in the way.

"I was a McDonald's All-American and I received hundreds of letters. But I visited only two colleges—this university and Providence. And I visited Providence only because my old high school coach in my freshman year had gone there as an assistant. I visited out of respect and loyalty. I figured I owed him that, but my heart was set on Duke."

The feeling was mutual.

Dawkins hardly looked like a savior when he arrived in the fall of 1982. But he helped put the Devils back on the map.

"Coach wanted me to be aggressive offensively," Dawkins said. "He would not allow me not to go out there in attack mode. I had to have it turned on. Always. Coach told me to shoot more. Jay Bilas still gets mad about that; he wanted me to pass it to him.

"I was a scorer from high school. I could put the ball in the basket, so it wasn't foreign territory to me. You miss a couple of shots, three or four, and you figure, 'Let me slow down, get in rhythm.' And Coach says, 'You'd better take the next one like you took the last one. If you have that same look, I want you to take the shot.'

"I got a lot of my confidence from him. People look at it like I would have the green light or Christian [Laettner] had the green light or Jay [Bilas] had the green light; but everyone has that. He's looking for guys who are capable of creating offense pretty much once they cross halfcourt. If they can put the ball in the hole some way, he'll give them the opportunity to do that."

For as good as Dawkins was, Duke struggled initially. The Blue Devils had signed the best recruiting class in the country, but they won only 11 games their first year.

"Talk about competition. In 1982, Carolina won the national championship. In 1983, N.C. State won it all. Can you imagine living 25 miles away from one school and eight miles away from the other? As a young player, you're going, 'Everyone around here has won a national championship and everyone is going to Final Fours.'"

And the competition wasn't just external, either.

As a freshman, Dawkins naturally looked to the upperclassmen on the team for advice. But it wasn't forthcoming. There were no tips for the rookie from the veterans he had replaced in the starting lineup.

"So it was a tough time," he said.

It was tough on everybody, especially Krzyzewski, who was under pressure for a good year and a half before A.D. Tom Butters quieted the wolves by giving him a five-year extension midway through the 1984 season.

But he never stopped fighting for the players he recruited. "K was the perfect guy to coach us," Dawkins said. "He was ready. And we were his guys. He never differentiated between us and the guys who were here before us. I never felt that. But I just know, from my experience, that we were his guys. We came in and, from freshman year on, there was no other influence but him in our lives."

Despite his problems, Krzyzewski never stopped competing, as evidenced by the comments on double standards he made about Carolina in 1984.

Earlier that season, Duke had played Maryland; and the normally creative Cameron Crazies temporarily lost their minds, throwing condoms on the floor after news broke that a Maryland player, Herman Veal, had been charged with sexual assault.

The national media took a hard line, accusing the students of being over the edge. Terry Sanford, Duke's president at that time, and Krzyzewski tried to calm tensions, with Krzyzewski urging them to "Cheer for us, not against our opponents."

Their efforts weren't too effective.

When top-ranked, undefeated Carolina visited the next week, some of the Duke students were seen wearing coat hangers fashioned into the shape of halos with silver foil and they chanted, "We beg to differ," any time they disagreed with an official's call.

The game was close—with Duke clinging to a slim lead late in the second half.

With five minutes left, Carolina coach Dean Smith wanted to buzz in a sub. When Tommy Hunt, the ACC head of football officials who was working the clock, refused to do it because the ball was already in play, Smith reached over and attempted to hit the buzzer himself. Instead of hitting the substitution horn, he hit the scoreboard buzzer, giving Carolina an extra 20 points. Bedlam ensued, but Smith was never hit with a technical.

But Krzyzewski eventually got one for arguing with officials.

Carolina eventually rallied to win 78-73 in a contentious game.

Afterward, Krzyzewski was incensed.

He was upset at the way Duke had been treated by the media in the Veal incident and how Carolina was treated with kid gloves in this instance. He went off in the postgame, claiming that there was a double standard in officiating where the Heels were concerned.

Smith reportedly wrote Krzyzewski a letter and claimed later that Lou Carnessecca told him that Krzyzewski had done the same thing against his St. John's team when he was at Army.

But Krzyzewski never backed down.

"He was only doing what any coach would do in that circumstance," Dawkins said. "He stood up for his players and his program. If a coach is willing to fight for you, for what he feels is right, you have his back 100 percent."

Duke lost another heartbreaker to Carolina in the regular-season finale at Carmichael Auditorium, in double overtime.

But revenge is sweet.

The Blue Devils broke their six-game losing streak to the Tar Heels by defeating Carolina 77-75 in the 1984 ACC semifinals.

This win set the wheels in motion for Duke's program to take off.

Dawkins's career blossomed when Tommy Amaker arrived the next fall, allowing Krzyzewski to move Dawkins to the off guard spot, where he could more easily take advantage of his scoring skills.

That year against Carolina, Dawkins went off for a career-high 34 points, eight rebounds, four assists, four steals, and a single turnover in 40 minutes. The Blue Devils blew out the Tar Heels 93-77, marking Duke's first win in Carmichael in 20 years.

Dawkins blew up in his junior and senior years, saving much of his best work for the final two months of his career.

When Dawkins was a senior, Georgia Tech, North Carolina, and Duke were all ranked No. 1 at one point in the season. Duke had won 17 straight to start the season and then lost to Carolina and Georgia Tech on the road.

"It was a tight race for the ACC title, and we had never won one," Dawkins recalled. "We were playing Georgia Tech at home in a big game February 9. Coach just chewed on me about being more competitive, tougher, against Mark Price, their great guard. He got me so charged up, fired up to go out and play. No inhibitions—just put everything on the line and see where it all falls."

Dawkins played like a man inspired, scoring 22 points and combining with Tommy Amaker to hold Price to just 12 points—six below his average—and only four shots in the first 30 minutes. They also forced Price into an uncharacteristic eight turnovers. Duke executed nearly flawlessly in the second half, shooting 60 percent during a 75-59 victory at Cameron.

Dawkins recalled, "I'll never, never forget the lesson I learned from that. No one can get there, reach levels of success, without having other people be a part of it. You don't do it by yourself.

"You watch movies, see *Braveheart*. You watch those clips. All those guys are part of something bigger than they are alone. That's what made their accomplishments so great. They always knew the pecking order. If you're part of something bigger than you, you always have a lot better chance to do great things than if you think everything revolves around you.

"He gave me what I needed to get by in that moment."

Dawkins had two spectacular back-to-back games against N.C. State and Notre Dame Saturday and Sunday on national TV that kick-started his National Player of the Year candidacy. While Walter Berry of St. John's won most of the major Player of the Year awards and was recognized as the consensus National Player of the Year in 1986, Dawkins was the Naismith Player of the Year.

He scored 24 points and made two clutch free throws at the end of a 72-70 victory in Raleigh. Then he made a sensational block of Notre Dame's All-America guard David Rivers's final shot just before the buzzer, the next afternoon in Cameron—just 16 hours later—to preserve a 75-74 victory.

Dawkins won the MVP award at the ACC Tournament after scoring 60 points in three games and making two critical free throws in the final moments to ice a 68-67 victory over Georgia Tech in the finals. This gave him a 6-5 edge over Price in their personal career series.

And he threw a huge life preserver to the Blue Devils in the first game of the NCAA Tournament. Duke was matched up against seemingly beatable 16th-seeded Mississippi Valley State from the SWAC and its colorful coach Lafayette Stribling in his white suit and periwinkle blue tie.

Duke trailed for the first 30 minutes. The Blue Devils were tight and almost totally unable to function against a smaller, quicker team. Finally, Krzyzewski put the game on Dawkins's shoulders and asked him to win it.

Dawkins would take the inbounds pass, dribble through the press, and then attack the basket. He scored 16 points in five minutes, and Duke won 85-78, but Krzyzewski recently said it was the scariest moment of his coaching career.

In retrospect, Krzyzewski established himself as a great coach due to his NCAA Tournament success. But going into the 1986 tournament, he was 1-2 in NCAA play and had never reached the Sweet 16.

If Duke had lost to Mississippi Valley State—to date, no No. 1 has ever lost in the first round—history might have been altered.

He didn't lose because Dawkins almost single-handedly saved Duke that day.

Dawkins was on fire that March. He was named Outstanding Player in the NCAA East Regional after scoring 28 points during a 71-50 victory over David Robinson and Navy at the Meadowlands.

"Our last year: we were like, 'Man, this is our year,'" Dawkins recalled. "'We got to go to the Final Four.' We had played pretty well in the preseason NIT. We had won it. The teams in the final four at the [Madison Square] Garden were Duke, Kansas, Louisville, and St. John's; and three of those teams made it [to the NCAA Final Four]."

Duke advanced to the NCAA Tournament finals, but Dawkins's 24 points were not enough to get a tired Duke team, which had extended itself during a 71-67 victory over Kansas in the semis, past Louisville.

"I always say the same thing to young people: if you get an opportunity to perform on that kind of stage, always remember one thing—the winners are going to remember that for the rest of their lives," Dawkins said. "The only thing you can do as a player is know that when you walk off that court, you gave it your all."

Dawkins certainly did that.

Dawkins will always remember his classmates—Bilas, Alarie, Henderson, and Williams—fondly. They combined to score 7,537 career points, the most of any class in NCAA history. In addition to Dawkins's 2,556 points, Alarie had 2,136; Henderson, 1,570; Bilas, 1,062; Williams, 126; and Bill Jackman, a kid from Nebraska who was supposed to be the next Larry Bird, scored 86 points as a freshman before transferring to Nebraska after one year.

"The beauty of all that was I thought we were a microcosm of society," Dawkins said. "He brought all these different guys from different nationalities, different locations together. To succeed, we all had to get along. We had to trust one another."

Dawkins graduated with a degree in economics and was selected by the San Antonio Spurs in the first round of the NBA draft. He played for nine years— with the Spurs, Philadelphia 76ers, and Detroit Pistons.

He may have gone on to the NBA, but he never really left Duke.

Dawkins spent the offseasons in Bahama, a suburb just north of town, and he and his wife, Tracy, and their four children—Aubrey, Julian, Blair, and Sean—still live there.

"The NBA season would end, and I'd come back here," he said. "I was on campus every day, basically working out in the gym. I'd see Coach all the time. He'd be going to work out, play racquetball. He'd come on the court, shooting around, working with the players. So it was home. It wasn't like he didn't know where I was."

Obviously, Krzyzewski had noticed his presence.

After Dawkins retired from the NBA, he talked to Krzyzewski about becoming a teacher and athletic director. "I was a management intern with the athletic department," he said. "I worked in the ticket office, the business office, alumni affairs—in different areas. That's the program they set up for me.

"Well, I didn't get that far because after six months, I was doing radio with the team. Now, you get to feel the court again: 'Man this is great.' You want to get back out there. You want to be a part of that. But there was nothing available. I assumed Tommy [Amaker] would be here forever. He was here as a player, here on the staff. So I was thinking, 'I'll never have an opportunity.'"

All that changed in 1997 when Amaker took the Seton Hall job and Krzyzewski asked Dawkins if he wanted to fill the spot.

"I had been with the team," he said. "I knew the players. So from that point, the transition was easy. I went in with Coach; we talked and I said, 'Hey, which one of my arms do you need me to give you?'"

That must have done the trick.

"He gave me the opportunity. I'll never forget it."

To Dawkins, "Coach is grounded. Has he changed? Yeah. But his values haven't. He's still a going-to-church-early-Sunday-morning type of guy. He's still the same coach who coached me. He's still a believer in where this program could be and what it could represent. He's always had a vision. He still coaches like he has something to prove.

"The lesson our young coaches are learning by being a part of it is that here's a man who is just as passionate about something today as he was when he first started. You can only dream about being passionate about something 25 years later."

5

THE GURU

HOWARD GARFINKEL

Five-Star Camps

Howard Garfinkel has been the director of the Five-Star basketball camps for the last 40 years. During that time, 264 future NBA players have passed through the outdoor courts in venues like Radford College, Robert Morris, and Camp Bryn Mawr in Honesdale, Pennsylvania.

He has seen all of the great recruiters: David Pritchett, the blue-suited Maryland assistant who once pulled out a cross-country airplane reservation for Thanksgiving with six stops on it and who became famous for his pursuit of Moses Malone; George Raveling, the former Villanova and Maryland assistant, who established an underground railroad for black players from Alabama and Florida to the Philadelphia Main Line before it was fashionable for the ACC and SEC to recruit them; and Rick Pitino, who used to fly from Hawaii to New York every week so he could recruit guard Reggie Carter from Long Island Lutheran.

But he has never seen anyone like Mike Krzyzewski of Duke. "He has to be at the top of the list," Garfinkel said. "Look at the players he got, then coaching them. It's very difficult to have seven, eight, nine players and keep everyone happy.

"You've got to be a—I hate to use the word—genius. There are no geniuses. I was once told that by Everett Case of N.C. State, and Vic Bubas of Duke agreed. That's what they said. They were wrong.

"There's at least one. K-r-z-y-z-e-w-s-k-i.

"So was John Wooden.

"So there are a few geniuses."

Photo courtesy of Howard Garfinkel

Krzyzewski has plucked five National Players of the Year—Johnny Dawkins, Danny Ferry, Christian Laettner, Grant Hill, and Jason Williams—out of Garfinkel's camp; and four more All-Americans—Bobby Hurley, Elton Brand, Mike Dunleavy, and Chris Duhon.

"It's him. It's his personality," Garfinkel said. "That's what recruiting is, anyway: picking the right player. A lot of kids now recruit Duke. They're recruiting him. His choices were excellent, but he gets them with his personality. Parents just love him. What's there not to love? He made Duke the place to go in the 1980s.

"He can talk to you or 1,500 coaches in a room or 500 Five-Star campers, and his secret is, like all great show-biz people—Frank Sinatra, Fred Astaire, Judy Garland, Streisand, the supers—you always think they're singing to you.

"And you think he's talking to you.

"What's amazing to me is how he's been able to entice kids to play at Cameron. I don't want to knock Cameron Indoor Stadium—it's a great court for mid-majors. But compared to the palaces some of these teams have—to play in a 9,000-seat arena when he's surrounded by the Dean Dome and N.C. State's 20,000-seat arena—it's Little Cameron."

The 75-year-old Garfinkel—one of the most influential voices in the history of New York City basketball—first met Krzyzewski through Hall of Famer Bob Knight—when Krzyzewski was just a young coach at West Point. Knight, the one-time Army coach, formerly was in charge of the Five-Star counselors and invented the concept of teaching stations at the best teaching camp in the country.

"I didn't know any of this would happen," Garfinkel said. "He was just another coach, coming up, watching players. But when he got the Duke job and he started signing those kids, I could see it was just a matter of time."

"He has two great character traits. I call them, 'F and F.' You know what they stand for? Focus and Forthcoming. I can't think of two better words; these two words sum up this guy.

"He's the most focused man I've ever met. In fact, there's a graphic on ESPN. It's called 'The K Zone.' The 'K Zone' in baseball is the strike zone, where they want to throw the pitch. That's what I think about when I think of him: The Krzyzewski Zone for the perfect strike.

"And the forthcoming part, I saw that when I first got to know him well. I watched him at camp with all the people when he'd come to recruit for Duke and how open he was to everybody—coaches, high school coaches, me.

"I first got to know him well when he was recruiting Johnny Dawkins in the camp, but we got very close in 1990 when Bobby Hurley Jr. was a freshman at

Duke. Bobby came from St. Anthony's, attended our camp, and his father coached there. Anyway, he was having his problems.

"Duke came up here to play in the Garden, and I remember his loyalty to Hurley. Everyone wanted him to get Hurley off the point. And he didn't do it. He stayed with Hurley. And it turned out, as you know, pretty well. He never hurt the kid's confidence."

Over the years, the two have become close friends. Garfinkel has attended the weddings of all three of Krzyzewski's daughters and watched Krzyzewski emerge as one of great coaches of all time. He also got a chance to watch Coach K's future stars make names for themselves.

Garfinkel has always been one of the game's great talent evaluators. He can still remember the first time he saw Johnny Dawkins—Krzyzewski's first star—play. Dawkins was a rising senior at Mackin High School in Washington, D.C., in 1981.

"It was raining, so some of the camp's NBA games were being played indoors. I'm standing next to Eddie Fogler, who was an assistant from North Carolina, in the lower gym at Honesdale; and they're playing cross court. We're watching this guy, and Fogler's eyes were popping out of his head. Every time he got it, he'd go up and shoot. And there was no defender there. He just went up so quick, it was like he was playing by himself. That's when I first recognized his greatness."

No one had to tell Garfinkel about Danny Ferry when he was a senior at DeMatha Catholic in 1985. Ferry was the most skilled big man in the country.

"We were getting ready to play the Orange and White Classic," Garfinkel recalled. "This was his game. He was going to be the man.

"I remember that was the night of the tremendous storm. It was the only time the All-Star game was not played. The lights went out. I remember Digger Phelps was trying to get all the coaches to line up their cars on the top of the hill and shine their lights on the court so we could have a game. We actually talked about that for about five minutes and then the trainers vetoed it.

"Every time I see him, he reminds of the fact that he never got a chance to play in the All-Star game the summer before his senior year at DeMatha."

Christian Laettner, who graduated from the Tony Nichols School, outside Buffalo, New York, in 1988, followed in Ferry's footsteps.

"He is still in the top 10 of all time in our development league for rising sophomores," Garfinkel said. (One of the other guys in that top 10 is LeBron James.)

"Then he went to Duke. We stayed very friendly. He came back as a counselor. When he was playing in the NBA, I ran into him one day and I said, 'Would you come back and do a lecture at camp?'

"He looked at me and said, 'No.'

"And he said, 'I don't want to do a lecture. I want to come back and coach in the NBA league for a week. And I want to do a station: one-on-one moves.' He came, showed up, did a major lecture, and coached a team. He did it for six years until his wife had a baby."

Garfinkel could see greatness in Grant Hill from South Lakes High in Reston, Virginia, long before the six-foot-eight forward could.

"I remember he used to get down on himself," Garfinkel said. "A lot of times when he didn't play well, I kept telling him, 'You don't know how good you are.'

"I also remember Clark Francis, the guy from the 'Hoop Scoop,' was at our June session and showed me his list of top 30 seniors. And Grant Hill was 27. I said, 'See that name. That name will be in the top 10 by the end of the summer.' Then Francis comes back in August, shows me the list, and Hill is third.

"Hill came back. He did a lecture three years ago. He laid $500 on the table and said, 'If anyone can answer this question, I'll give you this.'

"And the guy answered it. I grabbed the kid afterward, took the money off him, put it in the canteen fund. But Hill has been great. He's done charity work with the Special Olympics and work with child abuse prevention.

"They're all like that. Most of them give back. And one of the reasons is K."

Garfinkel has always prided himself in discovering sleepers. And he was the first one to put the word out on Steve Wojciechowski, a spunky point guard from Cardinal Gibbons in Baltimore, Maryland.

"That was easy," Garfinkel said. "Wojo played for Ray Mullis at Cardinal Gibbons. He was at camp for four years, and he had won all these Mr. Stations awards. He won five of them in eight sessions.

"Then he comes back as a rising senior to our June session in Honesdale. I'm watching him in a game, and I can't believe it. He's playing like a tiger. He's actually even shooting the ball, driving, and diving on the cement.

"Then I see another game, and he does the same thing. And I say to Tom Konchalski (the most prominent scouting guru in the East), 'Tom, you've got to come over; you've got to watch him. Tell me: what am I watching here? Is this kid as good as I think?' And we watch him, and he has another great game. And Tom likes him.

"So I ask the kid where he's thinking about going to school. And he says, 'I'm thinking Ivy League. I like Princeton, but I've got to pay.'

"So I said, 'Well, you're not paying anymore.' I called around, and one of the calls was to Duke and I said to K, 'Watch him at the Nike camp, because I think he's a Duke-level kid.'"

And bingo.

"They watched him play, started recruiting him—and they got him. Otherwise, he goes to Princeton."

When Krzyzewski comes to Five-Star, he makes a point of going to stations to see how a player responds to teaching and how he interacts with his teammates.

That's how he became sold on guard Jason Williams from St. Joseph's of Metuchen in New Jersey.

"Here's how K tells it," Garfinkel said. "We're in St. Louis and there are 1,500 coaches in this room; and he's speaking about player-coach relationships. He gets up and talks for about 45 minutes and then there's the question-and-answer part. I'm sitting on the right-hand side—second row, all the way over to the right—and he's working the other side and the center, so he has no idea I'm there.

"A guy asks a question: 'How do you determine attitude and character? All your kids are great.' And this comes out of his mouth. I couldn't believe it. 'What I do, I go to the Five-Star basketball camp, the best camp in the country. My good friend, Howard Garfinkel, runs it.

"'And I like to watch the stations to see if the kids get involved. This one day I'm there, it's raining. The stations are outdoors and they had to be postponed. So I'm watching the kids play.'"

Garfinkel explained that Krzyzewski got to watch Williams play in one of the greatest games in the history of the camp. His team was down 22 points going into the final quarter and they won. And it was an eight-minute-quarter game.

"Then K says, 'Garfinkel won't end camp until the stations are completed. We got to finish the stations.'

"He's exaggerating," Garfinkel said.

Then he picks up Krzyzewski's version of the story again:

"'They start the last station at 10:30 at night. So I stay around. I want to see Jason Williams. And, sure enough, he's doing the stations. They had a thing at this camp: at the end of the stations, the kids get together and they give a cheer.

"'I wanted to see if Jason was too cool to get into the thing. Sure enough, the station ended. And Jason got involved. That's when I knew I wanted him.'

"So now, the p.s. to the story. K goes on and the guy sitting in front of me has his hand up. He comes walking over to our side and he points to the guy.

"And he says, 'Howard, I didn't know you were here. Stand up. I want a nice round of applause for Howard Garfinkel.'

"I'm sitting there, dying. I'm shaking. I stand up and I wave. As I'm standing up, the guy stands up, too, and he says, 'No. No. Not you. Him.' And he points to me. That's one of the great stories of my life."

Garfinkel invited Krzyzewski to give the guest lecture at his 200th session in Pittsburgh last year. "I wrote this blurb, which I used on this year's brochure. And there are two pictures—one of him shooting, another of him standing up and talking," Garfinkel recalled. "And I wrote this little dig. I knew he wouldn't get mad at me: 'After proving Bobby Knight was right in not letting him shoot at West Point, Mike Krzyzewski of Duke—named 'America's greatest active coach in any sport' in 2001 in a poll conducted by CNN and *Time* magazine and the winner of 12 major coach of the year awards in eight different seasons . . . midseason favorite for No. 13—delivers masterpiece on life on and off the court at historic 200th session July 14, 2004."

Krzyewski's legacy has already been ensured. He has won three national championships. "He's going to be the Olympic coach," Garfinkel said. "That's a no-brainer. And he's going to have the record. Bobby Knight's going to break Dean Smith's record for career victories, and K will stay around and break Knight's record. But I don't think he's in it for records.

"You know, that American Express commercial he does says it all: 'I am not a basketball coach. I am a teacher who happens to coach basketball.'

"No matter what he would have gone into, he would have landed on top, whether he was a corporate executive, priest, coach, announcer. Whatever he did he would have been the best because of his 'F and F' and his brain. He's a brilliant politician. He could be president. Don't laugh.

"I don't see Duke's success story stopping. He's got players again. And he just recruited two more great ones—Josh McRoberts, a six-foot-10 forward from Indiana; and Greg Paulus, the point guard from Christian Brothers in Syracuse, New York.

"You've heard of Y.A. Tittle to Del Shofner and Montana to Rice. You're going to hear Paulus to McRoberts for three years. He'll find him every time."

Garfinkel had Paulus play in one of Five-Star's spring tournaments in 2004 before his junior year.

"He wins the MVP and I'm introducing him," Garfinkel said. "And I say, 'I thought I was looking at a combination of Bobby Cousy and Dick McGuire.'

"He comes up and whispers in my ear, 'Who's Dick McGuire?'"

Garfinkel made a point of introducing Paulus to the Knicks Hall of Fame guard last spring at one of the practices before the Jordan Classic at the Garden.

Krzyzewski has become one of, if not the biggest, celebrities in college basketball. But he is not always the biggest name at Five-Star camp. Three years ago, Krzyzewski was lecturing and he came into the mess hall at 12:30 to eat lunch with Garfinkel and Will Klein and Lee Klein—the camp's other co-owners.

"The kids see him, applaud politely, and there's a buzz," Garfinkel said. "We're having lunch. There's a door out of our sight; and, all of a sudden, there's a huge hubbub there. It's a roar. It's a fight. Something. Kid comes running over. 'Michael's here. Michael's here.' In walks Michael Jordan into the dinning room, looking for his son, Jeffrey, who is a camper.

"And the roof comes off.

"So he comes in, sees his son, comes over, and hugs Coach K.

"I saw a writer a couple of hours later and I say, 'Geez, I'm having lunch with the Pope, and God walked in.'

"It's true."

6

THE OVERLOOKED STAR
MARK ALARIE
Duke Class of 1986

I n the 1980s, geographical boundaries were fast disappearing in the world of college basketball. The high school gym was, at most, a plane ride away from the college arena. And coverage in the national media made the distances seem even shorter.

Everyone knew the hot programs and the up-and-coming prospects. So when a newly minted coach at an ACC school—whose program was on the prospect's wish list—traveled west to visit a would-be recruit, it was a reasonable expectation on his part that the player would call him by his name.

Or was it?

Mark Alarie, six foot eight, who had played for Brophy Prep in Phoenix, Arizona, had no idea how to address Krzyzewski when the Duke coach first visited him.

Alarie remembers that at their initial meeting, "I can tell you from that first recruiting trip—which would have been in 1981—I had no idea how to pronounce his name."

Not too promising a start.

"I wouldn't understand anybody who could look at that name and pronounce it," Alarie said. "You'd have to be from Poland to understand that whole 'zyz' thing.

"And I grew up in the West, in Arizona."

Alarie was an academically gifted student who graduated second in his high school class. His final three schools were Stanford, Duke, and Notre Dame.

Duke Photography

Notre Dame was a personal favorite of his father, who died right before Alarie's high school graduation.

"When my father was alive," Alarie said, "he wanted me to go to Notre Dame. But to be honest, I was never convinced that I was really that good. I had never played against great competition in my state. I had never gone to the national camps. That wasn't part of the status quo at the time.

"I was really a local kid with only local experience playing basketball. The one time I went outside Arizona for a summer invitational tournament in Utah [at BCI], it wasn't like I was tearing it up.

"To be honest, my father had passed away two or three weeks prior to me going up there, and I wasn't really in a great frame of mind.

"I wasn't a super confident kid on the court."

Apparently, Krzyzewski had seen something different in Alarie's level of play—and his attitude—something he liked.

Krzyzewski initially tried to sell Alarie on the idea that distance shouldn't be a factor in Alarie's decision. "It's a plane flight away whether you end up in Palo Alto, South Bend, or Durham," Krzyzewski told him.

But there were pressing concerns why Alarie should stay closer to home. His younger brother Christopher had cerebral palsy, and Alarie knew he had family obligations.

In the end, he agreed to come to Duke because he trusted Krzyzewski.

"He told me, 'If you didn't question your ability, you wouldn't be the player you are today,'" Alarie said. "'I wouldn't be coaching at Duke if I didn't have some of those same questions about myself and my ability to execute. But that's what pushes the envelope. That's what makes a great coach or a great player better.'"

That did it.

"I felt a little bit of a kinship, and I could identify with Coach K and his current situation," Alarie said.

"He convinced me I'd be a very competitive ACC player. I believed him. He'd watched me enough and he was excited about what he'd seen. He's very perceptive and he remembered plays from my high school career that I certainly remembered. There wasn't another coach out there who remembered a specific move I had made in a particular game.

"He told me that he hadn't seen a big man with my kind of footwork. He gave as an example the game he'd watched the night before when I'd cut a guy off at the baseline: then after he'd passed the ball, I was still able to recover and go up for the shot."

"There was no one else giving me the play-by-play of what they'd been impressed with. I just got the feeling that there was something special about Coach K."

So Alarie took a chance—a big chance—and went 2,500 miles away to school.

But not before he had a phone conversation with one of his prospective teammates: "Jay Bilas and I had spoken on the phone before I got to Duke. I had actually gotten Jay confused with Len Bias because their last names were only one letter apart. So I had to make sure who it was. I really knew about Jay only from Street and Smith and all the other scouting publications that were out there then.

"I wasn't sure: Was he the guy from D.C., or was he the guy from L.A.?

"Of course, once I spoke with Jay and saw him play, I knew the difference.

"Talking on the phone with Jay before committing to Duke gave me some confidence that at least I'd be going to school with somebody like-minded. I felt Jay and I had a lot in common."

Although the two freshmen were not roommates their first year, they became fast friends and roomed together for the following three years.

Joining Alarie and Bilas on that team were Johnny Dawkins from Washington, D.C.; Weldon Williams from Chicago, Illinois; David Henderson from Drewry, North Carolina; and Bill Jackman from Nebraska.

They all hit it off—on and off the court.

Krzyzewski had seen that they had great potential as a group. And he was not alone in that assessment. They were heralded as the top recruiting class in the country.

It's very heady to read about yourself and your teammates in recruiting publications. Young players are impressionable and tend to believe what they read. In this case, it worked out well because, as Alarie recalls, "I felt we had a lot of potential because of what other people were saying about us.

"That was a very positive thing."

And Krzyzewski accentuated the positive.

Alarie remembered, "One of first things Coach K said was, 'If you commit to this group, if you are Duke, then you're going to be something great, because Johnny Dawkins is a great player.' Then he talked about Jay, Bill, and Weldon and said, 'We have something great here. And you have a chance to be part of it.'"

And he was right.

But it would take some time.

In the fall of 1982, even before they played their first game at Cameron Indoor Stadium, the freshman members of the Duke squad showed up at Woollen Gym, where the North Carolina Tar Heels played their pick-up games. The Dukies' fame had preceded them because everyone had heard about the great matriculating class at Duke.

Alarie recalled the day: "We're sitting there, holding up the wall, waiting for our chance to play in a pick-up game. We're watching Jordan. We're watching Worthy, who was back getting himself in shape.

"We're watching all the great Carolina players and a lot of their very good pros, playing in this pick-up game. We were particularly focused on Jordan, because even back then, as a rising sophomore, he was just the man, doing incredible things on the basketball court. We're sitting there holding up the wall and then we finally get in the game.

"There were a lot of people watching.

"And they're thinking, 'These are the new guys at Duke. Let's see how they play against Carolina.'

"Well, they just kicked our ass. And Jordan was as good as he was in any NCAA game. He was so much better than anybody else on a pick-up court. He'd take the ball and dunk on the whole team.

"It was intimidating."

For the first time, Alarie had doubts about Duke.

He remembered, "The questions that were running through my mind were: 'Did I really make the right decision? And will we ever win a game against guys like that?' We were really overmatched."

During the regular season, Duke lost both games against North Carolina. And worse was to come.

Among the more memorable moments for the Blue Devils during the 1983 season was their 84-77 defeat by Wagner at home.

Alarie still remembers it, 20-plus years later: "That was the real low point if we were looking at the potential of this group. That was a loss during finals of our freshman year to a school that had no business being on the same court as us. And they beat us on our home court convincingly. It wasn't like a one-point game where they beat us at the buzzer.

"I remember alums and members of the Iron Dukes [a booster club] leaning over the concourse rail and shouting, 'You're out of here, Krzyzewski.'

"That's something I had never really expected to hear. It happened in January. It felt like if we didn't turn things around, Coach K wouldn't be there. And he was the whole reason why we had come; we wanted to play for him. We felt like we were putting his job in jeopardy.

"All those issues started to rise up, at least inside of me."

Krzyzewski stayed on. And the season went on.

The team made some improvement over the course of that season. They were surprisingly competitive against a great Louisville team January 12 at Cameron. They lost 91-76, but there was an eight-minute stretch when K's kids ran with that great Cardinal team that later participated in the now famous dunkathon against Houston in the Final Four. That was a flash the freshmen could play at a very high level. A week later, they beat Maryland, 86-67, in College Park, offering another glimpse into the future.

Then came the game against Virginia in the opening round of the ACC Tournament in Atlanta.

Humiliating is one way to describe it.

"We knew we were a better team," Alarie said. "Although we thought we could win that game, in the first half, we realized we couldn't. We just fell apart in that game."

Thanks, in part, to Ralph Sampson, Virginia beat Duke 109-66. Duke finished seventh in the ACC that year with a 3-11 record. What made it worse was the fact Sampson, the Cavaliers' National Player of the Year, accused Duke of being a dirty team, which set Krzyzewski off.

Krzyzewski was now 0-7 against the Cavaliers. But that would change.

A good leader learns as much from defeats as he does from victories. And Krzyzewski is a very good leader. And an excellent motivator.

According to Alarie, Krzyzewski used that loss to Virginia as "a motivator going into our sophomore, junior, and senior years. Virginia had a horrible record against us after that. We never lost to them again while I was there.

"I think Duke has a better than 90-percent winning percentage against them now."

But that loss has stayed with Alarie, as Coach K figured it would.

"I remember the bad things probably better than the good things," Alarie admitted. "I've always been that way as a person. I don't know if this is good or bad; but I respond to negative stimuli better than to positive. Coach K found this out about me. I won't say he abused that fact but he understood that's what made me tick.

"Mentioning that I had a really substandard performance or that so-and-so had kicked my ass: those were the kinds of things that really got under my skin and stayed with me. To this day.

"He also knew that it did not work with Johnny. But it worked with Jay, so Jay and I spent a lot of time feeling like we were being singled out. Coach K knows what buttons to push for each guy."

And push he did.

"I remember one game we lost to N.C. State my junior year," Alarie said. "I had made first-team All-ACC as a sophomore, and I was becoming maybe a little content with myself.

"When we got back from Raleigh at about 11 o'clock, he called a team meeting in the locker room. He had a picture of me there, grabbing for a loose ball. He took the picture and threw it down, as hard as he could. Glass flew everywhere. He took the picture and ripped it up, threw out a lot of expletives and said of the picture of me hustling, 'This is no longer true.' He knew how to push my buttons.

"I responded to that very well. That was the only time in four years that he exploded on me, but I always knew there was a possibility it could happen again."

All in all, Alarie considers that "This is a managerial gift. A good leader knows how to motivate."

And he doesn't exempt himself.

Alarie felt that "Coach K used different events in his life to motivate him. Sometimes it's hard to motivate yourself when things are going well. But I can guarantee that for years that ACC loss to Virginia kept him up a few extra hours preparing for Virginia and motivating his team."

The 1984 season was to be pivotal at Duke, but it did not begin auspiciously. The Blue Devils were 14-1 at the start of ACC play. They had played one league game—a win over Virginia. Then they lost three league games in a row. And Krzyzewski was called into Butters's office.

When the team learned that Coach K had gotten a five-year contract extension, it took some of the pressure off them and gave them a boost of confidence, even though they lost another league game that night—to N.C. State—and fell to 1-4 in the ACC.

And once again, they lost their two regular-season games with North Carolina, including one that went to double overtime at Chapel Hill.

But the Blue Devils finished the season 7-7 in league play and scored an upset 77-75 victory over North Carolina in overtime in the second round of the ACC Tournament.

It was a long-anticipated, well-earned victory.

The Duke team had a great feeling about the game, and Alarie recalled that Coach K was very excited before they started to play.

"I remember being in the huddle," Alarie said, "and Coach K said, 'Okay, when we beat these guys, let's pretend like we've been there before.'

"He told us to be calm, because we were going to win."

And they did. The Dukies were able to execute and so beat the No. 1-ranked team in the country.

"The horn sounded," continued Alarie, "and I'm thinking, as excited as we are, let's pretend that we've been there before. And then I look over at Coach K—and he's jumping all around like a little kid.

"We all went crazy after that. It was true vindication after having lost a double-overtime game."

When is a game more than a game?

When it's a harbinger of things to come.

Even though Duke lost the ACC Tournament championship game to Maryland, the Blue Devils had made their presence known in the league that year.

"I really think that was one of the critical wins in my career," Alarie stated. "And, by law of transference, I think it was one of the critical wins in Coach K's career. That win really built the foundation for going forward. It showed that Duke would be able to compete with Carolina and that the old guard might be crumbling."

But nobody guessed how quickly.

And their season hadn't ended just yet. They were playing in the NCAA Tournament.

Even though they lost in the second round to the University of Washington, the team had started on its path.

And when Alarie and his teammates were seniors, in the 1985-1986 season, they finished their journey—in Dallas at the Final Four.

Prior to that NCAA Tournament, the Dukies had only two defeats in the regular season—unfortunately, in back-to-back losses to North Carolina and Georgia Tech.

And they had to play their last game at Cameron Indoor Stadium.

It would be intense.

It was with North Carolina.

Alarie remembered, "The last game in Cameron as a senior was with Carolina. I couldn't reconcile myself to the idea of losing that game. I couldn't imagine what that would have meant. I don't think I could have lived with myself if we had lost.

"Good thing we won."

They were on a roll. They were the ACC champions. They had won 37 games, including a victory over the No. 2-ranked team, Kansas, in the semifinals of the Final Four.

So it's understandable that they thought they were going to win it all.

But Louisville had a different agenda.

And it prevailed.

"We thought the Kansas game was the national championship," Alarie said. "Not to downplay the Louisville game—but 1 versus 2 were playing Saturday and Louisville played LSU, an 11th seed.

"I can make all the excuses in the world, but they were better that night. We shot 34 percent to their 59 percent, and it went down to the last possession. We did everything but make shots."

But they had made it to the Final Four. And finished the year 37-3.

As for Coach K, Alarie said, "I think it was validation that his system worked. All along, I've thought that great organizations and great people are very simple. There's beauty in the simplicity of a model or of the values a person lives by.

"And I think the beauty of us having the season we had was that it validated the core of what Coach K believed in, which is: 'Look, we're never playing zone, guys. I don't care how badly Virginia's beating us. We'll still play man to man, because that's what's going to bring us a championship ultimately. So take your ass-kicking now, guys, and figure out how to be a good defensive player, because that's what we're all about.'

"On the offensive end, we didn't have plays. We were expected to learn the ropes as freshmen and sophomores: learn to run the offense; understand what your teammates' strengths and weaknesses are; get them the ball when they need to get it. We didn't run sets, except very sparingly. Ninety percent of the time, we were just running motion.

"And we were able to take those simple concepts he had learned playing under Knight and coaching with Knight and incorporate them in our playing.

"That model works if you get the right people in the system."

Obviously, Coach K has.

That appearance in the NCAA Tournament gave Coach K a lot of confidence to continue to have faith in those core beliefs, Alarie thinks. Especially his belief in man-to-man defense.

And history hasn't proven him wrong.

They were the highest-scoring class in Duke's history and believed to be the highest-scoring class in NCAA history.

No wonder the late Jim Valvano said of them, "They will go down as the greatest not-great team ever.'

And deservedly so.

Looking back at that time, though, Alarie remembered more than the points scored and the games won.

"We all felt like we were part of a family and part of something bigger than ourselves. Earlier on, it was harder to look at the Duke situation and say that. We were, but it wasn't necessarily anything to be proud of.

"That's what changed. The foundation was built. And what Coach K stood for meant something. It was easy to see. You could just watch our team play, look at the makeup of the individuals and the coach who was teaching them. It was very easy to identify with. It was the platform everything else was launched from.

"I think we're always shocked. There was just no way to know that it could become what it's become.

"Now I say that I was a young, naïve man when I made this decision. I was a boy. It's an easy decision now. But then, not only was I a boy, it was also impossible to look at Coach K's track record.

"He was an average player at West Point, although I think that Bobby Knight had a very high regard for him. His track record as a coach was mediocre.

"But the one insight we as players had of Coach K was that he was very passionate. Also, we thought he was a very sincere person.

"Obviously, he was the man."

After he graduated from Duke, Mark Alarie played one year with the Denver Nuggets and five years with the Washington Bullets.

He also coached one season at the U.S. Naval Academy with Don DeVoe.

"I never had a basketball experience like I had at Duke in the NBA," he said. "Not that I would have expected to, because you cannot replicate in the NBA what my experience was in college. I suppose it would have been possible if I had played on a championship team.

"But it was lucrative and a dream come true to be playing professional basketball, even though it was hard to lose the way we did in Denver and Washington.

"It was very unfulfilling relative to my college experience."

Alarie earned his MBA from the Wharton School of the University of Pennsylvania in 1995. He had majored in economics while at Duke.

He thought it would be fun to work on Wall Street after he finished playing basketball. Currently, he is a partner in Crosshill, a financial investment firm in Washington, D.C.

And he's still using the lessons he learned from Coach K.

"We interview a lot of management of technology companies; and at the end of the day, the investments we make are really bets on people. And I learned a lot of people skills from Coach K," he said.

He and his wife, Rene, have three children: six-year-old Isabella; three-year-old Christian; and an infant, Alexander. Alarie says that Christian is not named after Laettner. But it's okay if people think so, because "if he becomes half the player Laettner was, I'd be a happy father."

Wonder where he'll apply to school?

From the beginning, Alarie could tell that Coach K understood the game.

"There was such a passion with him. You love to be around him if you love the game of basketball. It's his life. He may not be the funniest guy in world. He may not be the kind of guy you want to have a beer with.

"But if you want to pick a head coach, he embodies that."

7

THE PRIDE OF DREWRY, NORTH CAROLINA

DAVID HENDERSON

Duke Class of 1986

D avid Henderson has been the head coach at the University of Delaware since 2000. But he showed up at his office in the Carpenter Center in the winter of 2004-2005 wearing a blue and gray Duke sweatshirt.

Some habits are hard to change.

Henderson was the last player to sign in Mike Krzyzewski's first big recruiting class that laid the foundation for Duke to become one of the elite programs in the country. He still keeps in touch with Johnny Dawkins, Jay Bilas, Mark Alarie, and Weldon Williams, who is now a minister in Collegeville, Pennsylvania.

"The most remarkable thing to me is we were able to create friendships and bonds that have lasted and, hey, will last a lifetime," Henderson said. "We still play golf every summer. We had a match down at Congressional last summer, and Johnny and I beat Jay and Mark. They were kind of upset about that."

Henderson is a small-town kid from Drewry, North Carolina, who made it big: a six-foot-six forward who scored 1,570 points during his career and was the co-captain of the team that won the ACC Tournament and reached the national championship game in 1986, his senior year.

He just never envisioned it would work out this way.

Growing up, Henderson was a huge North Carolina State fan. As a kid, he idolized David Thompson and dreamed of playing for the Wolfpack.

"I used to follow David and I loved him. In my area, you were either for N.C. State or Carolina."

Photo courtesy of University of Delaware Photo Services

Those were big dreams for a kid from an economically disadvantaged mill town of less than 300 inhabitants, located near the Virginia border. When he was growing up, his family home was on a dirt path, off the town's main road; Warren County was ranked among the lowest of North Carolina counties in terms of per capita income.

But there was an upside.

"You get into the South, you got all these small communities," he said. "There were 15,000 in the county. It was very family-oriented, a real community. When people say it takes a village to raise a child, I lived that. I knew everybody."

And everybody knew him.

Henderson is the third of four children, and the youngest son, born to Harold and Cassie Henderson. His father worked construction. To help his family financially, David Henderson drove a school bus during the academic year. During the summers, he and his two brothers had odd jobs.

But he still found time to play basketball.

Soul City, where he played his summer hoops, was a federally funded magnet community that was started to attract minority investment that never materialized. It was three and a half miles from his home. He would bike there, play, and bike back.

Henderson also found time for academics.

He was almost a straight-A student at Warren County High School, and he held a position on the student council. He also did volunteer work with the Special Olympics.

Henderson led Warren County High to the 3-A state championship. He averaged 26.9 points and 11 rebounds a game.

He was the first person in his family to attend college, although his brother, Marvin, had been offered a football scholarship to Guilford College.

Duke had recruited Henderson before Bill Foster left for South Carolina and Krzyzewski, who discovered him during his junior year in high school, picked up the process.

"I wasn't really in a hurry about making a quick decision, because I felt confident in who I was and what I was doing," Henderson recalled. "I knew we had a team that could win the state championship, so I wanted to concentrate on my senior year with my teammates. And we did win the state championship.

"Duke knew I was going to sign late.

"But they kept recruiting me.

"My mom said she felt very, very comfortable with Krzyzewski," Henderson recalled. "She said, 'I really like him.'

"There was something about the way Coach K delivered during the home visit. He spoke with great confidence, even though the program wasn't there. But you could feel that he knew what he was doing and he knew where he wanted to go.

"He talked about the fact he was building something special. I never forgot that statement. Then he asked me, 'Do you want to be a part of it?'

"His insight was amazing, because when you look at what's transpired since then, it was truly something special.

"One of the other things that really sold me was when I went to a game on my visit. Duke was playing Wake Forest. And you could see Coach's intensity and his passion for his players.

"Carl Tacy was coaching Wake. I was sitting in the stands watching. Tacy bumped Chip Engelland. And Coach K went livid. He was like, 'How dare you.' That was one of his players. He was fired up. And I thought, 'That's the guy.'"

Some people in Henderson's community had doubts. North Carolina was the state university and had mass appeal. It also had 25,000 students. Duke was a private school with a population of 6,000 and had a preppy reputation for kids from the Northeast corridor.

"They were like, 'You're going to Duke?' Duke was kind of an outside place for North Carolina folks. They were like, 'How are you going to deal with those wealthy people, with kids from that background?'

"I was like, 'I fit in wherever I am.' That's what I always believed. I wanted to be in an environment where every athlete is faced with what I'm faced with, academically and athletically."

Duke actually got lucky with Henderson.

Krzyzewski's primary recruiting target at that position that year was Curtis Hunter, a McDonald's All-American from Durham. Krzyzewski was recruiting Henderson, too, but wanted him to attend prep school for a year so he could be part of Duke's next recruiting class.

Ironically, Henderson clearly outplayed Hunter in the state semifinals that year at the Greensboro Coliseum, which is where Jim Valvano of North Carolina first saw him.

When Hunter chose North Carolina and Krzyzewski discovered that Valvano was ready to offer Henderson a scholarship, he changed his timetable and made an offer to Henderson, who committed.

Henderson quickly discovered he was not the only star in the gym.

"I remember meeting Johnny Dawkins the first time. He was this little, scrawny guy. I thought, 'Wow, this is the guy they were talking about?'

"This is a true story. I'm down at the other end of the gym, and he started jumping up and grabbing the rim. And I said, 'Lord.' I walked down, shook hands, and said to myself that this guy can really jump.

"What a terrific competitor. He was very driven. He always wanted to win. He had this side to him. Johnny wasn't as social as the rest of us. He always kind of stayed back.

"We'd be walking, and he'd ask me, 'Why do you speak to all those people?'

"I said, 'It's like that in North Carolina. We always speak to people.'

"He couldn't fathom that."

All six freshmen came in with great reputations. But there was a transitional period in the ACC. When Duke first traveled to North Carolina, the Tar Heels blistered the Devils 103-82 in Carmichael.

Henderson remembers almost committing assault and battery on one of his teammates on the bus trip home.

"I was upset at Bill Jackman, one of our freshmen, who was from a small town in Nebraska. The guy was from Duke—and he was looking to get Michael Jordan's autograph. We were like, 'Uh, uh, that's not happening.' We were not about that. We were competitive. We were winners.

"We didn't care who it was."

Jackman eventually transferred home to the University of Nebraska. But the survivors of that massacre got a measure of revenge a year later when they stunned North Carolina 77-75 in the 1984 ACC semifinals.

"For me, a kid growing up in North Carolina, that win was more important to me than to any other kid on that team, because I truly understood the Carolina-Duke-Wake-State rivalry," Henderson recalled.

So did Krzyzewski.

"There was a standard in the league that had been set by Dean Smith. If you wanted to be great at your trade, you had to reach that standard. So Coach K started to work in that direction, and he never looked back.

"Dean was sitting there. And all these other guys were looking to knock him off," Henderson said.

"Now, Coach K is that guy. He's everybody's big game. Everybody's looking to knock him off."

Krzyzewski, drawing from his military background, pushed his players hard from the start.

"For me, freshman year was the most difficult," Henderson recalled. "Before that, I had never really lost. I was 17. Each of us came from winning programs, so it wasn't like he had to sell us on winning. He just had to teach us how to win at that level.

"We had it. He just had to enhance it. I think that's why we were able to come together so quickly.

"Sometimes, today, when you coach, you push a kid—and it's like fighting him tooth and nail, because he's never worked that hard. We embraced it right away. There was no resistance. It was like, 'Keep giving it; we can take more.'

"He kept pushing. He kept giving it. And you could see it developing. We grew up. We got our heads beat in as babies. Then those babies became men.

"It's almost like being a songwriter. When you want to write, you want to write from your gut. When you experience more pain, then you become a better writer. When you experience great adversity, then you become a better coach or a better player.

"I think his greatest trait is that he's able to persevere in any situation. I think he has great flexibility. He's constantly making adjustments to fit his personnel. I think that is so insightful in a coach, because you can run a system and feel so good about your system that you try to fit your players into that system.

"He taught me how important it is to coach your best players. A lot of people just let their best players play and don't coach them. But you've got to coach them, too, because they need it.

"It's all connected to the team. That goes back to his sense of detail. I think that's why he's been able to have the run he's had. And I think that's why players love playing for him: he coaches everybody the way they need to be coached. You can't coach this guy the same way you coach that guy, because they're in different places. But when you're talking about the team, it's all the same thing. And I think players understand it."

When the class of 1986 were freshmen, Krzyzewski was being criticized for his refusal to play any zone. He only played man to man because he was using that to teach his system to a young team. By the time they were seniors, Krzyzewski still preferred the idea of playing man to man but would play a little zone when it was warranted.

"He had his vision," Henderson said. "We had to be committed to something. We were going to win with team defense. We stayed with it, and we learned how to help one other. People talk about individual play, but we had tremendous team defense and rotation, communication. We spoke each other's language; that's why we were so much in synch. That's why teams that may have been more talented couldn't beat us because we were a better team."

Duke was the most experienced team in the country in 1986, Henderson's final year, with four seniors and a junior in the starting lineup. They were also the most balanced.

"Dawkins scored over 2,500 points—and we didn't have a three-point line," Henderson said. Most of the time, anyway. The ACC actually experimented with a 19-foot three-point line for conference games in 1983 when Henderson was a freshman. Dawkins hit 19 of 54, and Henderson hit nine for 33. The line was dropped next year and not reinstated until the NCAA adopted the modern three-point line in 1987.

"It was a sharing experience," Henderson said. "We shared the ball. Johnny scored a lot of points, but nobody cared, because it was about winning.

"We made plays for one another, and everybody was efficient. We were all good players. We came from good programs, and we all knew how to play. We were able to fit into different roles and still, at times, shine bright. On any given night, it would be a different guy. That's what made it so good. We knew how to play off each other."

Henderson made his own sacrifices. He started at guard as a freshman before moving to sixth man for the next two years. He moved back into the lineup as a starting small forward his senior year.

"I could really score coming out of high school," he said. "What happened was Johnny was our best outside player. My ego didn't suffer, because I knew he was a better perimeter scorer than I was. Mark was a better interior scorer than I was. So I'm looking at myself and I'm saying, 'How do I fit into this puzzle?'

"I learned my role from Coach K just by listening. He told us when teams are planning to stop you, they're looking to stop your best players. So I said, 'Hey, they're going to try to stop Mark inside and Johnny on the outside. There's a spot for a guy who understands this stuff.' I accepted it right away and said, 'There's a spot for a third wheel to take advantage of this thing.'"

Henderson had a knack for coming up big in critical situations. He came into his own as a senior, winning the MVP of the preseason NIT and scoring 27 points when Duke defeated Carolina 84-72 in the last game of the 1986 regular season. That clinched the Dukies' first outright ACC championship in 20 years. This was a season in which North Carolina, Georgia Tech, and Duke took turns being No. 1.

Then he took the game over down the stretch when the Devils defeated Virginia 75-70 in the semifinals of the ACC Tournament that year and gave Duke the momentum it needed to win that title.

"It was a dream season," Henderson said.

Duke won its first 17 games before losing to North Carolina and Georgia Tech on the road; then won 19 more, entering the NCAA championship game against Louisville with a 37-2 record.

Henderson thinks, "If we'd have won that game, people would have been talking about us as one of the great teams of all time."

But it didn't happen.

Louisville freshman center Pervis Ellison put an end to Duke's dream, scoring 25 points during a 72-67 victory in the finals in Dallas. The Blue Devils, who shot just 40 percent, had no legs down the stretch and couldn't protect a narrow lead late.

"I still can play it through in my head," Henderson said. "As an athlete and competitor, I always think about what I could have done to make the outcome different. I look at different plays. I always criticize myself, because I'm a winner. And I missed a shot late in the game right at the basket. Pervis Ellison had rotated over—and he had those long arms—and I shot it a little bit high to get it over him. I missed it. I made a strong move baseline. We were down 66-65 at the time. I believed I could make a play. I was never afraid to be that guy. And when I didn't make it, it's stuck with me.

"It hurt. We had learned so much from Coach K about how to handle close games. I didn't believe we felt we'd lose. We played games believing we were going to win, no matter what was going on in the course of the game."

In retrospect, this was still a beloved team at Duke, much like the 1978 and 1994 teams.

"When people talk about the class of 1986, they talk about Coach K's impact on the university, because one of the things we had was a real connection with the people around the program," Henderson said.

"We were very approachable, very articulate, interactive. I think people felt a real bond with us. I think my class received the most attention as a group, and I think that gives Coach K a good feeling because of where the program had been and where it had come from.

"Coach K still tells us how much he learned from us. That's a great feeling, because as 18-, 19-year-old kids, you don't think you're soaking up everything he gives you. But then down the road, he sits down and talks to you as an adult and says, 'I learned a lot from you guys, too. Going through that time period, being able to say I'm a better coach than I was and if I was coaching you guys now, who knows what things we would have achieved.'

"I know for a lot of people on the outside, when Coach K talks about his family—especially the Duke haters—they'll say, 'I bet that family's not that close.' But it's real. I was 17 years old. I'm 41 now. That man has been part of my life for that long. It's been a positive thing, and you can't shake that."

Henderson played professional basketball in the NBA, CBA, Europe, and Asia over the 10 years after graduation. He always told himself he would never coach. But all that changed when he got back to the states from Turkey in 1996.

"I didn't have the passion for playing, but I still loved the game. So after taking a year off, I still felt a strong urge to be around it. I started to think about how do you impact the game now? Well, coaching.

"Then I started looking at it from another standpoint: dealing with young people. You see, in a lot of programs, kids are not managed the right way. It's unfortunate, because they need that guidance at that time. I had gotten such great guidance from Coach K. And I felt I could give some of that to some young guys. I felt I could have an impact on another young person's life so that down the road I could make a huge difference. It was just something I couldn't pass up."

Henderson broke into the profession as a Duke assistant in 1997.

"The timing was unbelievable," he said, "because Tommy Amaker was leaving at the time to take over at Seton Hall, and Tim O'Toole left for Fairfield. So Johnny Dawkins and I came in the same year as assistants.

"We laugh about it now. We came in the same year; now we re-committed to the same school. It was really something for the two of us, being best friends during that time."

They arrived at a time when Krzyzewski, who had missed most of the 1995 season with a physical breakdown, was trying to re-energize the program on a national level. "Coach K was just going full throttle, full throttle, when he came back," Henderson said. "It meant as much to him as it did to us, because we were his first guys. Everything he was about, we were about."

By the time Henderson left to go to Delaware, the Blue Devils were back on top of the NCAA and had made another trip to the national championship game in 1999. "I never imagined the program would be where it is at this point," Henderson admitted.

"I knew his passion for the game; that he loved what he did. He was very committed. He was driven so much. And he never took the time to enjoy what happened in the past, because there was more in the future. I just think you can be driven to a fault because sometimes your great strength can become your greatest weakness. But without that, he doesn't become who he is.

"I always say he is true to the game, to everything involved in it. He is true to college basketball, true to his athletes, true to his family. When you look at where his convictions are, you say that though some people are wooed by the almighty dollar, it's always about the game for him.

"Money is not the motivating factor in his life. People matter to him."

8

THE QUARTERBACK
TOMMY AMAKER
Duke Class of 1989

Tommy Amaker was the final piece of the puzzle for a near-perfect Duke team that reached the NCAA championship game in 1986.

He was recruited by Mike Krzyzewski in 1983 as a point guard and wound up being the perfect complement to high-scoring All-America Johnny Dawkins.

Their relationship on the court gave Duke its finest backcourt ever.

But then again, Amaker was all about relationships. That's why he chose Duke in the first place.

When Amaker—who is now the head coach at Michigan—was growing up, his mother was a teacher in the Fairfax, Virginia, school system, so he had the option of attending any public school in Northern Virginia because of her job status.

Amaker wanted to play for the legendary Red Jenkins at W.T. Woodson, who developed him into one of the best point guard prospects on the East Coast during the four years he coached him on varsity. Amaker also played AAU ball for Reginald Kitchen.

He trusted both men.

"I had had great coaches from the time I was in Little League," Amaker recalled. "In high school, you hear about big-time college sports, and it's a business. I am always very leery. I knew I wanted to play at a place for a coach I really believed in and had a relationship with.

"This was a guy who started recruiting me."

Duke Photography

Krzyzcwski first saw Amaker play with his high school team in the high-powered Jeleph summer league in Washington, D.C. He was actually there to watch Johnny Dawkins, a sensational talent from Mackin High School.

"I played in the next game," Amaker said. "My AAU coach was at the game and he said, 'Hey, you're the coach of Duke. Who you here to see?'

"Coach Krzyzewski told him, 'I'm watching Dawkins.'

"So he said, 'You might want to check out the next game. There's a guy playing the next game who's just as good, in his own way.'

"Krzyzewski told him, 'No, I've got to catch a plane.' But he started to watch the game a little. And I guess he cancelled his flight and kept watching me play.

"He always tells this story and he always prefaces it by saying, 'At this time, you could talk to kids.' He said he went up to my mom—this is a true story—and said, 'Your son is going to look great in Duke blue.'

"From there, he felt I was a guy he really wanted to recruit. And he really recruited me. I always felt comfortable with him. He made it known I was a guy he wanted."

Dawkins was a year ahead of Amaker in high school. When he committed, there were some questions about how the two would blend in. "Everybody said, 'No, you can't go to Duke because he's there,'" Amaker said. "We were small guys, small guards. He was the only one who ever said, 'My feeling about it is you guys are going to play together.'

"No one had ever said that."

Amaker got to know Krzyzewski when he was just 15 years old. "He really put in the time with me," Amaker said. "He would come to my games, come to the school. We developed a relationship, and I played under his guidance from that time until I went with him. I've known him and his family half my life.

"He was a guy I believed in. It wasn't fashionable to believe in the whole Duke situation at the time. The year before I got there, they were 11-17. So it wasn't like you see it now.

"I always felt I made my decision based on people; more specifically, I made a decision based on him. I say this now: I believed in him then; I swear by him now."

Amaker got Jenkins's approval the night Krzyzewski made his home visit.

"When coaches would come in, we would do those visits at the coach's house and we'd sit around in the coach's kitchen afterward and talk about the presentation: 'What did you think? Do you like this guy?' And you'd give your impressions about the visit and the coach.

"We were getting something to drink out of the refrigerator, and Red turned around to me and said, 'You know, Tommy, I'm just going to tell you, I got a good feeling about this guy.'

"I always tease him about that now. I say, 'You had a great feeling about that. I wish you'd tell me about something in Vegas. We could all go ahead and retire.' He felt this was a really good guy, he was going to make it happen, he was relentless. He said, 'This could be the guy for you.'"

Amaker chose Duke over Virginia, Wake Forest, and Maryland. As it turned out, it was the perfect choice. Amaker was a four-year starter who played on four straight NCAA teams, made All-American and was selected National Defensive Player of the Year his senior season in 1987.

More importantly, he allowed Dawkins to shift from the point to a more comfortable shooting guard position, where Dawkins flourished.

"I knew Johnny before I got there," Amaker said. "We first met at the University of Maryland basketball camp in sixth, seventh grade. We kind of knew each other, and then we went our separate ways. I always followed him in high school because he was one of the best players in the nation by the time he was in his senior year in high school.

"But it wasn't like we were close. The guy I grew up with in terms of playing together was Michael Jackson from South Lakes, who played at Georgetown. He was in the same class at Johnny.

"I think, for the most part, Johnny was a natural scorer. He scored over 2,500 points in his career. He could flat out put it in the hole. To me, his style, the way he played, I thought he was Allen Iverson before Allen Iverson. That wasn't necessarily fashionable or acceptable at that time for a guy his size to be that type of scorer.

"But he was a freak of nature in terms of his ability to score. People don't realize how great an athlete he was. He could jump out of the gym. We'd throw alley-oops to him. He was the guy we put it up to more than anyone else on our team.

"That's what Coach K saw. That guy really needed to have the freedom to do his thing and not worry about quarterbacking or running a team or setting things up. He needed to be set up. I cherished that role, to be that guy who could help him score. We needed him to put it in the hole. And, boy, could he ever."

Amaker fit right in with the young stars on Krzyzewski's team.

"We had some nice pieces to the puzzle when I arrived," Amaker said. "We had Dawkins and Mark Alarie and Jay Bilas in their second year. They had really gone through some tough times. They welcomed me in. And I loved playing for Coach K, because I knew, deep down, it didn't matter what anybody else said. Deep down, I knew he really appreciated me.

"Players need to know Coach believes in you. That's a special quality of leaders. They make everybody feel important and appreciated. I know he made me feel that way, and I'm sure if you ask the other players, they'll tell you the same thing. I always felt he was a great communicator. You might not have liked your role, but you always knew where you stood with him.

Amaker also discovered how important family was in Krzyzewski's life.

"They were invested in it as much as the players," Amaker said. "As a matter of fact, Mickie's dad—who just passed away this fall—would come with Krzyzewski to watch me play in high school. She's from the Alexandria area. He would pick up Coach K at the airport, and both of them would come to my games.

"And I'll always remember the kids coming in on Halloween, bringing little bags of candy for everyone on the team. They had their costumes on, ready to go trick or treating, but they'd stop by practice to give everybody on the team candy."

Krzyzewski finally began to turn the program around during Amaker's freshman year in 1984. The Blue Devils finally beat North Carolina, won 24 games, and reached the NCAA Tournament.

"Honestly, when I look back, I think I look at things a little differently," Amaker said. "I think back to two games: Vanderbilt and Virginia."

Duke defeated Vanderbilt 78-74 in Amaker's first game.

"I think that was such a monumental win for us," he said. "I don't think I realized it at that time, as a 19-year-old freshman. Vanderbilt was a good SEC team with a strong academic reputation, much like Duke, and was coached by C.M. Newton.

"Any time you're starting out and you have a pretty young team and a freshman point guard, you're trying to gain confidence and gain an identity. Looking back on it, maybe if we'd dropped that game, we'd have lost confidence and things might have gone in a different direction.

"Anyway, I made a couple of free throws late in the game to help keep us ahead. I remember Coach K coming into the locker room and he was drenched with perspiration. Typically, all the media were around Dawkins asking questions. He comes up to me—and he's got this little smile on his face—and he said, 'I told you I'd make you a star.'

"Then he just walked off."

The other game Amaker remembers was Duke's 78-72 victory at Virginia, the same team that had beaten the Blue Devils by 46 the previous season in the first round of the ACC Tournament.

"It was our first ACC road game," Amaker said. "That was a big game for me personally, being from the state of Virginia, and I had looked at going to school there. I remember going against Othell Wilson, Rick Carlisle, and Ricky Stokes. That was their guard line. Three seniors—and I'm a freshman.

"The opening tap, they come up with the ball. They had something set up. First play they run, I'm guarding Othell Wilson up top and he passes to the wing. And the next thing I know, I get banged on a back pick, and then as I'm turning and looking, I see Wilson going up in the air for an alley-oop dunk. That was my introduction to ACC basketball.

"The crowd was going crazy. I'm waiting for the ball to be inbounded and being a typical freshman, I'm not paying attention, not seeing the whole floor. I received the ball on the inbound pass, and Ricky Stokes comes running at me. I'm trying to do three things at once—and I shuffle my feet. The crowd goes crazy, a whistle blows, and it's a travel.

"I was like, 'Maybe I'm in the wrong place.'"

I remember Krzyzewski pointing his finger and motioning me to come over. He said, 'Look, get the ball, and go by him.' That's all he said to me. That calmed me down, gave me confidence. From there, we went on to win. That gave us the confidence to compete successfully in our conference as a young team."

By Amaker's junior year, the Blue Devils were ready to establish themselves as national contenders. They won 21 straight games en route to the national championship game against Louisville.

"Coach just wanted to make sure we had fun," Amaker said. "I'll tell you another story. He had coach [Bob] Knight come speak to our team the day before the championship game. I'll never forget it.

"Coach K came and said, 'Guys, everybody sit down on the bench. I've asked a special person in my life to speak to you about what it means to play in the national championship game.'

"So we all sat down—and in walks Coach Knight.

"His presence is still amazing. You can't take your eyes off him when he's around. He walks onto the floor; he paces up and down in front of us. It seemed like forever. It was like time stopped. Eyes were popping open, and everybody was waiting to hear what he had to say.

"'I've watched you guys in the semifinals against Kansas and I wanted to just say...' Then he stopped in front of me. I was sitting next to Johnny, and he grabbed my arm. And he continued, 'I thought you guys played tight,' and he squeezed my arm.

"'Then,' he said, 'you guys started to play like this.' And he kind of gingerly held my arm and moved his arm up and down softly. So he made his point about being tight and relaxed.

"And I'm terrified. I'll always remember how meaningful it was to me to hear him say a few words, the impact of listening to a great coach."

The next night, Duke ran out of gas against Louisville. "We ran into a kid who played the game of his life—Pervis Ellison," Amaker said. "But I thought that was still a monumental achievement, that we were able to make that run, to win the regular season, the ACC Tournament, and then go to Final Four.

"It was almost like we were supposed to win it all. We lost by three. It was a gut-wrenching loss, but I thought it put Coach K in position for his career to skyrocket.

"In all honesty, the next year was almost as important as my freshman year in terms of whether we were going to keep this thing going or improve it."

Duke won 24 games and reached the Sweet 16 that year with a relatively inexperienced team. Amaker was the lone starter. Krzyzewski also had Billy King and Danny Ferry, who was just coming into his own.

"No one thought we were going to be that much. I thought that was when Coach K really showed his greatness as a coach, because he was able to retool, revamp, tweak, and elevate the players he had."

Krzyzewski asked Amaker to be a little more offensive-minded. "That was never truly my game," he said. "I don't know what I averaged—12, 13 points— my senior year. I just know, going to the Sweet 16 that year equated to the Vanderbilt, Virginia wins my freshman year."

After graduation, Amaker tried out for, but was cut by, the Seattle SuperSonics. He returned to campus, became an intern in the athletic program, took classes for his master's degree, and then joined the staff as a graduate assistant in 1989. He moved up to full-time assistant the next year.

"I'll never forget when he offered me the job," Amaker said. "I said, 'Thanks.' And he said, 'All right. One of the first things you've got to do is get yourself up to Washington, D.C. We've got to get Grant Hill.'

"Grant wound up at Duke, but it wasn't because of me. I went to see him because we were from the same area. But certain kids are the right fit for the school and the coach.

"His parents were so worldly, so organized. He had taken all his visits by the spring of his junior year. They were so advanced in knowing what they wanted, so they weren't wasting time."

Amaker did not know if he wanted to be a full-time coach, but he caught the bug from being around Krzyzewski. "I loved the fact he was a great teacher," Amaker said. "My mom was a teacher. I viewed that as a chance to have an impact on kids' lives. I know how he impacted mine, and coaching gave me a chance to be a part of that. I think he cherishes that now even more, seeing what guys are doing with their lives and families."

Amaker got his first head-coaching job at Seton Hall in 1998. He has since moved on to Michigan. "I'll always remember him telling me about being a head coach. Before I got to the press conference, he said, 'Listen, just be yourself.' That was it.

"I watched the movie *Ray* recently. I love watching fact-based movies and documentaries. It's real, not like you're making it up, like you had a script and a book and everyone wants to make it into a movie, make it into a play.

"To have something based on what is true touches you. I'm telling you what was in my heart and what I was thinking when he said it."

9

THE MINISTER OF DEFENSE

BILLY KING

Duke Class of 1988

B illy King has been the president and general manager of the Philadelphia 76ers for the past seven years, but local sports fans still ask him about the 1988 NCAA Eastern Regional finals between his alma mater, Duke, and Temple University.

That's how King first made his reputation in that town.

The Owls, an Atlantic 10 commuter school located in North Philadelphia, were 32-1 and ranked No. 1 in the country by the AP that year and looked like they were on the verge of making their first trip to the Final Four since 1958.

But King helped pull the plug on that idea when the six-foot-six senior forward turned Temple freshman star Mark Macon, a six-foot-five guard who was a consensus All-American, into an invisible man during a 63-53 victory at the Meadowlands in East Rutherford, New Jersey.

Macon had been unstoppable all season, but King completely took him out of the game, limiting him to six-for-29 shooting and only 13 points. Macon shot six air balls, made just one of 13 three-pointers, and Temple's halfcourt offense was never able to get into synch.

"I still hear about it in Philly all the time," King admitted. "It's time to let it go. It's been a lot of years.

"Coach K really didn't say anything. I knew I was going to have Macon. Everybody else knew I was going to have Macon. The night before the game, Danny Ferry, Quin Snyder, Kevin Strickland—almost the whole team—were in my hotel room watching TV and they all were saying, 'Billy, you've got to stop this guy tomorrow.'

Duke Photography

"I watched film. I had a lot of tapes. I knew that whenever he looked to score, he always dribbled left. If he went right, he really came back to his left to shoot that stop-and-pop jumper.

"Coach K never really said, 'You've got to do this or that.' He just said, 'Billy, you got Macon. He's going to take a lot of shots.'

"A lot of times, I knew when to switch. Temple set so many screens for him, and a lot of guys would switch out, so the team helped out a lot.

"I tried to push him out of his range, and there was no way for him to go backdoor, because they had those double stacks. I wanted to contest everything. It was a game where I was just so focused. I don't know if I ever shot the ball. No, I take that back. Coach K moved me to the top of the zone as we were penetrating the middle, and I got a couple of jumpers. Then they flashed to the ball."

King was one of the first in a long line of defensive stoppers to play for Krzyzewski when Duke was establishing its credentials as a national power.

That was the reason Krzyzewski became so interested in King when he played for Parkville, Virginia, High School, in the D.C. suburbs.

The first time Krzyzewski saw King play was in an all-star game at Red Jenkins camp at George Mason University. Jenkins, who coached Tommy Amaker, and Krzyzewski were standing on the sidelines, watching Amaker play. "I'm dribbling up the court and I hear Red say, 'Dunk it on him,' so I went up and dunked on a guy on the break," King recalled.

"I remember the next day I got a letter from Coach K saying, 'I enjoyed watching you play.'

Krzyzewski became sold on King when he watched him play at the Five-Star basketball camp in Pittsburgh. King remembers, "Will Ray from Chicago was coaching me and he said to me, 'Billy, you got this guy, Reggie Williams. Just guard him. Don't let him get the ball.' I didn't know who he was before he got to Georgetown, and so I held him to 11 points. I think that's when Coach K saw I had it in me to become a good defensive player."

It would be nice to say King's feeling about Krzyzewski and Duke was mutual.

But King grew up a diehard Maryland fan. "I remember going to Maryland's camp when I was 10 years old," he said. "Tommy Amaker and I were at the camp together, and I got to know Lefty Driesell and his son, Chuck, and I was close with his family. From that point on—and because I think it was in 1980 in the ACC Tournament title game when Kenny Dennard undercut Buck Williams, and Maryland loses the game—I hated Duke. I said, 'I would never go to Duke.'

In the game King was talking about, Duke was up one when Maryland's star forward, Albert King, launched a 15-footer that just rolled off the rim. Williams went up to tap it in, and Dennard took his legs out from under him. No foul was called, and Duke won the title.

Krzyzewski eventually won him over, the same way he won Johnny Dawkins over: with constant attention.

"Coach K used to come see me play personally with his father-in-law. He'd fly in; they'd drive over and see me play. The thing about him is, when he would call me after games, he wouldn't say, 'You played great.' He'd say, 'I remember this play. I thought you could have done this.' He was always coaching me when I was in high school. He never said, 'This is great.'"

King was recruited by Duke, Virginia, Kansas, Syracuse, and North Carolina.

What sealed the deal with King was the way Krzyzewski dealt with King's infatuation with rival Carolina. King's high school coach, Kit Edwards, was a huge Carolina guy. "Looking back on it, our system in high school was more of a Carolina system," King said. "We did the run and jump, motion. But he never once said to me, 'That's where you want to go.'"

King made his official visit to Chapel Hill with two of his friends—both football players who were also being recruited by the Tar Heels.

"Back then, I was in love with Carolina. Eddie Fogler, Dean Smith's assistant, took me around. I loved Michael Jordan. I even had an autographed picture of him.

"I remember talking to Coach K when Carolina stopped recruiting me because they knew they were going to get Kevin Madden in the middle of the year. I told him that Carolina was one of my programs, and they had stopped recruiting me. I don't know why I told him that.

"And he said, 'Billy, I may be crazy, but if you really want to go to Carolina, then you need to start recruiting them. You should call them, let them know you're interested, if you feel that strongly. From that point, I said, 'No, I'm going to go to Duke. Anybody who would tell me that has to be concerned about my welfare.'"

With King, a lot of it was a matter of family ties.

"My father passed when I was five," King said. "He's sort of been that replacement.

"I remember my visit to Duke, because Tommy Amaker and I knew each other. We grew up 15 minutes apart and knew each other since we were 10. We played AAU basketball together and won the AAU 12-and-under national championship.

"When I visited Virginia, I stayed in a hotel. At Kansas, I was in an apartment with Kevin Walls, another recruit, from Camden High in New Jersey.

"My first night at Duke, I stayed at Coach K's house. I slept in his daughter Lindy's bed. His daughters were little then, and they made a poster that they hung on the wall. It said, 'Billy, please come to Duke.'

"Then the next night, I slept in the same dorm room with Tommy Amaker and Martin Nessley. They gave me a blanket and a pillow, and I slept on the tile floor. I lay there and I said, 'I'm coming to Duke because they treated me just like they treated a normal student.'"

King still remembers Krzyzewski telling him not to commit to any school on his visit, but wait until he got home. But King, who had an official visit to Syracuse scheduled the following weekend, didn't want to wait.

"I was at Cameron for the Blue-White scrimmage and the fans did the chant 'Bill-y King.' I remember going to breakfast with Coach K. His assistant, Chuck Swenson, was going to fly back with me—at that time you were allowed to fly down and back with a prospect. He went to pay the bill, and I said, 'Coach K, I'm coming.'

"And he stopped and said, 'Oh, great.' But he forgot to tell Coach Swenson.

"So on the flight back, he's still trying to recruit me. He was going on and on. He didn't find out until the next day when he got back to the office."

King didn't realize until he got home that Duke was coming off back-to-back 11-win seasons. But, like Krzyzewski, he could see the future. And it looked bright.

"Johnny, Mark Alarie, Jay Bilas, and David Henderson were juniors when I got there," King said. "They had just gone to the NCAA Tournament for the first time, lost to Washington. The one thing I'll always remember about my freshman year was their leadership.

"They sort of said, 'This is what we do. You do this, do that.' I remember one time in practice we were scrimmaging, and Coach K yelled at me for something. And I said it wasn't my fault. Tommy Amaker grabbed me and said, 'Not now.'

"The upperclassmen taught you the right things. We used to have dinner and they'd talk. It was more of them teaching you. And that's why I think Duke has always been so good. They've always had leadership.

"When I was a junior and Tommy was a senior, we taught Robert Brickey and those guys. It was always somebody older who taught the younger guys."

Duke reached the Final Four King's sophomore year. "The thing about that team was we all enjoyed one another," he said. "If there was a Friday night party, we all would be there. Everybody knew their role. The first subs, Danny Ferry and I, were going in for Jay and David. And we knew we needed Johnny to score. It was the best experience I ever had in basketball. And we didn't even win the championship."

King quickly learned that defense was an important part of his game. "In high school, I played as much defense as I needed to play," he said. "But when I got to Duke, it was something I needed to do if I wanted to play. I wasn't as good a scorer as Johnny, so I concentrated on defense."

King made a reputation for himself in that area during his freshman year when Duke defeated Georgia Tech 69-68 in Atlanta.

"It was a close game, and he took Johnny out and put me in," King said. "I didn't play the first half—and I always played the first half. He said, 'Billy, you got Mark Price.' And there was a four-minute stretch when they scored only two points. Then he put Johnny back in, but everybody was talking about, 'Billy King's four minutes of defense.'

"He's very good at teaching you your role, telling you your role, and not insulting you. Instead of 'You're a freshman. Don't shoot,' he would say, 'Billy, you're such a great defender.' He doesn't come right out and say, 'All right, Billy, you just play defense.'

"I remember, my junior year, he was talking to me, telling me, 'Billy, we're going to start playing you on some of the smaller guards.' Then my senior year, it was like, 'You got a tough matchup.' By the end of my senior year, I knew which guy I had. He didn't have to say, 'Play them this way, that way.' A lot of times I'd watch film at home. And I'd come back and say, 'Coach, I know you're watching film. This guy really likes to go left.'

"Then the next day in practice, he'd come in and say, 'Billy, this guy really likes going left.'"

King also remembers the Blue Devils' 70-61 victory over Notre Dame his senior year, when he shut down All-America guard David Rivers.

"He was another one of those guys you had to guard. I took two charges in the open court. The thing that probably meant the most to me was I scored more than he did," King said.

King became like another member of the Krzyzewski family during his time at Duke. "I was probably closer to him and his family than most of the players," he said. "I remember I was down at East Carolina speaking at a camp, and I would just drive over to his beach house. I would just show up, ring the door bell, and say, 'Here I am.' Or on Sunday, I would just drive out to the house and see what they were doing.

"When I had my tonsils out in the summer of my junior year, I just went there and stayed there, and his wife took care of me. I went to the dance recitals of Debbie and Lindy and went to different things with the family.

"I remember one time, we were staying overnight after the Maryland game, and a lot of the guys were going different places. I knew he had friends in from Chicago—some of his buddies. I went to dinner with him, Debbie, and his wife. I just wanted to hear stories.

"They were talking about Bobby Knight and West Point. I asked, 'Think I could have survived at West Point?'

"Coach says, 'Yeah, you could have survived at West Point.'

"Our relationship grew my junior year. We were playing Maryland at home and he took me out at the end of the game. I couldn't shoot a free throw, couldn't score, and we ended up losing the game 72-69. He called me Sunday and asked me to come over to his house. He said, 'Billy, I made a mistake. I took you out of the game because I didn't think you were getting it done offensively. And we ended up losing the game.'

"Then he said, 'It will never happen again. I have to have guys like you in the tough games.'

"And he said, 'I apologize again.'

"He told that story this summer. That's where I think he's secure and confident. He doesn't mind telling a college junior he made a mistake. He's confident enough to build the trust factor."

Five days after the Maryland loss, Duke went to Carolina and defeated the second-ranked Tar Heels 70-69. In that game, nobody scored in the last four minutes. It was a total commitment to defense. Then Duke defeated North Carolina in the ACC title game that year. Nobody scored in the last two minutes. Again, total defensive domination, particularly against North Carolina point guard Jeff Lebo, who was an outstanding player but could not run the Carolina offense against the pressure he faced from Duke. The Blue Devils defeated Carolina three times in King's senior year with Lebo at the point.

"He knows what buttons to push. He knew he could yell at me sometimes, I would get upset, and I would motivate the guys. He would blame me for lack of leadership, and he knew I was going to go out and do it. Some other guys, he had to hug."

When King graduated, he went to work in the management program with WRAL in Raleigh, but he also did halftime on the Duke Radio Network, speaking with alumni groups, and finding time to do the Ohio Valley midnight games for ESPN. King then took an assistant's job with Bob Bender at Illinois

State before joining Larry Brown's staff with the NBA Indiana Pacers. When Brown took the 76ers coaching job, King went with him, eventually working his way up the front-office ladder.

"I've never made a decision without talking with Coach," he said. "When I had to hire a coach, I'd call him, or if I had to fire a coach, he'd call me. He'd say, 'I heard. I just wanted to call and tell you it's tough, but you gave him an opportunity when nobody else would. Now you'd made a decision, you've got to move forward.'

"When I got engaged, I called my mom and then I called the Duke basketball office. I said, 'I know he's busy, but this is important. I need him for five minutes.' He was in the locker room. I said, 'Coach, I need you for five minutes. I just wanted to let you know I got engaged.'"

King has had long conversations with Krzyzewski on various occasions when the NBA came calling. "We sat with his wife in Vegas and talked about the pros for a real long time during a two-and-a-half-hour dinner one time," King said.

"I told him, 'I think you'd be great because you're a people person. The pro game is about individuals—and motivating them and talking to them. A lot of times, coaches don't communicate with them. I think you'd be great at it.'

"He was thinking about the Lakers last year, but I didn't think he would go. I'd just talked to him the year before about our job, when Larry Brown left.

"And I called him.

"I said, 'Coach, I got to ask you ...'

"Before I could finish he said, he wanted to stay at Duke.

"'You sure?' I asked just wanting to double-check.

"I think he enjoys the challenges of putting together a team every year and trying to keep college athletics at a high standard. He's in it—and a lot of coaches are—mainly to make sure the players get an education, that they practice hard every day but they have a good college experience. I remember we had one rule when I was at Duke: don't do anything to embarrass yourself, your family, or the university. That was our team rule."

Krzyzewski certainly exemplifies that.

10

THE PRIZE

DANNY FERRY

Duke Class of 1989

D anny Ferry was arguably the best prospect in the country when he played for DeMatha Catholic, the fabled high school program located in Hyattsville, Maryland, just outside Washington, D.C. He was the latest in a long line of great ones to play for legendary coach Morgan Wooten: a six-foot-10, 230-pound center with Larry Bird-like skills. He had a sweet hook shot, great passing skills, and the ability to face the basket, put the ball on the floor, and make mid-range jump shots.

Ferry had grown up around professional basketball. His father, Bob Sr., was a first-round pick of the NBA St. Louis Hawks, a 10-year pro who later became the general manager of the Washington Bullets. Danny remembers attending Bullets practices from the time he was five. He was on a first-name basis with stars such as Wes Unseld and Elvin Hayes, and it seemed like just a matter of time before he would follow in their footsteps.

No wonder so many ACC coaches were salivating when he entered his senior year. University of Maryland coach Lefty Driesell was so excited about the idea of signing another Tom McMillen, he had assistant Ron Bradley charter a small airplane and fly Ferry to campus to get a bird's-eye view of Cole Field House, where the Terps played their home games.

As the plane approached, there was a 40-foot sign stretched across the roof that read, "Danny's House." Ferry was suitably impressed by Driesell's creativity, but not impressed enough to sign with the Terps. Maryland was just two miles away from his home and he wanted to go away to school.

Initially, that school was North Carolina.

Duke Photography

"I used to watch Maryland play all the time and really followed North Carolina," he said. "Two teams, not Duke at all. At the time, Duke hadn't really been good as regularly and as consistently as Carolina had been. That was my dream, kind of—to go to Carolina."

Carolina—the school of Dean Smith and Michael Jordan—was blue heaven. The Tar Heels owned the ACC in those days. The Tar Heels won the national championship in 1982, and Smith had been to the Sweet 16 nine times before Ferry made his decision.

The Blue Devils were on the outside looking in at first. That's why when Ferry announced April 1 that he was going to Duke, it caught so many people by surprise. Ferry was the National High School Player of the Year in 1985.

He became the most coveted prospect to sign with Duke since Gene Banks from West Philadelphia in 1977. He was the first player to select Duke over North Carolina in the Mike Krzyzewski era. Krzyzewski had tried for Jordan and Buzz Peterson his first year, but they had limited interest after Carolina offered. He tried with Curtis Hunter from Durham in 1983, but Hunter also wanted to wear Tar Heel Blue.

But the climate on Tobacco Road was changing.

It took a while for Krzyzewski to establish his recruiting turf. But he got into Washington, D.C., his third year for Johnny Dawkins, a McDonald's All-American. And then he became competitive by signing Mark Alarie and Jay Bilas from the West Coast.

Duke had a young team that was starting to grow up in the ACC. The Blue Devils had finally beaten Carolina 77-75 in the ACC semifinals in 1984, finished 23-8 in 1985, were selected to the NCAA Tournament for a second straight year, and lost to Big East power Boston College 74-73 in the second round.

The Blue Devils had become more of a viable option.

And Danny Ferry took notice.

"It was a decision I took my time with," Ferry, now the assistant general manager with the San Antonio Spurs, recalled. "I was very deliberate in making it. Most people had signed early. I chose to sign late because I wasn't sure. My whole life I kind of wanted to play in the ACC. Growing up, that was a goal.

"The reason why I decided to go late was that one part of me was telling me, 'Follow your dream,'" Ferry said. "The other part was telling me, 'No, this other thing was much better, makes more sense to me.'

"And that was going to Duke.

"It was basically between those two schools the whole time. Duke just showed they really wanted me more than anybody else and I was more important to what they were going to be doing than anywhere else.

"They had someone at every game my senior year. They would have a Saturday afternoon game, and Saturday night their coach would be at my game. They were a constant presence."

Krzyzewski and assistant Chuck Swenson telephoned Wooten for four years. The two would fly to D.C. on a regular basis, then drive to Hyattsville to watch practices or games. They wrote to Ferry once a week and visited the home three times.

The Cameron Crazies even got into the act. During Ferry's senior year at DeMatha, Harvard played Duke in Cameron. Danny's older brother, Bob, was the Harvard co-captain, and the Dukies began chanting, "We want your brother! We want your brother!" throughout warmups.

Bob, who had a mischievous side to him, found a way to make them speechless for one of the few times ever. When the P.A. man announced the starting lineup, Bob sent Kyle Dodson, his black teammate, out in his place in introductions.

When Ferry decided on Duke, the toughest call he had to make was to Dean Smith. "But," he said. "I felt confident about my decision. And Coach Smith was great about it.

"He said, 'Are you sure? Then, good luck.'

"He was great about it. But there was no doubt about it: by the middle of my senior year, I really knew where I wanted to go. At that point, Duke had really started to establish itself. The year before, they went to the NCAA Tournament. My senior year in high school is when the team really started to take off, started to get good. So I watched that unfold and I loved how they played. I saw the opportunities, and I just sensed something special in Coach K. I sensed a guy who was a really good coach, a guy I really wanted to play for.

"I saw greatness."

Ferry saw it firsthand when he and Quin Snyder, who visited the same weekend, went to Krzyzewski's home. He was surprised to find out Krzyzewski was more than just a Bob Knight clone. He could be serious yet funny, intense yet warm, and, like Knight, driven to succeed.

Ferry was more than happy to go along for the ride.

There was no mistaking Danny Ferry when he arrived on campus. He fit right in on the Blue Devils' 1986 team that went 37-3 and went to the NCAA finals.

He started the first 21 games of his freshman year because Bilas was recovering from a preseason injury. Ferry was starting when Duke won the preseason NIT and in the losses at Carolina and Georgia Tech. Bilas actually missed only the first six games but came off the bench in the next 15. But Bilas started the last 19 games, and Ferry assumed the sixth-man role.

The star of that team was Dawkins, a senior All-America guard. Dawkins had played for DeMatha's Catholic League rival Mackin.

"I had played against Johnny in high school and had a lot of respect for him," Ferry said. "That guy is the most important guy Coach K has ever had—for a lot of reasons. Johnny gave the school and Coach K a chance to be very good, but he also did it with a style and substance that were cool.

"Grant Hill watched Johnny growing up. Had Grant Hill watched me growing up, he may not have wanted to go to Duke.

"The way Johnny carried himself and the charisma he had made Duke a cool place. Johnny was the total package. For me, he was the guy who showed me what it took to be good, how far he had to work, how to be a teammate. After Coach K, I'd put Johnny second as the reason why Duke is still having success now.

"It was a great year. It just flew by so fast. There was a transition for me, but I had the opportunity to play for a great team.

"That was easily the best team I was on during my four years. Easily. The star power of Johnny, the quality players around him, the sense of purpose those guys had. They had been down, and to see how they went about things was a great learning experience for me. It trained Quin Snyder, Billy King, me, and all the younger guys on how to carry on."

Ferry found himself in a far different situation the next year.

"That was important because we didn't know what to expect," he said. "We lost everything, basically. And we were building a team on Tommy Amaker, Billy King, and me—and none of us had really done that much. Billy and I had been role players, and we were put in a position to carry this thing on. But that was part of the reason I chose to go to Duke. I saw that window there."

So did Krzyzewski, who expanded Ferry's role, allowing him to spread his wings offensively instead of just being an inside banger. Ferry emerged a star as a sophomore when Duke showed it wasn't just a one-year wonder, winning games and advancing to the Sweet 16.

Ferry proved that he was a keeper, too.

As a sophomore, he became the first player in the history of the ACC to lead his team in scoring, rebounding, and assists.

"I'd worked hard, and I was going to succeed no matter where I went, but not to the level where I did at Duke," he said. "I hadn't known what to expect, how good I was. I didn't even think about that stuff. I just went out and played.

"That was a situation where Coach was great. He empowered me, gave me the confidence, put me in the position to be really, really good. That may not have happened anywhere now, especially the empowering part. He just makes you feel so confident, so good and so important.

"His communications skills are off the charts. If he sits you down one on one—whether it's recruiting in the living room or in an individual meeting during the season in a good or bad time, or if he's trying to get something out of you—he's unbelievable.

"He did that with that team. There was a way to do things. And we were going to be good. And he instilled both of those thoughts into our heads.

"We played the Russians in an exhibition game that year. We didn't know what to expect. We walked out of that game thinking, 'Hey, we're going to be pretty good.' That year was really important because it kept us going. And we were able to build on that each year."

Ferry's career took off as a junior when he led the ACC in scoring. He was selected ACC Player of the Year for a team that won the ACC Tournament and advanced to the Final Four again.

And, if it hadn't been for Krzyzewski, he might have cut his college career short.

NBA scouts had projected Ferry as a top five pick if he declared early—and Ferry had made up his mind to leave.

"My dad, in some way, shape or form, plays a role in everything I've done because he's been such a positive influence on me in my basketball career," Ferry said, "but he also kind of tries to take a hands-off approach—whether it was high school, college, an agent, when it was a decision for me whether to go to Italy or to the Clippers. I think he just wanted to present the facts and allow me to make a decision from there."

After Ferry made up his mind to go, he called Krzyzewski.

"I was on the phone in my bedroom. I had told my mom and dad I was going to go. That was fine with them, whatever I decided. It all came down for me when I told him I could go. I said, 'Coach, I don't even know if I really want to do this, but I just can't pass up the opportunity. This is a lot of money. If I get hurt, if anything happens, I'm just not comfortable with it.'

"He said, 'Let me call you back.'

"I think, basically, he just wanted to collect himself, think through things. He called me back, and we just talked. He checked into insurance, all the things I could do. When Coach K is in the locker room or in the living room, he is unbelievable.

"When I was getting recruited, I had coaches come in. They acted sincere. I had one coach come in; show a school video; and at the end, he was crying.

"I was like, 'Come on.'

"But when Coach K came in, if he did the exact same thing, you'd be crying with him, even if you didn't know him. Because he has such a passion for what he's doing, you're pulling right with him.

"In talking to him, I just got excited about what our team could be. I got excited about being there for my senior year, got excited about the learning I could get from him, from playing, from being in college another year. He got me excited about getting my degree and just following the process.

"The decision was easy after our conversation. I never, ever thought about it again. He had me so convinced that I was doing the right thing; there was never a second thought. He makes a lot of sense, believes what he's saying. He's passionate and he listens."

One thing Krzyzewski did stress to Ferry was that he needed to spend a year being the man, playing against guys who knew they could make their careers if they stopped him. Ferry flourished in that role. He averaged 22.6 points, and was selected National Player of the Year as a senior, playing for a team that made a second straight trip to the Final Four.

Along the way, he set the school scoring record, pouring in 58 points during a 117-102 victory over Miami in that city's new pro arena to break the record of 48, set by All-American Dick Groat in 1953. He also set the ACC single-game scoring record, topping the 57 points David Thompson scored against Buffalo State in December 1974.

Ferry shot a near-perfect 23 for 26 in that game. He struggled with early foul trouble, picking up two personals in the first nine minutes. Ferry headed for the bench, but with Duke trailing 32-28, Krzyzewski re-inserted him.

Then Ferry went off.

"I don't remember much about that game when it was over," Ferry claimed. "You hear about being in a zone or whatever. I remember everything moving really slowly, the ball going in a lot. I remember, at halftime, in the locker room, somebody telling me I had 30 points.

"I remember I had pancakes before the game. That was a big deal, because we had been trying to get pancakes before the game for a long time and our trainer finally gave in.

"We served pancakes a lot after that."

Ferry entered school in the same class with Quin Snyder, John Smith, and George Burgin, a tall, skinny seven-footer from Fairfax, Virginia, and the first Krzyzewski recruit to redshirt. He and Snyder made an official visit together, developed a close friendship, and roomed together for four years.

"He was like a spiritual leader for that group, early on," Ferry said. "He was just a dynamic leader. When he was there, he probably had to play out of position. He was probably more of a two guard than a point guard. But when we lost Tommy Amaker, we didn't have a natural point guard until Bobby Hurley came along. We made it work. We made it work well enough to win an ACC championship, to get to a couple of Final Fours, to get us to be the No. 1-ranked team."

But that didn't stop Ferry from torturing his roomie and teammates with practical jokes.

When the two were seniors, Ferry lent Snyder his car for a date. When Snyder and his companion came out of the restaurant, they couldn't locate the car.

Ferry had a spare set of keys and he and a friend had moved the car up the street. When Snyder finally located it, there were streamers attached and tin cans tied to the bumper and a sign that said, 'Just Married' on the window.

Snyder wasn't about to get punked. He and his friend drove to the local convenience store, picked up a package of double-stuffed Oreos, opened them up, and stuck them all over Ferry's car.

Ferry can still laugh at that one.

But he still feels a tinge of sadness at not leaving school with a national championship. The Devils lost to Seton Hall 95-78 in the national semifinals at Seattle his senior year—something P.J. Carlesimo, the former Seton Hall coach who is now an assistant with the Spurs, constantly needles him about.

"I still get ***** from P.J.," Ferry said.

"I got off to a good start in that game. I was making shots early. We were not a deep team, similar to the 2005 team. We had four, five, six guys who could play or were ready to play then. Some of the guys were freshmen, still figuring things out. Then, Robert Brickey got hurt. When he went out, we were up 26-8, and the game turned right then. They got the momentum. I probably tried to do too much once that happened, and we ended up getting run off the court at the end. It was a sad experience."

Ferry finished with 34 points in his final college game, but without Brickey for almost the entire second half and Christian Laettner in foul trouble, Duke could not offer him enough help offensively. The Devils were outscored 62-40 in the second half.

His disappointment was tempered by the fact that Ferry had his number retired at the end of the season.

"It was pretty cool. It wasn't something I had ever thought about. That was something that Coach, when I told him I was leaving after my junior year, mentioned. He said, 'If you stay and you have a great year, that's something that would be possible.' It had nothing to do with my decision. But when it happened, it was a pretty awesome feeling. It's even more of an honor when I go back and show my kids."

After his senior year, Ferry was selected by the Clippers with the second pick in the draft, but he decided that rather than playing in a dysfunctional franchise, he would sign to play in the Italian Pro League.

The next year, he wound up in Cleveland. Ferry played in the league from 1990 through 2003. He won a championship ring with the San Antonio Spurs his last year and then moved into the front office.

Like father, like son.

"It was something I always wanted to do. When I finished playing, they really wanted me to stick around. It's a great situation. They're a team that does it the right way, also. It's interesting. Greg Popovich is an Air Force guy—like Coach K was an Army guy. There are definitely similarities between them. I think a lot of it has to do with a military background.

"When I think about my career, I got to play at DeMatha High School, which is the model program for high school. Duke is the model program in college. And San Antonio is one of the model programs in professional sports."

But he still treasures his Duke experience.

"Coach K had such a great influence on me about how I'm a dad, how I'm a husband, how I do my job now. I'm working in the front office of a team. That is a model for me, a model I've gotten to live through. I'm the coach of my family team, basically.

"The willingness to communicate, open up, show passion, the right way to do things—are all things I was exposed to at a very intense level in playing for him.

"I watched his family grow up. I'm still not used to seeing them as adults. It makes me feel old. I'm not old, but it makes me feel old. My wife, Tiffany, and I have four girls: Hannah, Grace, Sophia, and Lucky—8, 7, 5, 3. I beat him by one.

"I'm having the time of my life. I win all the votes. I'm a good politician around the house. I know which kids to bribe.

"Other than my wife and my kids, my time at Duke was the greatest experience I've had in my life—the whole four years, a learning experience, a fun experience, everything. It was so rich.

"Just playing for Coach K alone is such a rich experience because it's more than a game. When I say that, I don't want to blow it out of proportion, like it's life or death or anything. It's just that you learn so much more than basketball, and there's more depth to it than just Xs and Os and making shots."

Spoken like a true son of the sport.

11

THE RIVAL

BOBBY CREMINS

Coach, Georgia Tech, 1982-2000

I n the 1970s, the Atlantic Coast Conference was filled with high-profile coaches such as Dean Smith at North Carolina, Norman Sloan at North Carolina State, Lefty Driesell of Maryland, Terry Holland of Virginia, Bill Foster of Duke, and Carl Tacy of Wake Forest.

They gave the ACC its character and its tradition. Sloan won a national championship with David Thompson in 1974. Smith and Foster each got to Final Fours.

But the face of the league began to change in 1980 when N.C. State hired Jimmy Valvano from Iona, and Duke hired Mike Krzyzewski from West Point. The next year, Georgia Tech hired Bobby Cremins, a fast-talking New Yorker with a Bronx accent, who had played for Frank McGuire at South Carolina and was coaching at Appalachian State.

"We were the young guns," Cremins recalled. "And we were all after Dean Smith. That was our goal: kick Dean's butt."

Smith was the king of Tobacco Road. And Cremins, Valvano, and Krzyzewski were trying to make a name for themselves.

"My first year—1982—I think Mike and I played a game for last place," Cremins recalled. "When I think back on it, I have to laugh. I actually played against Mike in the NIT. There's a funny story connected with that tournament.

"We came in with South Carolina, and we were staying at the New Yorker Hotel. We had these big travel bags. We had gone through the revolving glass door and the end of one of the bags blasted through the glass. And Billy Walsh, one of our starters, cut his hand.

Photo courtesy of Georgia Tech

"So we lost him. Frank McGuire had only five or six players. We played Army the second game, and Bobby Knight was running that motion offense—and they had us all screwed up—and we put in a 2-3 zone. Finally, we were down eight with four minutes to go, and Coach McGuire said, 'All right, we're going to go man-to-man. Does everybody know who they've got?'

"'Bobby,' he says to me, 'Who do you have?'

And, I swear to God, I told him, 'I got the guy with the big nose whose last name I can't pronounce.'

"And that was Mike. That's a true story. Mike always reminds me of that."

Cremins and Krzyzewski met for the first time at the ACC spring meetings.

"Mike was Polish. I was Irish. He was from Chicago. I was from New York. And I always kind of respected him because of his Army background and the fact that we played against each other. We always kidded each other and we both played tennis.

"It was Les Robinson of N.C. State and Dave Odom of Wake against Mike and me. He was a good player until he hurt his back. He'd hustle, run. We'd all have long points, all of us running around the court.

"At that time, I had no idea Mike would accomplish what he has. I thought nobody would ever touch Dean Smith. But, in order to get ahead, you had to beat Dean.

"I didn't understand it at first.

"One time, we were at the ACC meetings. Dean went to the men's room, and Lefty said, 'We got to get that son of a bitch.'

"I said, 'Why do you got to get him?'

"And Lefty said, 'Ah, shut up. You don't understand.'"

Cremins viewed Krzyzewski as a good, solid coach. "Then he started to upgrade his recruiting, bringing in really good players," Cremins recalled. "What turned it around for him was when he got Johnny Dawkins in 1982."

Dawkins was Krzyzewski's first great player, the foundation of Duke's first Final Four run. His personal duels with Georgia Tech guard Mark Price during his four years were legendary—because both programs were ranked in the top 10 in 1985 and 1986. Dawkins won six games; Price five during that period.

As freshmen, Price beat Dawkins out for ACC Rookie of the Year and was the No. 9 vote-getter for All-ACC. Dawkins was No. 10. The next year, Price was the fifth man on the first team. He had 20 more votes than Dawkins, who was the No. 7 vote-getter. As juniors both made first team, but Price was the third leading vote-getter and Dawkins was fourth. As seniors, Dawkins finally came out on top—but he was the No. 3 vote-getter behind Len Bias of Maryland and Brad Daugherty of North Carolina. Price never made a recognized first-team All-America team. He was second-team AP as a junior and third team as senior. Dawkins was second-team AP All-American as a junior and made consensus first-team All-American as a senior. Dawkins was selected by San Antonio with the 10th pick in the first round of the 1986 NBA draft. Price went to Dallas with the first pick in the second round.

"It happened quickly for all of us," Cremins recalled. "Jimmy [Valvano] won a national title in 1983. We won the ACC Tournament in 1985. And Mike got to the Final Four the next year. When we were building our program, we weren't really that conscious of what Duke was doing. But when Mike brought in Christian Laettner, Bobby Hurley, and Grant Hill, he took it to another level."

The Georgia Tech-Duke games in the late 1980s were classics. The Jackets were good back then, making nine-straight NCAA appearances from 1985 through 1993.

"I remember one game in 1989," Cremins recalled. "The ACC used to introduce one player at a time before tip-off. The P.A. man would announce Danny Ferry from Duke, then he would introduce Tommy Hammonds from our team. And the players would go to midcourt and shake hands.

"Well, this time Tommy almost took Danny Ferry's hand off. Because of that incident, the ACC changed the rule so they now introduce one team at a time."

Cremins also remembered one intense recruiting battle with Krzyzewski over Bobby Hurley, a point guard from St. Anthony's of Jersey City.

"I went up to visit Bobby Hurley," Cremins said. "I flew up to LaGuardia airport Sunday evening for a Monday visit. I stayed at the Marriott there. I got my rest. I was all fired up, took a run, put my suit on. I was all ready to go out. And just as I was about to leave my room, the phone rings.

"It was Bob Hurley Sr., the coach of St. Anthony's and Bobby's father.

"He said, 'Coach, I was trying to track you down. Your secretary told me where you were. I'm sorry, but Bobby committed to Duke last night.' I think he had visited Duke that weekend. I'll always remember saying to Bob, 'Well, that's too bad. Congratulations.'

"Then I hung up the phone and said, 'That SOB Mike Krzyzewski.' So, instead, I went over to Queens and said hello to Jack Curran at Archbishop Molloy because he had Kenny Anderson."

Anderson, who set the New York state scoring record, came into the ACC the same year as Hurley. Both players wound up playing in the 1990 Final Four in Denver as freshmen.

"We were up seven at halftime against UNLV in the one semifinal game and we would have played Duke—which had beaten Arkansas in the other semifinals—for the national championship, if we'd held on," Cremins said.

"We had great guards: Kenny, Dennis Scott, and Brian Oliver. They were called 'Lethal Weapon III.' They all averaged over 20 points a game. I think we would have beaten Duke because UNLV beat them badly in the championship game.

"When Mike came back the next year and beat UNLV in the semifinals, that was it. That was the year he won his first championship. I think Jerry Tarkanian had the better team, but Duke found a way to win. That's when Mike started making a reputation for himself—when he beat a team that had better personnel than his team.

"That game was the one that left the biggest impression on me. I have been to every Final Four for the last 30 years, and I watched the game very closely. I was waiting for UNLV to jump ahead, take the lead. But Mike kept it close, really controlled the tempo. Mike was great at that. He can play a cat-and-mouse game or he can bust it open.

"To me, Mike is the most detailed coach I've ever coached against. He doesn't leave any stone unturned. He's very detailed; very meticulous—sometimes to a fault. When he got that second national championship, being so young, winning all those ACC championships, you could just tell he was going to catch Dean.

"I tell everybody this: Bobby Knight is going to break Dean Smith's record for career victories and if Mike stays healthy, he will break Bobby Knight's record."

Krzyzewski won another title in 1992 and got back to the national championship game in 1994.

"He did the same thing against Purdue in the Southeast Regional finals that year," Cremins said. "That was when Gene Keady had Glenn Robinson. Purdue had the better team. But he beat Purdue.

"Games like that defined him."

Cremins seriously considered leaving the ACC at one point during Krzyzewski's ascension. He accepted the job at South Carolina, his alma mater, in March 1993. Two days later—just when local merchants in Columbia, South Carolina, began selling "Welcome Back Bobby" bumper stickers—Cremins changed his mind and decided to stay put at Tech.

"During the South Carolina thing, I called Mike," Cremins recalled. "I said, 'I'm coming back.' He actually started laughing over the phone."

Krzyzewski hit a temporary bump in the road the next year—a back injury that forced him to miss most of a 13-18 season.

"I heard so many rumors," Cremins said. "I believe I called him when that was going on. He was pretty hard to reach. But what I remember most was when he came back. When he came back, he was like a different person. He was like totally focused. He was taking no prisoners.

"Something transpired during that time. He came back with more determination than I've ever seen. He had a fierce competitive mindset. He was gung-ho. He seemed more focused. He built a wall around himself. It was almost like he was mad about something. He came back and, *****, we couldn't beat him."

There was one exception: the 1996 snow game at Cameron.

"That was Stephon Marbury's freshman year," Cremins said. "We got there, and it was snowing like hell. I thought they were going to call off the game. But we were there already, so they played the game. They had only about 3,000 fans there, and we wound up winning."

Tech reached the finals of the ACC Tournament and advanced to the NCAA Sweet 16 that year and Marbury left for the pros. But things drifted downhill after that.

Cremins stepped down late in the 2000 season at age 52. He knew when it was time to get out. Tech had not been to the NCAA Tournament since 1996 and wasn't about to go that season.

"I remember a string of games at Georgia Tech," he said. "It seems like we always beat them at home. Duke won just one game in Atlanta from 1982 through 1989. I just knew it would be a hard-nosed, tough-played game. Then they started winning all the time."

Duke won 12 of 15 meetings in the series between 1989 and 1994. Then, after Krzyzewski came back, the Blue Devils won 15 straight over the Jackets from 1997 until March 3, 2004.

"I have great respect for Mike's players," Cremins said. "The Bobby Hurleys, the Danny Ferrys. I got to know a lot of these kids. I was an assistant coach at the Olympics. We had Grant Hill. Christian Laettner was a bit different. I coached him in a World Championships qualifying tournament. He was great, but he could be tough. Shane Battier: he was a nightmare for me.

"Mike gets the cream of the crop now. I don't know how he does it. I told him one time—I was kidding him—'Will you please get through recruiting quickly, so I can start. I'm tired of recruiting against you.'

"He has an empire, a complete empire. I do a recruiting show in Atlanta every Tuesday and it's amazing. When I did it this year—every year—it's Duke, Duke, Duke.

"I was just at the Nike Hoops Summit game in Memphis. I watched Greg Paulus play. He's absolutely one of the purest point guards I've seen. And then there's Josh McRoberts—six foot 10, top five in the country."

Both will be freshmen at Duke in 2005.

Cremins also respects the work Krzyzewski has done with The V Foundation for Cancer Research.

"I want to talk to him about Jimmy V, how they got so close at the end," Cremins said. "They were fierce rivals. Jimmy, Mike, and I didn't have a lot of words for each other. We respected each other, but we wanted to beat the hell out of each other."

Krzyzewski was sorry to see Cremins leave the ACC scene. The day after Cremins announced he was stepping down—February 18, 2000—in a press conference where some of his players were crying, Krzyzewski called Cremins to offer his condolences.

"I told him not to say anything," Cremins said.

Krzyzewski told him just to watch Duke's game the next day against N.C. State.

That day, Krzyzewski abandoned his normal attire and walked onto the floor wearing a blue blazer with a yellow tie—Cremins's trademarks at Tech.

"The best times were at the ACC meetings," Cremins said. "It took us a few years to speak up in meetings. Jimmy was fine. I was nervous. Mike was very quiet. He hardly said anything, but he took a lot in. He'd write a lot.

"But after a while, we all had fun. All that's changed now. It's all business. It was business back then, but we had a lot of fun, too. The world changes.

"Back then, Valvano would start drinking the wine. You never knew what he was going to say.

"I remember one time I was really mad at him about recruiting and I said, 'I'm not going to laugh at his stuff today.' Ten minutes later, I was laughing. He would do imitations of other coaches, bust on Dean.

"Now, Dean was always late for the ACC meetings. I think he did it on purpose. He'd come 30 minutes late to every meeting; he played those mind games. For the first 20 minutes, Valvano would bust on Dean.

"At first, we used to wait for him, but finally we said, 'Screw him,' and we would start the meetings without him.

"One time we even hid in the closet. Another time, we hid all the extra chairs so when he arrived, there were seven of us sitting around the table and no chair for Dean."

Those were the days.

12

THE DEAL MAKER

DAVE GAVITT

Basketball Consultant

W hen Dave Gavitt left his job as commissioner of the Big East after 11 years to become senior vice president in charge of basketball decisions for the Boston Celtics in May 1990, he inherited an NBA franchise that was just about drained of life.

But what a life it had been.

Hall of Famers Larry Bird, Robert Parish, and Kevin McHale—the catalysts for the Celtics' championship runs in the 1980s—were approaching retirement. Boston, which had fallen behind Detroit in the Eastern Conference picture, had not won a divisional title in two years. In addition, the franchise had just fired its coach, Jimmy Rogers, after a disappointing first-round playoff loss to the Knicks.

Gavitt was given a mandate.

He had to find a replacement who could recharge the batteries on an aging team that had fallen into a tailspin and who could eventually rebuild the foundation of a team that had won 16 NBA titles.

He attempted to address the problem by going to Durham.

Gavitt—the former Providence and 1980 Olympic coach and a college guy at heart—had known Mike Krzyzewski since he had coached at West Point and liked his competitive nature. The two had become good friends when Krzyzewski began coaching USA Basketball traveling teams.

Krzyzewski was the guy he wanted for the job. And Gavitt was intent on romancing him away from Duke. "Yeah, I was guilty," Gavitt says now.

Photo courtesy of The Big East Conference

Gavitt hopped on a plane, flew to Durham, and spent the day with Krzyzewski and his wife, Mickie. "I tried to entice him to come," Gavitt admitted. "Selfishly, it would have been great having him rebuild the franchise."

Krzyzewski, who had just coached the Blue Devils to a third-straight Final Four appearance and had seven-straight 20-win seasons, was initially intrigued. He had grown up in Chicago but had been a huge Celtics fan as a kid. He had enormous respect for Gavitt and the Celtics organization.

The two agreed to hold a follow-up meeting the next week in Washington, D.C. Also attending would be Red Auerbach, the Celtics' semi-retired general manager and president and legendary sage who had coached the Celtics to nine NBA championships.

Auerbach interestingly could have once been the Duke coach. He was brought to Duke in 1950 by Eddie Cameron with the idea he would succeed Gerry Gerard, who was dying of cancer. Auerbach never coached at Duke. He was there over the summer and left because he told friends he couldn't stand to wait around for another man to die.

Gavitt took the shuttle in from Boston. Krzyzewski flew up from Raleigh, and the two met at National Airport. Gavitt had asked Duke athletic director Tom Butters, a good friend, for permission to speak with Krzyzewski, and Krzyzewski made the school aware.

But otherwise, the meeting was supposed to be on the Q.T., or so both men thought. Auerbach had agreed to pick Gavitt and Krzyzewski up when they arrived. As the two walked out of the terminal, there was Red, sitting in a green Saab convertible with the top down and a license plate that had "Celtics" on it.

"I just started laughing," Gavitt said. "We jump in the car and Red decided we're going to have lunch at Blackie's House of Beef on Third St. in Washington, an extremely busy and crowded restaurant. Well, you can imagine what our table was like, with people coming by all the time."

So much for privacy.

The flirtation lasted a week.

"Mike and I talked a couple of more times," Gavitt said. "In the final analysis, he decided not to do it. The thing I always remember is Tom Butters. Butters is a good guy who stuck by Mike in tough times when he first hired him. When Mike went to see Tom and talk to him after he got the offer, Butters looked him in the eye and said, 'Mike, you need to decide whether you can make more of a difference coaching 25-year-old millionaires or young men who play here at Duke.'

"That did it.

"Tom picked the exact right words he should have picked."

Krzyzewski was smart enough to realize he had a chance to win a national championship the following year at Duke with Christian Laettner and Bobby Hurley coming back.

And they did.

The Celtics were not the only NBA team to make a run at Krzyzewski.

And suitors found Krzyzewski surprisingly willing to listen.

Even though Duke found a way to win 28 games in 1993, Krzyzewski was feeling restless. His wife, Mickie, wasn't happy either. There was some speculation she was upset that a lot of people at Duke, particularly new president Nan Keohane, didn't appreciate how much Mike meant to the school. The two talked about the moving on to the NBA or TV.

Krzyzewski, it seemed, was always on call—from the NABC, USA basketball, clinics, charities—time-consuming tasks that took him way from family and his team. Krzyzewski always had problems saying no, because he didn't want to come across like a big timer to his friends or coaches. But the growing number of obligations was wearing him down. It was also having an effect on his recruiting.

Krzyzewski coached the Blue Devils to the national championship game in 1994 then began looking for an escape hatch. He almost found it a month later when both the Portland Trailblazers and Miami Heat from the NBA came after him, and offered him lucrative contracts to coach their teams.

NBA commissioner David Stern wanted to get Krzyzewski into the league. When Hall of Famer Billy Cunningham was part-owner with the Heat, he made an inquiry. Then, Portland's billionaire owner, Paul Allen, fired in with a blank check.

Krzyzewski, who had become intrigued with the idea of coaching NBA players when he served as an assistant on the 1992 Dream Team, thought about it.

Duke had planned a summer exhibition tour of Australia, and Krzyzewski cancelled it when he discovered some of his freshmen had fallen behind academically and needed summer school.

G'day, Australia.

When promoters complained, Keohane asked Talman Task, her right-hand man, to investigate it. Krzyzewski was upset about the second-guessing and the oversight.

He was also upset that the administration was dragging its feet on putting air conditioning into Cameron and building an annex with a new locker room, weight room, and offices, although to be fair, A.D. Tom Butters had his hands full at the time with a protracted football coaching search. He also wanted an academic adviser for his team.

Keohane, who was politically savvy enough to understand Krzyzewski's power with the money people on campus, cut short a vacation and met with Krzyzewski over Memorial Day weekend. The two hammered out a peace accord and worked closely together from that point on. Krzyzewski stayed at Duke and eventually signed a new seven-year deal when he returned from back surgery in the spring of 1995.

Then in the summer of 2004, he was offered a five-year deal—reportedly worth $40 million—to go to the Los Angeles Lakers after that team and Phil Jackson parted ways following a loss in the NBA finals.

Superstar Kobe Bryant, who had been recruited by Krzyzewski and had developed a friendship with him when he was a senior at Lower Merion (Pennsylvania) High School, reportedly liked the idea of being coached by Coach K. The Lakers, wanting to please their free agent star, made a lucrative pitch.

Krzyzewski kept Duke fans guessing for four days over the July 4 weekend. More than 100 students showed up at a pep rally on campus, led by new president Richard Broadhead, urging Krzyzewski to stay.

In the end, Krzyzewski had built up too much of an attachment to the school to walk away.

So long, L.A.

"Mike and I laughed about the Celtics situation many times; most recently when he turned down the Lakers last summer for a lot more money," Gavitt said. "We were in New York—we're both involved in college basketball partnership with the NCAA—and we had a private conversation. I said to him, 'You know, as I've said to you many times before, thank God we weren't successful in 1990 recruiting you.'

"I remember saying to Mike and Rick Pitino later, 'You can coach anywhere—college, pro, anywhere. But one thing you need to understand. When you coach in the pros, the day you sign your contract, you put yourself in a position of not being able to have anywhere near the influence on the game you can have in college.'"

Certain people, as ESPN's Dick Vitale likes to say, are meant to be college coaches.

"Mike is so smart," Gavitt said. "He's a very smart guy who understands the college game and the pro game. Both play with the same-size ball. But they have developed into very different entities. The college game is still a sport. If you watch it on TV or go to a big ACC game, you're going to see big-time sport, where two squads are coached as teams—with emotion, defensive help, motion of ball, and motion of movement.

"If you go to an NBA game, you're not going watch a sport. You're going to watch entertainment. You're going to a contest where they have rules called illegal defenses. Think about that: not being able to help your teammates defend.

"I think Mike has an inner respect for the game. He understands that while the best players are in the pros, college has the best game, the purest game, a team game. It's a game, and it's not a game. The arrow hasn't tipped too far over."

Krzyzewski has become the face of college basketball. He won three national championships, dominated the ACC, and was voted into the Hall of Fame, which Gavitt used to help oversee, four years ago.

"He succeeded at the highest level at a school with high academic standards," Gavitt said. "I think people who stay at one school for a long time in their career and have success put themselves in a position of being able to carry a lot of weight. Mike has done that at the very highest level. And in doing that, he's proven himself over and over again as a really outstanding teacher who's been able to change with the times."

Krzyzewski has never been one to shirk responsibility, so it's no surprise that he has been heavily involved with the reform movement in college athletics.

"With all the success he's had, Mike has never changed," Gavitt said. "And he's always been willing to give back. He was committed to giving back while in the thick of the fire, while competing for the national championship. He hasn't said, 'No,' to NABC or the NCAA or the coaches. He's been all about the game. He understands that the game is the most important thing. He honors it, respects it, and gives back to it on a daily, consistent basis. I really admire him for that. I think it's fabulous."

They say if you want something done, ask a busy person to do it.

Krzyzewski's resumé has made him a logical candidate to become the 2008 Olympic coach.

"I've been involved in the movement, and I'm a big advocate of that," Gavitt said. "Mike gave of himself, coaching the World Championship team that finished third in 1990. He took on some tough assignments—particularly so a couple of times when he was saddled with P.J. [Carlesimo] and [Jim] Boeheim. That's some heavy lifting."

Gavitt laughed.

But the United States' weak sixth-place finish in the 2002 World Championships and bronze-medal finish in the 2004 Olympic Games at Athens are no laughing matters.

"We've had our troubles the past four years, and we need to straighten it out," Gavitt said.

Historically, the United States had dominated the Olympic men's basketball competition. But then came 1988, when the American team lost to the Soviets in the semifinals.

Talk about a wake-up call.

There was a push throughout the world to incorporate NBA players. The first Dream Team—with all-time greats like Michael, Magic, Larry, Patrick Ewing, Chris Mullin, Karl Malone, John Stockton, and Charles Barkley—set the gold standard. And took home the gold medal. They won games by an average of 43.75 points and defeated Croatia 117-85 in the finals.

"We had good people, world-class players and people," Gavitt said. "They understood what it meant to wear the uniform of the United States, what the team was all about. It was probably the best team ever assembled."

It was so good that in 2005, Krzyzewski motivated ACC Player of the Year, J.J. Redick, by telling him stories of Mullin spending all those extra hours in the gym shooting or Malone getting up at 6:30 a.m. to work out.

As a West Point graduate, Krzyzewski has always understood what it means to represent his country. He was also the head coach of the U.S. team in the 1990 Goodwill Games and the 1991 World University Games.

Six members of Krzyzewski's Duke teams—Laettner, Hill, and Carlos Boozer, Dan Meagher (1984) and Newton (2000) of Canada, and Crawford Palmer of France—all participated in the Olympics. Six—Tommy Amaker (1986), Laettner (1990), Trajan Langdon (1998), Newton (1998), Elton Brand (2002), and Jason Williams (2002)—played in the World Championships.

To whom much is given, much is expected.

Krzyzewski was actually a candidate to coach the 1992 Olympic team before the NBA asserted its influence during the selection process. Chuck Daly, a players' coach who spent time at Duke as an assistant to Vic Bubbas and went on win two NBA titles with the Detroit Pistons, was eventually chosen as head coach. The staff included Lenny Wilkins of Atlanta, P.J. Carlesimo from Seton Hall, and Mike Krzyzewski.

"Mike and P.J. were heavily involved with game preparation, with how we were going to play. They had a lot more knowledge of international play than Chuck or Lenny," according to Gavitt.

Wilkins and Rudy Tomjanovich of Houston coached the pros to gold medals in 1996 and 2000, although Tomjanovich had to dodge a bullet during a close call with Lithuania.

But it was obvious that the rest of the world was catching up.

Larry Brown of the Pistons did not experience the same type of success when nine members of the originally invited roster for Athens—including Kobe Bryant, Kevin Garnett, Shaquille O'Neal, Ray Allen, Jason Kidd, Mike Bibby, and Tracy McGrady—took a pass. Argentina won the gold, defeating a young NBA team in the semifinals and opening the door for the committee to take another look at a college coach who has been on the short list for so many NBA jobs.

"I think he's paid his dues," Gavitt said. "I don't think being the Olympic coach is the purview of NBA coaches alone. With all due respect to the number of fine coaches there are in the NBA, Mike knows more about the international game. He's been involved in coaching USA Basketball teams over the years, and he has a lot of his former players spread out in the NBA and overseas."

Maybe Beijing is closer to Durham than people think.

13

American Idol
CHRISTIAN LAETTNER
Duke Class of 1992

Any college basketball fan who watches the NCAA Tournament has seen "The Play" over and over on videotape. It has become the hallmark of March Madness.

As one writer eloquently described it, Christian Laettner flashes to the foul line, catches a long, looping pass from Grant Hill, drops his left shoulder, dribbles left, spins, and then shoots an 18-foot jumper that rips through the net at the buzzer, and then runs in a crazy half-circle, arms wide open, waiting to be embraced by his teammates.

Duke 104, Kentucky 103 in double overtime at the 1992 NCAA East Regional finals in Philadelphia.

"Yeah, I see it all the time and it makes me smile every time, even when I'm depressed because I got traded," the six-foot-11 former Duke star, who now plays for the NBA Miami Heat, admitted. "That means ESPN is on a lot around my house."

Duke was ecstatic.

Kentucky was in tears.

Laettner—who was once described as looking like he just came right off the set of *Beverly Hills 90210*—combined matinee idol looks with a testy personality on the court and the dark heart of an assassin. He made more big shots—and broke more hearts—than anyone who has ever played for Mike Krzyzewski.

Laettner was a two-time All American and the National Player of the Year in 1992. He started on four-straight Final Four teams, was the star of the Blue

Duke Photography

Devils' back-to-back national championship teams in 1991 and 1992, and was voted the Most Outstanding Player of the 1991 Tournament. The combined record for Laettner and senior teammate Brian Davis in NCAA play was an incredible 21-2.

Laettner also was the only college player selected to play on the initial Olympic Dream Team that had Michael Jordan, Magic Johnson, Patrick Ewing, David Robinson, Charles Barkley, and Larry Bird and cruised to a gold medal in the 1992 Games at Barcelona.

It is hard to question his resumé—especially at crunch time in Duke's biggest games.

If the Naismith Basketball Hall of Fame had spots open for players based solely on their college careers, he would be a lock for enshrinement.

Laettner was the most competitive player ever at Duke. He hated to lose in everything. He would routinely challenge his teammates in ping pong, pool, and air hockey. And he didn't mind rubbing it in when he won.

"It was nothing conscious on my part," Laettner said. "The only time it was conscious was when Coach K told me to do something. He didn't have to do much with me. I loved practice, the competitive nature of it. You could scrap a little, draw some blood.

"I wanted to go out and dunk on everyone and see if they could dunk on me. I wanted to beat [Bobby] Hurley in a three-point contest. We were just goofing around—the way I did against my older brother and my brothers on the team.

"But we loved each other, and we could go out to dinner afterwards."

The intense part of Laettner's personality dates back to his childhood in Angola, New York, a lakeside community 30 miles south of Buffalo. Laettner's father, George, was a printer with *The Buffalo News*. His mother, Bonnie, was a teacher. Christian got his name from Hollywood. His mother named him after Christian Diestl, the German solider played by Marlon Brando in the 1958 movie, *The Young Lions*.

"I got the intense side from my father, who coached me and my older brother, Christopher, for a long time," he recalled. "When I was younger, he kicked my ***** in just about every sport.

"Coach K took it to another level. I respect him so much for doing things the right way, coaching in a smart way, the best way, the fundamentally sound way. He knows you can be highly successful in anything if you have the spirit and the heart. You have to be involved. He knew how to push the right buttons with me.

"He would get Thomas Hill and me so riled up. It was something out of *Hoosiers*. We just wanted to kick ***** every time out. He knew how to feed our fire. He always recruited kids who had that fire."

Laettner led the Nichols School to two New York state championships and was a McDonald's All-American. His father liked Notre Dame for him, but the program had slipped. Laettner eventually selected Duke over North Carolina because it reminded him of Nichols, a small private school that was strong in both academics and athletics. "I'd wanted to go to Duke for a long time," he said.

Laettner realized how intense the Duke-Carolina rivalry was before he enrolled. During his official visit to Carolina, Dean Smith was taking the family on a tour of the campus dorms. When his mother asked Smith about the rivalry, Smith tried to downplay it as an overreaction on the part of the media.

Then the elevator door opened and she could see that the door to J.R. Reid's room was covered with anti-Duke slogans.

It's part of the culture.

Laettner wanted to experience it by playing for Krzyzewski.

"I love Duke. I love Duke. I love Duke. But I'd rather play for Coach K than Duke," he once said during an emotional speech at the team banquet his senior year.

"He isn't Hollywood," Laettner said. "He's honest and real. That being said, he places the highest degree of discipline and the highest demands on you. When you see the whole thing in action, you respect where he's coming from. He's charismatic. He attracts people to him, and you listen to every word he says."

Laettner had his first shot to be a hero when he was just a freshman. Duke was playing Arizona at the Meadowlands. The Wildcats had a 77-75 lead, but Laettner had a chance to force overtime if he converted a one-and-one at the end of regulation.

He missed the front end and was consoled afterward by his teammates and former President Richard Nixon, a Duke Law School graduate.

That was the one of the few times Laettner missed a big shot during a brilliant career.

Laettner took a huge step forward at the end of his freshman year when he scored 24 points, grabbed nine rebounds, and got the best of Georgetown's six-foot-10 freshman, Alonzo Morning, as the Blue Devils defeated the Hoyas 85-77 on the same court where he'd missed the free throw against Arizona three months earlier.

Laettner loved the Meadowlands.

He found himself in another critical situation there the following March with the game—and a trip to the Final Four—on the line. Duke was playing Connecticut in the 1990 NCAA Eastern Regional finals. Laettner's family had made the trip from upstate New York to watch him play. Connecticut had a one-point lead in the closing seconds of overtime. And it looked like they were going to win after Tate George stole a pass from Phil Henderson. But George was unable to control it, losing the ball out of bounds with 2.6 seconds left.

Krzyzewski called timeout to set up a last play.

"He had prepared a good out-of-bounds play. It was one of his 'end-of-the-game plays,'" Laettner recalled. "You have to prepare for it in practice. A team that never goes to the tournament never has to worry about them. But a team that knows it's going into a big-time situation has to work on them. We not only practiced a main play, but we also practiced the audible.

"Coach K was under control in the huddle. He told us we had time for only one play. Then he drew up a box set, side out-of-bounds play. We knew how to run it. But we were so well-drilled, he could call an audible. He called a special quick hitter where I inbounded the ball and they threw it right back to me because no one was guarding me. That's a mistake teams often make.

"Coach K didn't tell the rest of the team. He told only Brian Davis and me. The other three guys didn't even know it. We were giggling. I saw no one guarding me. It was the same play they used to run for Danny Ferry when he was at Duke.

"After that, I got lucky."

Laettner drained a 15-foot double-pump jumper to give the Blue Devils a 79-78 victory and propelled the Blue Devils into the Final Four for a third-straight year.

However, that season didn't have a fairy-tale ending to it. UNLV shattered Duke's dreams of a national championship with a 103-76 victory in the championship game in Denver. It didn't help that Duke's feisty point guard, Bobby Hurley, was sick with the flu for the entire game. "If Bobby hadn't been sick, we wouldn't have lost by 20," Laettner said. "I thought about that game all year."

Laettner got his chance for revenge when the Blue Devils met the Runnin' Rebels again in the 1991 national semifinals. Duke was a year older. They were a year better. "Coach K pumped us up as high as he could," Laettner recalled. "He showed us tapes of us doing great. He told us they were a good team, but he figured we could beat them.

"We had two or three guys on [six-foot-six All-American] Larry Johnson and got back in transition because they were the Runnin' Rebels. We left the other guys open. It was a good game plan. We had confidence in it. We had some success, so we were pumped up.

"He told us at halftime, 'We can do it. We're freakin' Duke. We can beat these guys.' The last thing he put in our heads was this: 'You've been in a lot of close games. We can handle it better than they can. They hadn't been in a close game all year.'

"Like Coach K said, it was a tight game."

The game came down to the final seconds. The score was tied 77-77, but Duke had the ball and held it until there were 15 seconds left. Then Thomas Hill missed a drive, but Laettner grabbed the rebound and was fouled with 12.7 seconds remaining. He calmly made two free throws to give Duke the lead. And the Blue Devils held on for the victory.

Laettner finished with 28 points in 40 minutes but was completely exhausted. Krzyzewski, cognizant of the fact his key players had no legs during the 1986 championship loss to Louisville, made sure to rest Laettner at key spots throughout the 72-65 victory over Kansas in the finals.

Laettner scored 18 points by getting to the line and making all 12 free throws and was named Most Outstanding Player.

It was Krzyzewski's first of three national championships.

Laettner thought about leaving for the NBA after his junior year. "A friend gave me a quote he found: 'A year you can put in your memory is better than a dollar you can put in your wallet.' That's how I felt," Laettner said.

The Blue Devils were the overwhelming favorite to repeat the following season.

"I remember Coach K saying he was hungrier than ever," Laettner recalled.

"There was a little cursing behind closed doors. We could see how hungry he was. He was passionate, serious. We had to match his intensity all season. He told us we weren't defending our national championship; we were trying to get another ring. That kept us on our toes. Instead of being defensive, we were coming after you. We were going out to get another. He was a genius.

"He knew how to keep us levelheaded with all the attention we were getting. If you were on your high horse, he'd tell you: 'You've got to play better. You're a good player. Don't get down.'

"If your head got too big—which mine did, occasionally—he would say, 'I wish you'd left your junior year. Don't be a punk.'

"He knew how to handle us."

That's not to say there weren't distractions.

The players on the 1992 Duke team were treated like rock stars wherever they went during that 34-2 season. "We were the hot item that year," Laettner admitted.

They were No. 1.

There was, for example, the girl at Clemson who dashed up to Grant Hill and screamed, "Oh, Grant, I just love your ears. Can I touch them?"

When Hill said, "Uh, yeah," she proceeded to stretch up on her tiptoes and kiss his right earlobe.

The Blue Devils couldn't get on the bus after that ACC game. The crowd was so large that the Littlejohn Coliseum doors were opened and the bus driven up to their locker room. One girl, wearing a "Christian Laettner Lover" T-shirt jumped on the bus.

The scene at Maryland was pretty much the same—with some of the players having to sneak out of a back window.

When Duke played at Boston University, a handful of girls were waiting for them when they departed a Boston hotel at 5 a.m. Some 6,000 fans showed up just to watch Duke practice before the sub-regionals. And, again, the players couldn't make their way safely to the bus. A police escort was needed to help them escape through a side door.

Not all of the receptions were love fests.

When North Carolina and Wake Forest pulled off upsets over the Devils during the regular season, their students celebrated by cutting down the nets.

When Duke played at LSU, the team bus was pelted with beer cans as it went to practice.

Laettner responded by outplaying LSU's seven-foot-one giant Shaquille O'Neal and scoring 12 of his 22 points in the final 9:06 as Duke won 76-67 in a nationally televised February 8 game at Baton Rouge. Hurley did not play because of a broken foot.

The mania had gotten out of control by the time the Devils reached the regionals. When Hurley was walking up the narrow corridor that connects the locker room and the court at the Philadelphia Spectrum before practice, a girl reached down from the stands, wrapped him in a headlock, and jerked him back to her.

"They've got to make the corridors a little wider," Hurley said.

That was nothing compared to the insanity of the Kentucky game.

After Sean Woods hooked the ball over Laettner to give Kentucky a one-point lead in double overtime with 2.1 seconds left, Hurley called timeout.

"You know, everyone knows what Coach K did," Laettner said. "He used his psychology training to reinforce positive thinking in our minds. He had taken psychology at Army and he could really rally the troops.

"He said, 'Grant, can you make the pass?'

"Grant said, 'Yes.'

"And I knew we were on the path. He said, 'You know how to run the play. We practiced the play. Let's run it.'

"We ran the play and, magically, things happened."

Laettner was the perfect player on a perfect night. He shot 10 for 10, made all 10 free throws, and finished with 31 points. "I didn't know I hadn't missed," he said. "No one told me. I just felt, 'Man, we're going to lose.' And I didn't want to lose.

"That's the genius of the Duke staff. When you go to Duke, if someone has 30 points, you've got to go out and get 35. My feeling was more like, 'Man, we're in a dog fight, and I want to go to my fourth Final Four in four years. If we lose, we won't be able to repeat.'"

Two games later, Laettner got his wish.

After the season, USA Basketball added Laettner to the Olympic roster. "They decided the 12th guy would not be an NBA guy; it would be a collegian," Laettner said.

"I was the best collegian that year. There was no one else who had done the things I had done. If people want to debate that, then go look at the cold hard facts. Alonzo Mourning didn't win anything. Shaq didn't win anything. I won two years in a row."

Before he left Duke, Laettner also had his number retired, although Krzyzewski warned that both his jersey and the 1992 national championship banner would come down from the rafters if Laettner did not earn his degree by July. Laettner took a psychology course to complete his degree work in the first session of summer school before he joined the Dream Team.

There was a huge fuss in Durham one day that June because Laettner was spotted in a wheelchair. It turned out he had to spend a day in the wheelchair for the course he was taking.

Laettner was the third pick in the 1992 NBA draft. He has played in the league for 14 years, and his pro career is winding down. "My family makes me think about quitting," he said. "I'm in Miami, and my wife, Lisa, and two daughters, Sophie and Sommer, are up in Jacksonville. Sophie will be eight. Sommer is six. They're into *Kim Possible*, *Lizzie McGuire*, and gymnastics. And I miss them during the season."

Laettner has learned how to count his blessings.

He and Brian Davis, close friends and co-captains of the 1992 championship team, recently donated $2 million to their alma mater—part of the Legacy Club, the organization that provided scholarships for Duke basketball players and provides support for the program, and part to help fund a new athletic facility.

As for Krzyzewski, he keeps pushing on. He is already in the Hall of Fame and Laettner thinks he is destined to become the best college coach ever, ahead of John Wooden, who won 10 national championships at UCLA.

"Everything in college basketball is different now," Laettner said. "Players play two, three years at most. When Wooden was at UCLA, freshmen weren't even eligible. How many games were they playing to reach the Final Four? Blah, blah, blah.

"What Coach K has done is more significant. Now he does get some players. You can't be as successful as he is without players. It's not like he's doing it with bums. But a lot of coaches get players and don't win big with them."

14

THE RADIO VOICE

BOB HARRIS

Duke Radio Play-by-Play

When Duke's radio play-by-play announcer Bob Harris took a job as a sales representative at WDNC in Raleigh in 1975 and began doing basketball play-by-play the next winter, he had no idea he would have such a big role in chronicling the Mike Krzyzewski era.

He had no idea he would even be broadcasting intimate details of a Hall of Fame career.

Harris was in the audience the day Duke A.D. Tom Butters hired an obscure coach from Army and then broadcast every important game during Krzyzewski's rise to power in the Atlantic Coast Conference.

"My opinions of him now and then are probably worlds apart," Harris recalled. "I remember the press conference. I knew about an hour before what the decision was and actually met him there in Cameron before he went over to the Duke news bureau on campus.

"I kept thinking, 'Where did this come from?' because, you know, Bob Wenzel, Paul Webb, and Bob Weltlich were the three candidates. Everybody kept talking about, 'It will be Coach W leading the Blue Devils.' In fact, the *Herald* wrote a story just that morning.

"That day, Duke stayed true to its word. It was Coach W—then in parenthesis [HO]. But knowing Tom Butters, knowing he was a man of conviction and action when it was warranted, I knew he had done his homework. He had talked to Bob Knight and several other people and made his decision on that."

Duke Photography

Krzyzewski got to the NIT his first year, when Gene Banks and Kenny Dennard were seniors. Then the roof looked like it was ready to cave in.

"The next two years were traumatic," Harris recalled. "It was kind of frustrating because like everybody else, I like to win, and I like to see the team I broadcast win, going all the way back to high school.

"But there was something about the guy.

"I'll never forget sitting with him back in the old coach's locker room up above the old dressing room his third year. I guess it was early February, and the wolves were out. Jimmy Valvano had done some good things at N.C. State and everybody was saying, 'Why didn't we hire this guy instead of him?' things like that.

"They were really getting on him because he would not play any zone. He did not even use the word *zone*. I can remember sitting there after one game. All the assistants had gone, all the players. I was talking with him and he almost had tears in his eyes, and his chin quivered and he said, 'If they just leave me alone and let me build it the way I know it can, it will work. I know this will work. Yeah, we could have won more games if we had played zone, but that would have defeated the entire purpose. I'm not building for this year or next year. I'm building for the long term.'

"I remembered that his entire career."

Especially after Duke beat Kansas to win its first national championship in 1991. "After we did our final daily radio show, he just kind of leaned back in his chair and I said, 'I'm glad they left you alone and let you do it the way you wanted.'

"He looked at me real funny and almost teared up again and said, 'You remembered, huh? I never forgot that.'"

Harris also never forgot the Devils' 46-point loss to Virginia at the end of the 1983 season. "I went back to the team hotel in Atlanta, and this Iron Duke who had given quite a bit of money to the athletic department grabbed me by the coat lapels and was screaming, 'When are we going to get rid of that SOB and the guy who hired him, too?' He wanted Butters gone. The veins in his neck were standing out. I thought he was going to have a coronary.

"I looked at him. I called him by name and said, 'I don't know. I don't have anything to do with it.' I later realized why people do things like that: it's because they can't get to those people. I'm the first one available.

"It was so funny: about 10 years later, I saw the same man and his wife having lunch with Mike's brother and his wife in Philadelphia before we beat Kentucky in the 1992 regional finals. It's amazing how things turn around."

Harris has watched up-close and personal while Krzyzewski pulled off miracles, including the one against Kentucky in the 1992 East Regional finals in Philadelphia. That was the game that immortalized Christian Laettner, when he caught a long pass from Grant Hill, then drained a jumper from the right of the key at the buzzer to give the Blue Devils a dramatic 104-103 double overtime victory.

"That was the defining moment for him, for Christian, for my call. That final 2.1 seconds got much more notoriety than any of us would have anticipated. You look back on that situation and see that here you've played a great basketball game, two great teams that slugged it out like heavyweight champions.

"All of a sudden, Sean Woods hits a runner over Christian—and he's going to be the hero. And Mike calls timeout. I remember leaning back in my seat during a commercial and looking up at the scoreboard and making sure I had the score right. Okay. It's 103-102. We either miss a shot or don't get one. Kentucky wins. They're going to the Final Four. Our string is through.

"So then I look at the team as they break the huddle to see who may get the shot. Grant goes to the baseline. Where's Bobby Hurley? Bobby comes up to midcourt. Where's Christian? He's in the far corner. And, all of a sudden, the light went on: the Wake Forest game in Winston-Salem.

"We'd had the same kind of situation. It wasn't overtime, but Laettner was in the corner to my left that night. Grant was going to make the inbound pass but he threw a curveball. Christian caught it. As he turned to take the shot, his heel hit the out-of-bounds line. And we lost the game.

"And I'm thinking, 'They're going to run the same play.' Out of the corner of my eye, I watched Christian come up, but he came all the way to the top of the circle.

"Going back to the timeout: when Mike called the timeout, when the guys sat down, he looked at them and said, 'We're going to win this ballgame—and here's how we're going to do it.' He never said, 'If you can do this, if you can do that, we've got a chance.' He is one of the strongest people I've ever been around—he almost wills things to happen.

"He willed 27 wins out of the 2005 team. It was his best coaching job, bar none. Billy Packer—and I don't always agree with what he says—said it was Mike's best job, the ACC's best coaching job, ever.

"And he said, 'Well, think about it. You've been around as many years as I have. Who's done a better job considering all the circumstances: all the problems he went through in the summer, getting the team harnessed back together with all the sickness, injuries, and kids leaving early for the pros? Who's done a better job, ever?'

"I still haven't come up with anybody."

After Laettner's shot beat Kentucky, Krzyzewski took time after the celebration to make his way over to the Kentucky radio booth.

"It startled their legendary broadcaster, Cawood Ledford," Harris said. "It was Cawood's last year, and Mike said, 'Can I go on and talk to the Kentucky fans?'

"Cawood told me later, 'That is the most unbelievable thing I've ever had happen. Here's a coach of an opposing team that had just beaten Kentucky and he's talking about the Kentucky seniors and said they had nothing to be ashamed of or disappointed in. It was a great game, and he was so proud to be a part of it. I think it caught everybody by surprise: that he would have the presence of mind to do something like that.'"

Harris still hears his call on ESPN and CBS every year around tournament time. "The Kentucky fans still hate me because of that. I'm kidding. I do a charity golf tournament with a friend of mine, Doug Flynn, in Lexington every year in June. The first year I went down there, they introduced me with all the celebrities, and I got boos and catcalls. Some guys said, 'Where's Christian Laettner?'"

"I said, 'He's backstage waiting to see if you all kill me.'

"That just defused the whole thing. As a matter of fact, the owner of the Pepsi distributorship out there told my wife, 'You know something, my opinion of Duke basketball has changed 180 degrees because of your husband.'"

Krzyzewski began changing the nation's view of Duke basketball when the Blue Devils reached Krzyzewski's first Final Four in Dallas during the 1986 season.

"Johnny Dawkins was the linchpin," Harris recalled. "He was the cornerstone for what happened that year. But that team had special players: Jay Bilas, Mark Alarie, Tom Amaker, and David Henderson. I can remember a guy in a press conference at the Final Four was sitting in the back, talking to his buddy, and he turned to him while the Duke guys were talking, and he said, 'Are these guys for real?' They were so intelligent, answering every question without giving you coach-speak. It was so much fun to watch that and see the reaction of the national media.

"During that same press conference, watching our guys, I was talking to a writer from Los Angeles, and he asked if this was my first Final Four.

"I said it was my first since we went in 1978.

"And he said, 'Enjoy it, you might not get back.'

"I said, 'Oh, we'll be back.'"

Krzyzewski coached the Blue Devils to the Sweet 16 the next year, but Duke went on an incredible run of five-straight Final Fours from 1988 through 1992, winning two national championships.

"That's when everybody began calling him 'Coach K' or 'Special K,'" Harris said. "He kind of piecemealed some things together with teams that were somewhat talented but didn't have the veterans like Laettner or Hurley. We got back there in 1990, but we got our heads handed to us by 30 by UNLV in the finals. Golly, it was maybe one of the low points of the Final Four."

But Duke avenged the loss the following season, knocking an unbeaten UNLV team off 79-77 in the national semifinals.

"I remember going into the locker room to do Mike's pregame show before that game like I always do. And when I went in, he was in a meeting in the back with Bobby Hurley, showing him the video of his freshman year, because he always was making faces. So I waited. It was halftime of the Kansas-North Carolina game, and the players were all lying around on the floor, watching the game on TV. All of a sudden, Thomas Hill jumps up and runs out the door and I'm saying to myself, 'What's going on?'

"'Just watch the monitor,' he said.

"Lesley Visser of CBS is waiting outside for a live shot with Kansas, and all you see is the door crack open and Thomas Hill's head come up. He kind of waves over her head, shuts the door, runs back into the locker room, and howls.

"So I finish up with Mike, go back out, and as I turned to go through the door in the hallway, the big door opened up—and there's the UNLV bus. The players get off, and I looked at their faces. They were tight as tight can be. I walked to our broadcast location, where my wife is keeping stats for me, and I said, 'We're going to win this ballgame.'

"'What have you been drinking?' she asked.

"I told her, 'You watch. The Duke kids are as loose as they can be, and UNLV is so tight, it's scary.' When it was over, she looked at me and said, 'You knew what you were talking about, didn't you?'

"After the final buzzer sounded, some of the Duke players began to celebrate. But Mike had the presence of mind to say, 'Calm down. You haven't accomplished a thing yet.' That was a great moment."

Krzyzewski's success has brought out suitors from several pro franchises.

"He has turned down blank checks from expansion owners, Dave Gavitt," Harris said.

"I can still remember 1990 when the Celtics came after him. I got a call from WBZ radio when the rumor was heating up in Boston. The guy says to me, 'I'd like to arrange an interview with you about the new Celtics coach.'

"And I said, 'What?'

"'Yeah,' he said, 'Krzyzewski's going to be named tomorrow. They're just crossing the t's and dotting the i's now.

"I said, 'You're crazy. It ain't going to happen.'

"He said, 'Will you go on the air and say that?'

"So we go on the air and he says, 'Our guest says it's not going to happen, Boston. Bob Harris, tell me why it's not going to happen.'

"'Well,' I said, 'there are a couple of reasons why. No. 1, he's a teacher. No. 2, he's a great family man. And No. 3, you have to play defense, or you don't play for Coach K. The last time I checked, none of those things is in evidence in the NBA.'

"So he said, 'Tell you what. On Friday morning, I'm going to call you back, and one of us is going to eat crow.'

"So it comes out the next day that it's not going to happen. He calls me back Friday morning, true to his word, and says, 'Well, evidently you knew Mike Krzyzewski better than I thought.'

"I said, 'Well, I'd like to think so.'"

Krzyzewski has poured himself into this program, even when he hasn't been completely healthy.

Harris recalled, "After he lost to Connecticut in the finals of the 1999 tournament, he was getting ready for a hip replacement. He was sitting back in that little cubicle, kind of slumped back in his chair, and he was ashen. He looked like he had gotten run over by a truck.

"I said to him, 'Mike, how in the hell have you done it?'

"'I just put it out of my mind,' he said.

"How can you put pain like that out of your mind?' I asked.

"And he said, 'I had to do it for this team.'"

Krzyzewski had won 721 career victories and should be the all-time-winningest coach by the time he retires. "He can coach as long as he wants to, as long as he's healthy," Harris said. "He told me felt the best he's felt in 15 years."

Krzyzewski has developed a new energy ever since he became a grandfather.

"He's a puppy. It's unbelievable to watch him interact with those kids," Harris said. "I know when the first one came around—Joey—he was like putty in that child's hands. He and I have talked about that. I have grandchildren of my own."

Harris was on the floor after Duke had just defeated Arizona 82-72 to win the 2001 national championship when Krzyzewski found out there was a new addition to the family.

"It's the middle of the interview, and Mickie tugs at him. I could read her lips: 'Debbie's on the phone.'

"Joey had just been born. Debbie did not get to go to the Final Four because of that. So she was back in Durham. She was on the cell phone. Mickie looked at him with such an expression, and I said, 'Coach is going to have to break off this interview because he's got a very important phone call. And, no, it's not from the president. It's from his daughter who just presented him with a new grandson.'"

Harris has felt Krzyzewski's personal touch in his work.

"For my 25th year, my wife had bought me a Waterford crystal microphone and had it engraved," Harris said. "She told Coach what she had done and wanted to know if it could be presented to me at a game.

"Mike said, 'No.'

"She looked at him funny, and he said, 'That wouldn't do him justice. Bob deserves better than that. I want my team to be there when it happens, and we can't be out there at halftime. Let's wait and do it at the banquet.'

"That was in 2001, the year when we won the championship, and he presents it to me. I get on the stage and try to say something and I start crying.

"He's that kind of guy."

15

THE GYM RAT

BOBBY HURLEY

Duke Class of 1993

N ot all of the players on Duke's back-to-back national championship
teams had blue blood running through their veins.

But Bobby Hurley Jr. did.

Bobby Hurley Jr.—an All-America point guard who has his No. 11 hanging
from the ceiling at Cameron Indoor Stadium—came from Jersey City, New
Jersey, a faded town just across the river from Manhattan. He learned to play
from his father, Bob Hurley Sr., who has run one of the most successful high
school programs in the country at St. Anthony's, a tiny Catholic outreach
school with an enrollment of less than 300 on Eighth Street, adjacent to the
fire hall and across the street from a senior center, for the past 33 years.

Bob Hurley Sr., a parole officer in the city, has won 847 career games and
lost just 97. He has won 22 state championships and two mythical national high
school championships and has had four undefeated seasons. The school consists
of one three-story brick building. Practices and home games are held at the
nearby Golden Door Charter School.

Hurley Sr. is the patriarch of the first family of Jersey City hoops. He lived
down the shore for a while but has since moved back to Jersey City and is living
with his wife in a building on the water, where gentrification has kicked in.

This is home.

With Hurley, coaching kids from what he calls "the belly of the beast" has
always been a calling. The nuns who run the financially strapped place can't
always afford to pay his $7,000 salary. Hurley used to run his practices at the
White Eagle Bingo Hall, where players had to stack the folding chairs before

Duke Photography

they took the floor—then put them back afterward. Scrimmages were survival-of-the-fittest challenges—with no fouls called and players fighting for possession of loose balls that may have gone down the stairwells. White Eagle has since been torn down.

But before the wrecking ball hit, Hurley invited all of his former players over for one last pick-up game.

There were a lot of tears.

Bobby Hurley Jr. grew up in that kind of rough-and-tumble atmosphere. He used to play tackle football with his younger brother in the living room of their old row house until one time, Bobby—pretending to Lawrence Taylor—nailed his younger brother, Danny. Danny required stitches.

"I spent a lot of time in that gym," Bobby said. "My dad would take us to practice with him all the time. He was a huge Celtics fan when we were growing up. I was a big Larry Bird fan when the Celtics had it going in the 1980s, and I can still recall watching those Boston-Lakers series with him."

When Hurley was younger, he used to play one on one against his father and Danny. Later, when he was old enough, his father used to give him bus fare, and the six-foot, 160-pound gym rat would travel to the parks and projects in some of the toughest parts of the city—like the Duncan Projects—to play pick-up ball.

"There were no refs, nobody to stop someone from beating you up," Hurley recalled. "I was a little nervous at first. I was the only white kid playing, but the guys I played with respected what I did on the court."

Hurley learned his lessons well.

He led St. Anthony's to 50-straight wins and a 32-0 record and a mythical national high school championship in 1989, his senior year.

Initially, Hurley had no intention of attending Duke.

"I was a big Carolina fan ever since Jordan hit that shot," he said. "I actually went to the Carolina basketball school when I was in the eighth grade. I wasn't that impressive as a physical athlete then. I was very immature and was a late bloomer physically. They didn't really take notice of me at that point.

"When I started playing, I wanted to go there. At that point, I think they felt they were going to get Kenny Anderson from Archbishop Molloy in Queens. They couldn't go wrong with Kenny at the point. I didn't recall holding any ill feeling toward them.

"But Kenny kind of surprised me by choosing Georgia Tech."

By the time Hurley entered his senior year at St. Anthony's, he was considering playing in the Big East at either Seton Hall or Syracuse.

"I had talked to Coach K a lot on the phone; but Duke being so far away, I figured I'd stay close. Actually, my parents were kicking me out of the door to make an official visit that fall. I wasn't that thrilled about going, but I completely changed my feeling when I got a chance to see it.

"I just loved the campus, and he had the kids out at the house, watching games, and I just felt everyone got along well. I just really got a good feeling about being there. I got a chance to watch the guys play pick up and I saw Laettner playing, and I thought that might be a good thing."

In retrospect, Hurley says Krzyzewski just wore him down. After Hurley's official visit, Krzyzewski and assistants Bob Bender and Mike Brey flew back with Hurley and guard Billy McCaffrey of Allentown Central Catholic, who had committed over the weekend.

They were getting ready to put on a full-court press during the home visit that Monday night. When Mike sat down to begin his presentation, Bob Hurley Sr. interrupted.

"Bobby," he asked, "do you have something to say?"

"And I said, 'Coach, I'd like to come to Duke,'" Hurley recalled.

It was a decision neither one would regret. The Cameron Crazies affectionately referred to Hurley as "Bart Simpson," because he looked like he was 12 years old. But Hurley was a four-year starter who set a school record and an NCAA Tournament record for assists and, more importantly, an NCAA record for career assists for all games, passing Chris Corchianni of N.C. State.

What made that so significant was the fact Krzyzewski tried so hard for Corchianni. After Amaker graduated in 1987, Krzyzewski was on the lookout for another point guard, but lost Corchianni to N.C. State. The next year, he wanted California point guard Derrick Martin. The recruiting battle went down to the wire, but Martin picked UCLA. Funny how things work out. Had Krzyzewski signed either one, he might not have worked so hard on Hurley.

"My father and Coach K were two of the best people I've ever been around as far as knowing the game of basketball," Hurley said. "But they were two different personalities.

"My dad has mellowed out a lot over the years. In younger days, he could be a little tough on you. He was a tough SOB. I think that's what I needed as a young kid. It kind of made me a tougher player when I got to that next level. Coach K was more of a calming influence on me. I was a little hot-headed when I played. Just looking over at the sideline and seeing how calm he was was a good influence on me."

Hurley had been the salutatorian of his senior class, but he'd had to work hard on his academics. And there had been an adjustment period after he arrived at Duke.

"I spent a lot of summers taking courses so I could take a lighter load during the season," he said. "Just managing that was pretty difficult. Then it was learning to live on your own for the first time. If you get a big pile of laundry that accumulated, you know Mom's not there anymore, and you've got to figure out how to do it yourself or try and sweet talk someone else into doing it."

There was also a transition on the court. "I don't know if I was ready to handle starting right away," he said. "Being a young player, being in charge of a team was hard for me. It was tough for me, just handling my emotions.

"I was yelling at officials, arguing with my teammates on the floor, like Laettner, sometimes. I was too hot-headed. I think that was my dad's personality. He has that fire and that emotion. I just needed to tone that down a little bit and use the energy a lot more positively.

"With the help of Coach K, I was able to solve that problem."

Krzyzewski realized that Hurley talked with his face. In order to cure him, Krzyzewski and assistant Pete Gaudet put together a one-minute videotape of Hurley sulking and complaining in various games.

"He showed me a film of times when I was doing it," Hurley said. "He said, 'You don't understand the negative impact it has on other guys who see you as the leader of the team. It doesn't really help matters.' When I saw that, I realized it wasn't that good and I had to do something about it. I think it was a maturity process.

"That helped. But what helped more was Coach K making a tape of the good things I did and showing that to me as well. I was down on myself enough as it was."

Hurley piled up 228 assists that year and played well enough down the stretch to help lead his team to 29 wins and a spot in the 1990 NCAA championship game against UNLV. But two days earlier, before Duke's semifinal game against Arkansas, he became violently ill with flu and diarrhea.

Hurley was so sick he had to leave the court with just 4:40 gone and the Blue Devils ahead 16-5. He ran to the locker room where he threw up and missed four minutes of playing time. He returned, played 36 minutes, and had just three points, six assists, and had six turnovers.

"I was on IVs," he recalled. "It got played out like I was nervous but that's not what happened. It was bad timing for something like that to happen for me. I'd always dreamed of playing in the Final Four, but to feel that way and not really enjoy being there, that was tough. And it wasn't good for me to feel that way and have to chase UNLV guys."

The Runnin' Rebels cruised to a 103-76 victory, making 17 steals and forcing Duke into a sloppy 23 turnovers. Hurley played 32 minutes and had just three assists and five turnovers in the embarrassing blowout.

"Losing to UNLV like we did made me tougher, mentally stronger, and ready to assume a bigger role the next year," Hurley said.

Duke finally got some measure of revenge the following year when they knocked off an unbeaten UNLV team 79-77 in the NCAA semifinals at Indianapolis en route to their first national championship.

Nobody gave Duke a chance in that game.

Except Krzyzewski.

"He told us, 'I'm going to be telling the media how good they are all week, but I think you guys are going to beat them.'

"He was so believable and so energetic. I've been in some of his pregames, even after I graduated. I've sat in those locker rooms when he's talking, and I get goosebumps all over, just listening to him. He's amazing."

Krzyzewski showed the team a tape of the 1990 final, pointing out that the Blue Devils were sick and tired. He also felt Duke had a chance as long as it could keep the game close at the end. UNLV had cruised to a 32-0 record that year. The Rebels' closest game was a 112-105 victory over Arkansas in Fayetteville.

"We knew we had very little margin for error," Hurley said. "We knew we had to play a nearly flawless game to beat that team. They were as close to an NBA team as I saw in my four years.

"We got off to an early 14-4 lead. That was huge for us. We knew we were going to make a game of it. We respected how good they were, and we knew if we weren't going to bring it right from the beginning, we could get embarrassed again."

The Blue Devils hung around long enough to create a specter of doubt. UNLV looked like it might pull away after the Rebels took a 76-71 lead. But then Hurley drained a three-point goal over the Vegas "Amoeba" defense to spark Duke's late rally. Duke historian Bill Brill claims it was the "biggest shot" in school history. The Blue Devils took the lead when Christian Laettner was fouled on a rebound with just 12.7 seconds left and made a pair of free throws to tie a 77-77 tie.

After Anderson Hunt missed a desperation heave at the buzzer, there was a wild celebration on the court. "I got the last rebound when they missed and the buzzer sounded," Hurley said. "I dribbled for three seconds after that. I couldn't believe the game was over. Grant had to grab me and say that we won it.

"I've never had a feeling like that in basketball."

Hurley was riding on Clay Buckley's back when Krzyzewski called for perspective, pushing his palms down. "You have to enjoy that moment, if Coach K wanted to calm people down," Hurley said. "But we also realized if we hadn't beaten Kansas, it wouldn't have been as important as it was."

Duke finished the job two nights later when the Devils defeated the Jayhawks 72-65 in the finals.

That was only the beginning for the Blue Devils, who pulled off a rare repeat the next season. This was the closest thing Krzyzewski had to a dream team, with Laettner, Hurley, and Grant Hill—all of whom had their jerseys retired. "Christian was obviously a huge draw wherever we went," Hurley said. "People went crazy over seeing him play. It was exciting. I was just like the baby-faced kid. I've gotten a little older since then."

Krzyzewski knew his rock stars had talent.

"He knew what we had, coming in, and he didn't push as hard on us, especially early in the year," Hurley said. "He was trying to gear us up for the tournament. He treated us like a team that knew how to handle adversity. That was a little different than the year before. The year before, he was a little harder on us, trying to get more out of us, constantly pushing on us in practice."

Duke was 34-2 and ranked No. 1, wire to wire in 1992, beating Seton Hall and his brother Danny in the East Regional semifinals before playing Kentucky in one of the greatest games ever to reach their fifth-straight Final Four. Neither of the brothers played well in that game. Bobby had one of his worst games—four points, seven assists, and six turnovers. Danny did not score.

Bobby heated up against Kentucky two nights later.

And he pulled off some unexpected heroics from Hurley to win a second consecutive title.

"Christian had used so much energy, had a perfect game against Kentucky, that I think he was sort of worn out. So for about a game and a half, there was more responsibility on some other guys to step up," Hurley said. "That's what kind of made us the team we were."

Krzyzewski specifically told Hurley that he needed to upgrade his offense. "I had missed three weeks with a broken foot that season and had just come back a few weeks before the ACC Tournament," Hurley said. "So I was able to freshen up during that time off. I was starting to get real healthy, feeling good. Especially in the Final Four. Once I saw Christian wasn't really there mentally, I had some opportunities to step up."

Hurley stepped up big in the semifinals, scoring 26 points during an 81-78 victory over Indiana while Laettner endured his worst game of the season, shooting two for eight and scoring just six points in 39 minutes.

Then in Duke's 71-51 championship victory over Michigan in the finals, when Laettner looked like he was completely out of gas at halftime, and Krzyzewski told Hurley to get him involved in the offense, Hurley was all over Laettner in the locker room.

It worked. Laettner scored 14 points in the second half and finished with a game-high 19.

"He demanded a lot out of me," Hurley says of Laettner. "Sometimes his expectations of me were too excessive. We butted heads sometimes, but he made me better. By the end of my career, as mature as I was and as good as I felt about my game, I had no problem telling him, 'Get out of here. I'm handling this.' We developed a good level of communication, and I would always look for him because I knew he could deliver."

Hurley scored only nine points in the final game, but he was still selected the tournament's Most Outstanding Player, primarily because of his performance against Indiana in the semifinals.

Hurley's senior year didn't turn out quite as well as he would have liked, largely because Grant Hill suffered a broken toe near the end of the season, missed six games, and was never the same when he returned. Cal eliminated Duke in the second-round game at the Rosemont Horizon in what was essentially a matchup between Hurley and Cal's Jason Kidd.

Kidd had 14 assists, eight rebounds, and 11 points on four-of-11 shooting. Hurley had 32 points, nine assists, and just one turnover. Cal built up a huge first-half lead, and Duke appeared dead when Cherokee Parks broke his leg late in the first half. But Hurley and Hill—who had 18 points—brought Duke back, and the Blue Devils actually had the lead. But, with Cal down one, Kidd picked up a loose ball under the Cal basket and scored the winning points.

After the game, Krzyzewski cried when he spoke about Hurley.

"I remember hugging him after the game," Hurley said. "It was just a long trip, that third year. After going back to back, trying to do it again became a burden. Maybe that was a release of all that had gone on. It was a tough day.

"But I remember a happier day, walking with him after the UNLV game, going to the press conference, seeing him, knowing we had done something special together, concluding with the championship.

"I just think he was the type of person who deserved to be an elite coach. And until he broke through and won that national championship, I didn't know if he was going to get to that level.

"I'm just happy to feel that I was a part in helping him get there, because now he's continually proven—year after year with the type of teams he has—how great he is. But until you get those championships, no one is going to put you at the top of the game.

"I know he's the best coach I've seen, had a chance to be around. His credentials could be stacked with anyone in the sport: John Wooden, in a different era; Dean Smith. And I think the world of Dean Smith."

Krzyzewski popped into Hurley's life later that year under more difficult circumstances. Hurley was the seventh pick of the Sacramento Kings that June.

Hurley was starting, averaging 7.1 points and 6.1 assists when his life changed forever. On the night of December 12, 1993, he was driving home from Sacramento's Arco Arena when a station wagon being driven without its lights on slammed into the side of his Toyota Four Runner.

Hurley wound up in a ditch, near death. He had his lung torn from the trachea. He suffered broken ribs, multiple fractures, and a torn ACL in the right knee. Twice he died on the operating table. Doctors had to have his heart started again. As soon as Krzyzewski heard the news, he got on the next plane and was out there, along with Hurley's immediate family.

"It was hard, because there was really no way to prepare yourself for what happened," Hurley shared. "Your life is one way and then it changes. I had to get used to being in a car again. I'd hear a car horn honk and I'd become so unnerved I had to pull over. I just don't know where my career went after that. It was all over the board."

Hurley recovered, but he never really made a dent in the NBA. He was relegated to a part-time player and was traded to the Vancouver Grizzlies before eventually being released in January 1999.

Hurley wasn't ready to leave just yet. He got back in shape and attempted to make a comeback in the Jersey Shore League that summer. But late in a game on a hot July night, he tried to make a move, and his right knee popped.

Hurley knew it was over then.

But true to his bloodline, he plunged into a new business venture shortly thereafter: racehorses. Hurley used to go to Monmouth Park while he was on summer break in college, and he and a friend brought their first horses in 1997. Then he and a minority partner plunked down $1 million for Songandaprayer, a two-year-old, at the Tipton Select Sale at Miami's Calder Race Course. "When I called my wife, Leslie, to tell her about it, she hung up the phone," he recalled.

Leslie felt better about the investment when the horse won the $50,000 Fountain of Youth Stakes at Gulf Stream and raced in the 2001 Kentucky

Derby. Hurley sold 40 percent of his investment for $1 million in 2002 and collected $500,000 in stud fees the following year.

"He's a stallion now in stud," Hurley said. "I own half of him. He's doing great. Some of his offspring are just about to make it to the races, and Bob Badford bought one of them for $1.9 million. It looks like it could be a really good horse. That would help."

Hurley is now co-owner of nine horses, a dozen broodmares, Songandaprayer, and his foals, which are housed at the Devil 11 Stables at Aqueduct.

He thinks about coaching once in a while and occasionally takes his ball to the local playground. But other than that and playing dribbling games with his daughters, Cameron and Sydney, he has said his long goodbye to a sport he loves.

Hurley did make it to the Garden in 2004 when the Blue Devils played there. "A lot of Duke students come from the metropolitan area," he said. "So there's a huge following. I was shocked the first time I went. I saw so many people I went to school with. Duke is a national program. Everywhere you go, people are interested. But it goes both ways. For as many people who like the Yankees or the Cowboys, the same amount hate them.

"It's the same with Duke."

16

THE FAVORED SON

GRANT HILL

Duke Class of 1994

C alvin Hill is still one the most familiar faces at Cameron Indoor Stadium, dressed in that same blue Duke baseball cap he brought during son Grant's recruiting visit, along with the white turtleneck and khaki pants.

Hill, who is on the board of visitors for the Duke Divinity School, and his wife, Janet, still make the pilgrimage from Reston, Virginia, in suburban Washington, D.C., to Tobacco Road for home games—11 years after Grant graduated in 1994.

The Hills are the closest thing Duke basketball has to royalty. Calvin graduated Yale and was a star running back for the Dallas Cowboys who attended Perkins School of Theology in that city while he was playing. He is now a consultant for the team. Janet was a physics major and suitemate of Hillary Rodham Clinton at Wellesley College, worked for the secretary of the Army, and is a lawyer who runs her own consulting firm in Washington, D.C.

But at Duke, they are Grant Hill's parents.

"They're Duke junkies," Hill admitted. "My mother went down this year, and my dad goes all the time. I think, for parents, it had to be a lot of fun watching your child for four years, witnessing what went on down here when I played, to be part of that fraternity.

"It's really great for them because Coach K is there. They know [assistant] Chris Collins, who played with me; the staff; and all the workers in the office. Everybody knows everybody. I could call right now and talk to the secretary

Duke Photography

and find out everything that's going on. It's nice. When my parents go down there, they feel like they're part of the family."

Calvin and Janet Hill were both there for their son's Senior Night when Duke retired his number and the Cameron Crazies started chanting, "One more son. One more son." Calvin fought back the tears the best way he could, quoting Shakespeare.

It was the ultimate compliment to the ultimate player.

Krzyzewski has called Grant Hill the best overall player he ever coached at Duke and claimed Christian Laettner and Bobby Hurley told him the same thing.

It's hard to argue with the facts.

The multitalented, six-foot-eight Hill was a four-year starter and consensus first-team All-American as a senior. He became the first ACC player to finish with over 1,900 points, 700 rebounds, 400 assists, 200 steals, and 100 blocked shots. He has two NCAA championship rings—from the 1991 and 1992 seasons—and played in a third national championship game in 1994 before he graduated.

Then he was selected with the No. 3 pick in the draft by Detroit that June and went on to play for both the Detroit Pistons and the Orlando Magic. He was selected Rookie of the Year and has made the NBA All-Star game seven times, despite never being completely healthy since 1999.

"I've always had to prove myself—probably for other reasons than other players," he said. "Coming from a family that has money, I always got tested. But the way I look at it, that keeps me going."

Hill, an only child, is extremely close to his parents. They gave him a global view when he was younger. He made educational trips to Asia, South America, and across Europe. His mother took him to see the pyramids in Egypt. Family vacations always included a trip to a museum. Hill got to meet the last three presidents. He still likes to tell the story of meeting Kingman Brewster, the ambassador to England who went on to become the president of Yale, when he was six and starting to do cartwheels in the office to impress him.

"I guess, in a way, I'm lucky," he said. "Part of it is genetics and DNA, but my parents have helped me in so many ways off the court, developing me into the person I am, exposing me to a variety of different experiences during my childhood and giving me two people I could lean on."

Calvin had no interest in his son following in his footsteps.

"I wanted to play football as a child," the younger Hill recalled. "But I wasn't allowed to. I think, deep down, he wanted me to play at some point. But at that point, I started to have success in basketball. I think he realized basketball was a lot safer and—I can't say for sure, but I think—he probably enjoyed following me as a basketball player in high school and college more so than if I had been a football player."

When Hill was younger, he used to attend Georgetown games with his father, and patterned his game after Reggie Williams, the Hoyas' six-foot-eight All-American with similar skills. When he was 13, he went to an AAU Tournament and developed a national reputation.

When he returned home, his father challenged him to a game of one on one in the driveway. "Think you can beat your old man yet?" Calvin asked.

Grant beat him. Twice.

"That was kind of the turning point," he said.

"I don't mean to brag or come across as arrogant, but I kind of feel like growing up around my father and around professional sports, I've almost been groomed for this," he said. "Just watching him, being around the locker room, hearing stories: it was almost like I was destined to be a professional athlete. I don't know if that's always the case."

"My father's helped me in so many ways, not so much with free throw shooting. He likes to remind me, as good an athlete as I am, that I have only half his chromosomes. Just imagine if I had the other half—because my mother's not athletic."

There was a time when Hill shied away from his parents' celebrity and access to power. "I just wanted to be normal," he recalled. "But I knew that wasn't possible."

When Calvin was scheduled to speak at Grant's junior high school, Grant pretended he was sick. When Calvin would drive him to practice, Grant would request his father leave the Porsche at home and take the family Volkswagen.

When Hill was in ninth grade, Wendell Byrd, the South Lakes coach, invited him to try out for the varsity. But Hill balked. He wanted to play JV with his friends. When Calvin told Grant to try, his son began to cry.

"If you make me do this, it's a form of child abuse," he told his father.

Grant eventually gave in, started varsity as a freshman, and became a McDonald's All-American by the time he was a senior.

"I got to know Coach K when I was in high school," Hill recalled. "At the time, he had just come up short in the Final Four, but Duke was emerging into one of the premier programs in college basketball. What really impressed me was the fact he was honest, and I felt like I would benefit off and on the court from being around a man like him for four years.

"Of course, Duke is a great school; of course, they had great teams—and I wanted to win. But there were certain qualities in him that really attracted me. He was really passionate.

"It came down to Duke and North Carolina. From the outside looking in, you think the programs are just alike. They are in the sense that they both win, they both had tradition—this was back when Coach Smith was there—and they both do things the right way.

"But as I got to know both coaches and both situations, I realized there were a lot of differences. I'm not saying one is better than the other, but I just felt more comfortable at Duke. It wasn't one of these flip-a-coin decisions. Duke was a perfect fit for me. This made sense.

"And, of course, Coach K was a huge part of that."

Krzyzewski had to like the idea Hill had a strong sense of discipline before he arrived. Although he did receive a Mercedes for his 16th birthday, he was raised by a family with a strict set of rules. No TV during the week. One phone call during the weekends. One time, after he missed curfew, his mother took his watch and flung it against the wall. "You don't use it," she told him, "so you obviously don't need it."

Janet Hill had the watch repaired and eventually gave it to Grant on his next birthday. "That was his present," she recalled.

Hill was shy and a little unsure of himself when he first got to Duke. A week before freshman registration, he remembers calling assistant Tommy Amaker and asking him, "Do you think I can play here?"

Hill started as a freshman and averaged 11.1 points, despite breaking his nose in a late-night practice early in the ACC season and having to play several weeks with a hockey mask on.

He was more than happy to blend in with stars Christian Laettner and Bobby Hurley. But, just like in high school, he couldn't help but stand out. He was a *SportsCenter* highlight waiting to happen.

There was, for instance, the vicious one-handed dunk he threw down off a high-arching alley-oop pass from Hurley to set the tone at the start of a 72-65 1991 national championship victory over against Kansas his freshman year that made it to the cover of *Sports Illustrated*. When Hill was asked about the picture, he complained that he's always embarrassed by his awful haircut that he had at the time.

Or the time Hurley broke his foot against Carolina the next year and Krzyzewski shifted Hill from forward to point guard for a big game at LSU and its massive seven-foot-one center Shaquille O'Neal. Hill responded with a spectacular 16 points, nine rebounds, and six assists during a 77-67 victory on national TV February 8, 1992.

Or the 75-foot inbound pass he threw to Laettner for the miracle shot that defeated Kentucky 104-103 in overtime in the 1992 NCAA Eastern Regionals that propelled the Blue Devils to a second national championship.

"That was a great moment in sports, as I like to call it," he said. "It's not like I watched the game. I watch that play because they play it every year at tournament time.

"What I do recall from that game was it was a tough go down the stretch. Sean Woods hit a big shot with 2.1 seconds to go. We knew we were playing to get to the Final Four, but I don't think any of us understood the significance of that long pass at the time."

Duke had been faced with a similar situation against Wake Forest earlier in the season. The Blue Devils were down three in the closing seconds when Hill attempted to make a three-quarter-court pass to Laettner for a three-point attempt during a 72-68 loss. "I threw the ball to Christian," Hill said. "He caught it at the sideline, but his foot went out of bounds. The interesting thing was we practiced that play all season. I used to take pride in the fact I was the best baseball passer on the team. So, Coach K, I guess, kept that in mind when we needed it.

"The pass was the easy part. Christian had the difficult part, catching it and making the play."

Of course, he made it.

Duke seemed destined for greatness that season when it became the first team since UCLA in 1973 to win back-to-back national championships.

"We knew from Day 1 we were the favorites to win it all. We wanted not to just win. We wanted to go undefeated. We wanted to beat everybody. We wanted there to be no question about who was the best team in basketball. We knew that when you're No. 1, when you're defending champions, you get everybody's best shot—and we had to be even more sharp.

"And we were.

"That team loved to play.

"And I think one of the things Coach K, in his brilliance, recognized was that each team is different. He sat back and let us play. He encouraged us to go out there and make plays and have fun.

"We had personalities, guys who were very talented, very visible. Duke has gone on to do some great things since, but I know, for me, the 1992 season was by far the most fun and the wackiest year I've ever been a part of.

"There was really nothing like it, not in the NBA or even the Olympics. That 1992 team, I never experienced anything like it. The reactions of fans on the road: they'd boo you, then afterward they'd be dying to try to meet you. Even our fans, we didn't understand how they could go crazy over a bunch of teenagers."

Hill could have left early for the NBA. "But," he said, "one of the most important things I learned was to honor your commitment. I made a commitment to Coach K, and he made a commitment to me for four years."

Hill took ownership of the team in 1994 when Duke made an unlikely run at another national championship before losing to Arkansas 82-76 in the NCAA finals. "My senior year, what motivated me was to win and to have a leg up on Christian and Bobby," he said. "I felt if we could win a championship, I'd have three to their two. That would be for bragging rights.

"I knew this team was a little different. I thought, in terms of how we progressed through the year, it might have been a lot like my freshman year. We knew we had to lean on the young guys—Chris Collins and Jeff Capel in our backcourt. They would ultimately get better during the course of the season. They were at their best when it really counted.

"It's weird, I was on some great teams in terms of talent and in terms of going out and accomplishing things on the court, but I thought in terms of togetherness, that was the best team I have been on at Duke. We needed to be. We weren't the most talented team, but we genuinely liked each other. We could be honest with each other. We didn't have agendas. That's the kind of environment Coach fosters."

Hill moved into Hurley's role at the point full time that season, averaging 17.6 points and 6.9 rebounds while filling up his line almost every game. He was the catalyst for a team that had no true point guard, no power forward, and limited depth, and won the ACC regular-season championship. On the road to the Final Four, Duke had to face Purdue, with its consensus National Player of the Year Glenn Robinson, who had just gone off for 44 points against Kansas in the Sweet 16 and was averaging 31 for the season.

Hill—the National Defensive Player of the Year in 1993—drew the assignment on the six-foot-eight "Big Dog."

"We were in the hotel the night before the game, and Cherokee Parks, our starting center, kept calling out, 'Big Dog! Big Dog!' and each time I would jump up and do defensive slides across the floor."

The next day, Hill consistently fronted Robinson and denied him the ball, and Parks blocked two of his shots during a 69-60 victory as the Blue Devils advanced to the Final Four for the seventh time in nine years. Robinson shot just six for 22 and scored only 13 points.

Upon arriving in Charlotte, Hill discovered that President Bill Clinton, a huge Arkansas fan, would be there to watch his beloved Hogs. Hill's parents visited the presidential box during the semifinals.

"I'm pretty sure Chelsea is a Duke fan," Hill countered.

For Hill, who studied African-American and American Indian history at Duke and actively pushed for more diversity at the school, basketball was only part of his college experience.

His mother had introduced him to fine art as a teenager and he purchased his first piece—a color print by Ernest Banks, a black artist, on the 1984 Olympics—and hung it over the mantel in his apartment. Hill has since made collecting African-American art his passion and has lent 45 pieces from his collection to an exhibition called "Something of Our Own" that is on an 18-month tour of the country.

That, along with numerous donations to charities, is his way of giving back to the community. Hill has also given back to Duke. In 1998, he and his mother made gifts totaling $100,000 to help fund a Duke Divinity School scholarship honoring Calvin. Two years later, he and his wife, Tamia, a five-time Grammy Award-nominated R&B artist, gave the school $1 million to establish an endowed fund for athletic support by providing financial aid for a Duke player each year.

It has not been all roses for Hill since he left Duke. In 1999, he injured his right foot and has gone through five surgeries in an attempt to regain his health. In March 2003, he spent one night in intensive care after an operation to realign his broken heel with his leg. Grant contracted a 104-degree fever after the operation that sent him into convulsions. He is still battling, though, and actually made the 2005 All-Star Game during his latest comeback attempt.

"I think when you go through adversity, you tend to fall back on your foundation," he said. "For me, it was my time at Duke. Really. In 2004, when I was out the entire season, I would have monthly checkups in Durham. I had a chance to go back and be around the program. It really reinforced what I love about the game. Sometimes you can get a little tainted in the NBA. But being back in the Duke environment, being back at practice, going to the games, having those values reinforced, really inspired me to get back.

"Also, I think Coach K was very helpful because he'd missed the 1995 season with a back injury. He had to fight to get back to the level and possibly even exceed the level he'd been at the year before. There were a lot of complications, but he wanted to come back and achieve greatness.

"It's like that *Rocky* movie—and I hate to use that movie to make an analogy—but it's almost like he lost that edge, and he had to go back and train with that Apollo guy to get back the eye of the tiger. Coach K is still in that frame of mind: boxing, training in that old gym. He's motivated. He's very hungry. And I think he will be as long as he still coaches. He wanted to prove people wrong, show that he could still do it.

"And those conversations with Coach helped me. For me, it wasn't just about coming back and overcoming the ankle. It was about being motivated to be better than I was before the injury."

17

THE COACH'S WIFE
PAM VALVANO STRASSER
Chairwoman, The V Foundation for Cancer Research

Even as experienced a coach's wife as Pam Valvano—as she was then—was unprepared for a fact of life in North Carolina.

Everyone, it seemed, was a member of the fashion police.

In 1980, her husband, the late Jim Valvano, had been named the new basketball coach at North Carolina State, and the family headed south. In the move, their TV set had gotten damaged, so Pam called a repairman.

Pam recalled, "When I first moved here, I had gone on a Nike trip. One of the gifts they had given me was a light blue warm-up. I had it on the day the TV repairman arrived.

"Well, I normally wouldn't have thought, 'I have this light blue warm-up on today.'

"He asked me, 'Mrs. Valvano, why are you wearing that light blue warm-up suit?'

"I said, 'Somebody gave it to me, and I'm going to wear it.'

"And he said, 'You don't wear that color anymore.'

"This was my first inkling of what it was going to be like down here.

"They expected me to wear red. Everything I owned had to be red."

But life as it was known in the ACC was about to change.

There were some new boys in town: Jim Valvano and Mike Krzyzewski.

Pam remembered, "In 1980, Jim and Mike came down at the same time. Jim got the job at N.C. State and Mike got the job at Duke. We all met at that point. We had a lot in common then. Jim and I had three daughters. And Mike and Mickie had two; then they had another one.

Duke Photography

"Now we each have four grandchildren. Unbelievable.

"When we moved down, we bought a beach house within a couple of blocks of each other. But to be honest with you, they were busy and we were busy—with our lives and our kids. Basically, we would see them just at games and ACC meetings."

Krzyzewski and Valvano had a little history on the court. They had played against each other in college, when Valvano attended Rutgers and Krzyzewski was a cadet at West Point. Later, they met as coaches when Krzyzewski's Army team played Valvano's Iona College.

But the ACC was a totally different world.

Pam said, "The league can be cannibalistic. It's unbelievable, just unbelievable. And the rivalry is absolutely fierce. It's unlike anything I've ever seen before.

"But that's healthy because the coaches are just being coaches and they don't dislike one another personally. They're just competitive on the floor. Off the floor, they're all nice to one another.

"The fans are the ones that can get pretty ugly at times with their allegiance to their schools.

"It was amazing. When we came into the league, there were some people who didn't like one another—and it was obvious. Everybody used to hate somebody. Originally, everybody hated Carolina. Then it was Duke hated Carolina; Carolina hated Duke. Because we didn't grow up here, we didn't have that animosity. We just came into it."

But a fierce rivalry did develop between Krzyzewski and Valvano. For their first two seasons, the two teams split four games.

Then came 1983.

While Krzyzewski was gathering the pieces for future Duke success by recruiting the highly touted Class of 1986, Valvano beat the Blue Devils twice and swept the other ACC teams off the board by winning the ACC Tournament and the NCAA championship with senior stars like Thurl Bailey, Sidney Lowe, and Dereck Whittenburg. The backcourt of Lowe and Whittenburg came from DeMatha Catholic, where Krzyzewski eventually recruited Danny Ferry three years later.

Actually, State was on the bubble when the ACC Tournament started. The Wolfpack were just 14-10 and looked like they would have to win at least two games so Valvano was able to ride the return of Whittenburg—who had broken his foot in February—and the ACC's experimental three-point rule and the 30-second clock, which was used in all but the final four minutes of ACC games, to win it all.

Along the way, they defeated the same Virginia team that had devastated Duke 109-66 two days earlier, in the championship game. N.C. State put four players—led by Bailey's 24 points—in double figures and built up a 75-66 lead, and then held off the Cavaliers with their seven-foot-four National Player of the Year Ralph Sampson 81-78.

The championship gave State an automatic bid. They were a sixth seed, playing in the West, in the same region as powerhouse Virginia.

The Wolfpack brought along a pocketful of miracles. And they needed them all to defeat Pepperdine 69-67 in two overtimes in the first round after trailing by six points in the final minute of the first overtime.

Then they had to rally from a 12-point deficit to defeat Nevada 71-70 when Bailey scored on a follow-up shot with four seconds to go.

The regionals were just as dramatic. State trailed Utah 32-20 in the Sweet 16 before shooting 79 percent in the second half to pull away 75-56. Then they rode the hot shooting of Whittenburg to rally from seven down with 7:30 remaining to beat Virginia 63-62 in the regional finals. Two free throws by Lorenzo Charles sealed the deal with 23 seconds remaining.

N.C. State made the most of its first trip to the Final Four since 1974. The Wolfpack defeated Georgia, 67-60, in the semifinals and then played highly favored Houston in the championship game.

No one gave them much of a chance. But Valvano decided his best shot was to hold the ball against Houston's seven-foot center, Akeem Olajuwon. The strategy worked in the first half when State grabbed a 33-25 lead. Then, after Houston stormed back to take a 42-35 lead, it looked like it might backfire.

But Houston coach Guy Lewis made a tactical error when he decided to slow down his high-flying team, which was at its best in transition. Valvano elected to foul the opponent and make them win the game from the foul line.

The Cougars couldn't do it.

They missed critical free throws, and State pulled to a 52-52 tie with 1:05 remaining. State fouled Houston guard Alvin Franklin, who missed the first part of a one-and-one with 44 seconds left, and State rebounded the ball, setting up a last shot.

It wasn't exactly what Valvano wanted. With 10 seconds left, Whittenburg wound up launching a 30-footer that fell short of the basket. But Charles caught the ball and dunked it to give State an improbable 54-52 victory.

Pam remembered that time, "The last nine games were unbelievable. To win the ACC Tournament and then the next six games. Every single game was just like a miracle. I said, 'This can't be happening: overtime and a double overtime. This is freaky.'

"Jim had a hernia that year, so he was coaching while wearing a bulging truss. On the day before the national championship game, he had a 103-degree fever. He was sick as a dog when he coached the championship game and nobody knew.

"And I thought, 'Oh my God, he's going to collapse between the hernia and being sick.'"

But Valvano didn't collapse.

And the Wolfpack beat Houston 54-52.

In the video flashed around the world, Valvano is seen running onto and around the floor of the Pit in Albuquerque, looking for somebody to hug—somebody to love—while the adrenaline just kept on pumping.

That was the highlight of his career. N.C. State won 20 games in each of the next five seasons, advancing to the Elite Eight in 1985 and 1986. The Wolfpack won the ACC title in 1987 and were always competitive with Duke. Valvano finished with a 13-9 head-to-head record against Krzyzewski before he left at the end of the 1990 season.

Valvano, who had dabbled in TV while still coaching, joined ESPN as a full-time basketball analyst in the 1990-1991 season, teaming with Dick Vitale.

He was a natural. He'd found an outlet for his enthusiasm, his spirit, and his basketball knowledge.

And his wit: the man was a master of one-liners.

In 1992, while covering the Final Four in Minneapolis, Valvano started complaining of a backache. He needed to stand and stretch between on-air segments.

Dr. Vitale recommended aspirin.

When Valvano went to the doctor in June, he thought he had a disc problem. But he had a rare and aggressive form of cancer.

The unimaginable had happened, and Valvano's world had changed forever. He was taking treatments and still trying to work in pain.

His illness changed the lives of those around him—including Krzyzewski's.

Pam said, "Jim and Mike always had a nice relationship—and a competitive relationship. But when Jim was sick, everything really changed.

"I think the *Sports Illustrated* article really made a big impact. I was very against Jim doing the article because I thought, 'God, we live in such a fishbowl. Why does his sickness have to be so public?'

"He decided to go ahead and do it. And after he did it, so many people's lives were changed.

"What was so wonderful about that article was that it showed a different side of Jim Valvano—a side that maybe a lot of people didn't see. Everybody saw this fast-talking New Yorker who probably wasn't sincere. But reading what he wrote, people could see the real person inside him."

And they liked what they saw.

Pam remembered Mickie Krzyzewski's reaction:

"Mickie told me that she read the article and it changed her life.

"She said she didn't know if Mike would take the time during the season to read it so she highlighted the sections she wanted him to read.

"She found Mike reading the article, and they got to know the real person who was there. Mickie said Mike kept it in his nightstand next to his bed.

Every once in a while, she would find him taking it out and reading it.

"Mickie said that article really, really changed Mike when he read it.

"Their daughter, Debbie, told me that Jim's death really had an impact on Mike. Afterward, he was a better husband and a much better father than before.

"Mike just realized that you can have it all taken away in the blink of an eye. No matter how much fame or money you have, it doesn't matter. If you don't have your health, you have nothing."

Krzyzewski did have his health and he was ambulatory. He started visiting Valvano at the Duke University Medical Center regularly—in the middle of basketball season.

Pam's reaction to Krzyzewski's frequent visits?

"Was I surprised? Yes.

"Mike would come to the hospital every single day after practice over at Duke. It was just incredible.

"My daughters and I would be sitting in Jim's room. Jim would be hurting because the cancer had gotten into his bone and it was very painful. There would be a knock on the door, and Mike would be there. And all of a sudden there's a smile on Jim's face.

"The girls and I used to say, 'What are we, chopped liver?'

"Mike would sit there with him and talk about practice, talk about an upcoming game or about a game he had just played.

"And it was as if, all of a sudden, the pain left. The pain went away for the time that Mike was there, because Jim just forgot about it and was able to focus on what Mike was saying.

"It was very, very special to watch this. At that time, it was an acquaintanceship—more than a true friendship—of two men who had a lot in common.

"It was unbelievable. Thanks to that article, Mike saw a different side of Jim that he hadn't really known. He found out who the real person was and he liked him. He visited Jim because he knew what Jim was feeling and wanted to try to help him.

"Jim's situation made Mike realize that nobody promises us tomorrow."

Meanwhile, Valvano was using his time to devise a strategy to defeat cancer.

He wanted to set up a foundation that would raise funds for cancer research. Grants would be given to doctors and researchers who were trying to find new ways to fight the disease.

And with the assistance of ESPN, The V Foundation for Cancer Research was formed.

Then Valvano started his recruiting.

Pam recalled his one on one with Krzyzewski:

"Jim told Mike about ESPN establishing the foundation and said that he needed people on his team who were going to get the ball and go run with it. And he knew Mike would be that type of person."

But one person does not make a team.

"Jim went to his college roommate, Bob Lloyd. He went to his brothers, Nick and Bob. He went to John Saunders from ESPN. He said to all of them, 'You know, I'm not going to be here to do the work, so you guys are going to have to do this for me and make my team up.'

"So that's what he did before he died. He just set in place all these people he knew would be able to help him."

On March 4, 1993, ESPN inaugurated its American Sports Awards—the ESPY. One of the categories was the Arthur Ashe Award for Courage.

The first recipient was Jim Valvano. Pam and Jim Valvano flew to New York with Mickie and Mike Krzyzewski. And that's when acquaintanceship became friendship.

Pam recalled, "When we flew up to the ESPY Awards with them, Jim and Mike talked during the whole flight. Being in Mike's world and talking to him took Jim away from the pain for a while. And the relationship became unbelievable."

That day, Jim's doctor had given him the worst news of all: the cancer had spread throughout his body.

The other video clip with which most people associate Jim Valvano shows him standing on the stage of the ESPY Awards and saying, "Don't give up. Don't ever give up."

Pam shared the efforts required for him to say those words:

"It was a very hard day. He was very, very sick. We were in the hotel room all day, and he was sick. When we got to the Paramount Theatre, the staff said, 'Coach, it's a really long walk to get to your seats. Do you want a wheelchair?'

"Well, of course, I piped up and said right away, 'No, no. He doesn't need a wheelchair.'

"And he turned to me and said, 'Pam, if it's a long walk, maybe I do need a wheelchair.'

"Well, my heart just sank to think that he had to go in a wheelchair. He got in, and I pushed him there, and that really hit me hard. We sat down in our seats. I knew how sick he was. I didn't know what was going to happen.

"Then I couldn't believe it. If you had watched him or listened to him, you'd never have known anything was wrong with him. That he was able to go some place in his soul to deliver a speech like that was absolutely incredible."

James Thomas Valvano died on April 28, 1993. He was 47 years old.

But his legacy, The V Foundation for Cancer Research, is very much alive.

Pam Valvano married Dr. John Strasser, a veterinarian, in October 2003. They live in Chapel Hill, North Carolina. She is the chairwoman of the organization.

When asked about the foundation's success, she said, "When we started this project, did we think it would be this successful? Absolutely not.

"There's no way in the world that I would have thought we would be able to raise the money that we have. It's absolutely incredible, because people who did not even know who Jim was have jumped on the bandwagon because they're friends of Mike Krzyzewski's or Dick Vitale's or Bob Lloyd's.

"That's the thing that's amazing to me. We go out to the wine event, and these people didn't even know who Jim was. They're doing it because of the cause. They're touched by this horrible, horrible disease. They say, 'If we can do something to make a difference, we will. It's great that Jim was able to start it, and it's horrible that he had to lose his life.'

"Everybody always asks me, 'What do you think Jim would say? Would he be amazed?'

"I answer them, 'He'd say, "How come you raised only that much money? Raise more money until you find a cure."'

"That's what he would say."

In the years since Valvano's death, Krzyzewski has proved he was worthy of the confidence Valvano had in him.

He is a member of the board of directors of The V Foundation. He was a co-chairman of the annual Celebrity Golf Tournament for nine years.

Since 1999, Mike and Mickie Krzyzewski have hosted the foundation's annual wine festival in Napa Valley, California.

"They're great, great people," Pam said. "I always see them at the wine event; they take all their kids to Napa. I see Mike and Mickie through the year at other events. And I see Mike at a lot of the board meetings.

"What Mike has done for the foundation is incredible," Pam said.

"When George Bodenheimer of ESPN, Dick Vitale, or Mike Krzyzewski talks, people listen. And they dig deep, believe me.

"As a speaker, Mike is the best. The older he gets, the better he gets. He can get people to do unbelievable things."

18

The Apprentice

MIKE BREY

Duke Assistant Coach 1987-1995

N otre Dame coach Mike Brey has a special appreciation for Mike Krzyzewski because Krzyzewski has never forgotten his roots.

Krzyzewski was part of that long gray line at West Point and coached Army from 1975 to 1978, long before he was winning national championships at Duke.

"He's been in this fight a long time, and he's seen it all," Brey said. Even though he's been at Duke 25 years, he can relate to the guy at Delaware, the guy at Army, because he was that guy.

"I think people respect that. He was that guy at Army. He was the graduate assistant. He was poor at one point and he drove around to recruit. He talks about the U.S. Army-issued cars that he used to drive. He talked about changing pants before he'd get to a home visit. He got so good, he changed pants in the car. He'd be driving and he could change pants.

"One year he and his wife, Mickie, drove to the Final Four in a U.S. Army-issued car. They get to the coaches' hotel, and the car breaks down right there in the valet parking area, with all the coaches there. Tires are falling off. The tailpipe is falling off."

Times have changed.

But, in many ways, Krzyzewski is still the same person. Brey—who spent eight years as an assistant at Duke—first saw it when he was an assistant coach to Morgan Wooten at DeMatha Catholic and Krzyzewski was recruiting Danny Ferry in 1985.

"Back in that time, they did not miss one of Danny's games," Brey recalled. "That was back in the day when there were no limits on how often you could watch a kid play. Mike or his two assistants, Chuck Swenson or Bob Bender, made 34 DeMatha High School games his senior year.

"Danny was a late signee. He wanted to watch the teams play. Jeff Lebo, the McDonald's All-America guard from Carlisle, Pennsylvania, had signed early with Carolina, and they thought they were going to get both. Danny watched the whole year, and he and his dad got into the GM mode: we're going to evaluate. So I got to know Mike pretty well.

"I joined the staff in 1987. Ferry was going into his junior year, so he had been there two years already. Obviously, it was great to play at DeMatha, because you get great exposure. It was also great for a young coach, because Morgan didn't want to deal with the recruiters. I'd deal with Lefty Driesell, Terry Holland. And then, at practice, Morgan would let me run a half practice sometimes. Well, you got three of those guys up there and a Hall of Fame high school coach is letting some young sucker, some 25-year-old guy, run practice. And those guys are saying, 'If Morgan is letting him do that, he must be good.'

"So that was unbelievable for me.

"With Mike, he took a personal interest in everybody at DeMatha in that recruitment. He knew the principal. He knew the priests. He had his focus. Obviously, Danny was the biggest one to get. That was the one. That kind of swung the Carolina thing, beating them on somebody they really wanted.

"Yeah, you had Johnny and Tommy and Alarie, but to beat somebody on the High School Player of the Year in 1985, that was the one.

"I saw that focus and attention to detail, but Mike was a really personable guy. I thought some of the other guys in the league were older, a little more like CEOs. They sent their assistants. Mike was a little more hands-on. He was a young Turk, a young assassin. He'd come down, sit with me for half of a practice. That was pretty darn good—the Duke head coach. When he asked me to come, that was the grand slam."

Ironically, Swenson, who Brey replaced at Duke, originally offered him an assistant's job when he became the head coach at William and Mary.

"You would think that would have been most likely if you had been a high school assistant and you really wanted to get in. I talked to Chuck about it and told him I was involved with Duke. I told him, 'If I can't get that one, I'm going to stay here.'

"In this business, it's all about who you hitch your wagon to, and I'm with Morgan. Even though it's a high school situation, it was a trump card. And I didn't think I needed to play it for William and Mary. I think Mike respected that.

"It came down to Stu Jackson, me, and Mike Hanks—who was just fired at South Alabama and was at Indiana. So I'm thinking [Bob] Knight is pushing that one. Stu was with Rick Pitino at Providence. Both of them were more experienced.

"I think what helped me was he wanted someone who was going to be with him for a while. He didn't want someone who was going to come in, get one last stamp on the resumé and move on to a head job.

"He felt because of the relationship I'd built with Danny—and I know Danny was very helpful with this—I could go out and talk to kids. I think Mike respected the fact that I'd said if I couldn't get the job there, I was going to stay at DeMatha, because Knight told him to talk to Iowa State when he was involved with Duke. It was on the table.

"Knight said, 'You'd better take it. It's a bird in the hand.' But Mike was young and obviously had his own mind and said, 'I'm going to roll the dice for Duke. I have a feeling I can get this thing.'"

Brey arrived at Duke in the summer of 1987. His family had not arrived yet. Brey got his first sense of Krzyzewski's competitive nature when he was invited to join the staff for a little three on three on the outdoor courts.

"It was Mike, Pete Gaudet, Bob Bender, me, and two managers," Brey said. "Mike had just turned 40, and he's playing like it's all on the line. I'm like, 'I'm younger. I can still move pretty good.' I'm feeling my way; I've been on the job only a month. He was bone-knocking the hell out of me, going after it. Bender, who'd been on the staff, was just rolling his eyes: be ready. It's 100 degrees in late May. We play for an hour. He gets in his car, goes. Nobody says anything.

"Bender and I go get a beer and I say, 'So that's...'

"Bender says, 'Oh yeah, we'll be doing that a couple of times.'

"And you know, no students are coming up, stopping and watching. You're just playing ball, beating the hell out of each other, calling some fouls, and guys are looking at each other. You would have thought there was a lot of money on the line if you drove by."

Krzyzewski always believed in competing every day, whether it was for recruiting, public relations for his program, or preparing to play North Carolina or Maryland, according to Brey.

"I think I had a feel for that because I was a college athlete and, in the offseason, I wanted to make myself better," he said. "I wasn't a great athlete, so I had to really work hard to be a good college player. But nobody lives by that more than this guy. He had a focus that was almost maniacal."

Krzyzewski needed it to battle neighborhood rival North Carolina and Virginia. "As he's always said, 'Those guys really made me go,'" Brey said. "Dean and Terry Holland of Virginia. He missed that for a while once they retired.

"Living in close proximity to North Carolina, you really experienced the competition every day.

"Mike's daughters—Jamie, his oldest, in particular—really experienced it every day. She went to the public school, and she really had some hard times with Carolina people. I didn't experience it until my son was in kindergarten. If we got beat by Carolina, if they got us, I'd tell him—I'll never forget he was six; he's 17 now—'Kyle, today, you may catch a little bit.'

"And he said, 'Yeah, Dad, I know. They'll be on me.'

"'Just be prepared,' I'd tell him.

"Durham has a lot of Carolina people, so you lived it all the time. You couldn't let down, because when you got on the plane, you looked over, and [assistant] Phil Ford was on the same plane or Roy Williams was on the plane. You'd walk into the gym, and there's Phil or Bill Guthridge.

"You saw it, read about it, or heard it every day through third parties that they had so-and-so on campus, or this is what they're doing. It really drove you to work hard and be good."

Krzyzewski beat Smith on two key recruits when Brey was there: Christian Laettner and Grant Hill. Those two and point guard Bobby Hurley were the nucleus for two national championships in 1991 and 1992.

"Laettner's dad was a huge Notre Dame guy," Brey recalled. "His dad wanted him to come to South Bend if things were better. I'll never forget: Lacttner made his visit to Carolina the weekend Scott Williams had a murder-suicide at his home in California. Dean left the visit to fly west.

"After Laettner committed to us, Dean's assistant, Roy Williams, was really down. He asked the high school coach, Jim Kramer, 'What did I do wrong?'

"The other thing that pushed Krzyzewski's buttons during that period was Jim Valvano of N.C. State, who came to Tobacco Road the same time as Krzyzewski—after the 1979-1980 season—and who won a national championship in 1983.

"His first three years at Duke, Carolina wins and N.C. State wins," Brey said. "Jimmy V was, in some way, a worse rival than Dean, because he was a personality guy. That didn't play well with Mike early. Mike was not an entertainer and a quotable guy.

"Those two guys in the triangle, both of them had you moving pretty well. They had you on edge on a daily basis. They had him on edge. And if he was on edge, we were on edge.

"The atmosphere, when I think back to it, was absolutely dysfunctional. There were days when we'd say, 'How crazy is this?' and we were the voice of reason. I'm sure the assistants now say, 'Those guys were psycho.' We had a lunch spot we'd go to, but there were just certain days of the week, we didn't go. You just don't go out in the fray."

Brey was at Duke when the Blue Devils made five-straight trips to the Final Four. "Talk about spoiled. Mike used to tease us all the time. He still calls me 'Final Four Mike,'" Brey said. "We go to five Final Fours in six years, play in four championship games.

"The year before I got to Duke, I'm at the Alhambra Classic in Cumberland, Maryland. That's my Final Four. The next year, I'm in Kansas City. My son is two years old. I told my wife to get on the plane. I told her, 'You know what, you should write everything down, because do you know how many coaches never get this experience as a head coach or an assistant?'

"Then we go the next four years and she's like, 'Don't we do this every year? We're so spoiled.'"

The streak finally ended in 1993 when Duke was eliminated by Cal in the second round.

"I had never experienced a Final Four Coaches Convention, and I don't know what to do," Brey said. "We get to the Hyatt in New Orleans, and I have no idea what to do. Eddie Fogler, who used to work for Dean and is now the head coach at Vanderbilt, sees us. We're at the desk and he says, 'What do you mean you have no idea what to do?' He's killing us. 'All you guys know is the Final Four.'"

Krzyzewski was in constant demand during that period. "He's absolutely essential for the men's basketball movement," Brey said. "He's the only guy who spends time with the issues that face our profession. He really wants to fight for coaches—like the year he went on a mission for the restricted earnings coaches and he flew to Dallas.

"But the NCAA was not that receptive. They ignored him. So when that didn't work out, he kind of backed off a little bit and said, 'I'm just going to coach my program.'

"We were ***** off at him as a coaching staff, because we were in the midst of an NCAA run and they went to the well too much. This is when he wouldn't say no. He gets on a private plane and comes back, gets on all of us because he hadn't slept, and we got Wake the next day. But that's who he is."

Eventually, it caught up with Krzyzewski, who missed most of the 1995 season with complications from back surgery. Brey ventured out on his own at the end of that season when he took the Delaware job, but he did have to spend some time in purgatory.

"I looked and watched Mike be pulled all over the place, watched his physical breakdown," Brey said. "The only road win we had that year was Notre Dame. That's how bad the Irish were. We lost to Clemson—Rick Barnes's first year—in Cameron with Mike on the bench. We're going to play Georgia Tech in Atlanta, and we get the call. Mike is probably not going to make the trip, and he can't move. The worst thing was you had some young guys on that team— Steve Wojciechowski and Trajan Langdon. It was a heck of a blow. He was the leader, and we were already in crisis.

"We were just a beaten-up group.

"The thing you try to do is keep kids' heads up, make practices fun, and try to get through it. After three, four games, the reality is we're not going to play for anything serious. We're not going to get into the NIT. So let's try to keep the kids in the right frame of mind so that next year we don't lose anybody. And let's make sure there aren't too many fractured psyches when Mike comes back.

"There was a lot of pressure on the staff. 'Hey, are they going to hire somebody else?' No one really communicated with us at that time, and we had parents of players calling us. It was damage control to the hilt for three months on a daily basis."

Brey actually had a chance to move on in 1994. He received an offer from Auburn.

"Mike was caught up with winning a third national championship that year," Brey said. "He said, 'You've got to look at it.'

"I had questions about some of their boosters, but I was still interested in the job after I had my interview the day after Duke won the regionals in Birmingham. I wanted to wait until after the tournament was over. But Auburn wanted to run with it, jump on the publicity of the Final Four.

"When I flew back to Durham, my wife, Tish, said to me, 'You must have taken the job. I had three reporters call.' Apparently, the Auburn president got on the phone and started to let it out.

"I go to practice the next day. Instead of Duke going to the Final Four, I was the story. I was really uncomfortable. I'll never forget riding the bus to Charlotte. I was a basket case. I felt this wasn't me. I didn't feel good about it.

"Mike walked to the back of the bus, and we talked for about an hour. He said, 'If you don't feel good about it...'"

"By the time we got to the Embassy Suites, I realized I'd be a fish out of water in the SEC. That's not how I was trained. I called the A.D. and withdrew. Later that day, some Auburn people called me. They blamed my decision not to come on one of the school's biggest boosters.

"That's when I knew I'd made the right decision."

The next year, the Delaware job opened up. Brey liked everything about it, but the timing was crazy again.

"When I got the call, we were in the Greensboro Marriott and we had just beaten N.C. State in the eight-nine game of the ACC Tournament," Brey recalled. "Poor N.C. State. We're walking around the locker room, and Tom Butters is hugging me. Wake Forest hammers us the next day, and I'm thinking, 'I'm ready. It's time.'"

Krzyzewski tried to convince Brey to stay. "He was a little ticked off because he was coming back. And I don't think he wanted to deal with staff changes," Brey said. "It was like, 'You're patient. You can do better.'

"My feeling was it was the right fit. I never looked at it like a stepping stone. I looked at the success Tubby Raymond had in football there and the quality of life."

Brey transformed Delaware into an NCAA program and then left for Notre Dame in 1999. He has taken many of the lessons he learned from Krzyzewski with him, especially the importance of academics.

He remembered that Krzyzewski refused to hang the 1990 Final Four banner in Cameron because the whole senior class—Alaa Abdelnaby, Robert Brickey, and Phil Henderson—would not graduate on time.

Eventually, all three graduated. Henderson was the last to earn his degree, in 1999.

And that banner joined the others in the rafters.

"I thought that was a great thing for Phil," Brey said. "Mike held that banner until Phil graduated.

"Mike was very plugged into Chris Kennedy, our academic guy, and what was going on. When the mid-term grades would come out—about the second week of practice—he would sit down with the guys. We would run the first 30 minutes of practice, maybe some individual workout, then he'd call them all over to the scorer's table. He'd have his notebook there with their grades and he'd go over it with them, like their high school counselor.

"He just wanted accountability."

When Brey thinks back to his time at Duke, he still has an image of his working out a player in Cameron one day in the spring of 1992 and watching

Krzyzewski walk through after finishing a game of racquetball. Krzyzewski stopped and looked up at the banners hanging from the ceiling.

Then he paused and said, "We never really take enough time to reflect and enjoy it."

"It was very typical of the pace we had down there," Brey said. "Eight years just flew by."

19

THE BALL BOY

CHRIS COLLINS

Duke Class of 1996

C hris Collins has always had a strong bond with his father.

Doug Collins had been an All-Star guard with the Philadelphia 76ers who got the rare opportunity to coach Michael Jordan with the Chicago Bulls when the legendary guard with six championship rings was just coming into his own.

Chris always had a front-row seat.

"I still remember growing up in the Philadelphia 76ers locker room, being a ball boy with the Chicago Bulls," he said. "You just end up learning so much about basketball. You don't even know you're learning by being at practice and in coaches' meetings. You're just sitting there and listening. I've been doing that since I was maybe four, five years old. That was my time with my dad. I loved the game. I would tag along. He would speak at camps, and I would demonstrate."

When Collins was a six-foot-three senior guard at Glenbrook North High in suburban Chicago, he was considered one of the best pure shooters in the country and one of the best prospects in the state. Collins was recruited by many of the Big Ten schools—most specifically, Illinois and Iowa.

But there was a mystique about Duke that had always intrigued him.

"My dad had input," he recalled. "He wanted me to come to Duke. He just wanted me to figure it out for myself."

The light bulb went on during Collins's official visit in 1992.

"I had always been kind of a Duke fan, because I had always identified myself with the Duke players," he said. "I grew up watching Dawkins and Amaker and

Duke Photography

Hurley and that group of guys. You saw the way they played together, the emotion they showed. I always viewed myself like that as a player.

"I was always such a basketball junkie, and I have a great respect for the history of the game—just from being with my dad. And I'm a pretty outgoing guy. So when I came for my visit, the first thing they did was take me for lunch on campus. And all the guys were there. I'm not really saying a whole lot. Grant Hill greets me. We go to lunch. Here comes Laettner; here comes Hurley. Here come Cherokee Parks, Coach K, and Tommy Amaker.

"And I'm just looking around.

"'Where am I? What am I doing? Why am I here?'

"It took me about an hour to realize that these are really guys like me, down-to-earth guys who love playing ball. But I was in awe."

Collins felt an immediate, strong bond with Krzyzewski.

"We got along really well right off the bat," he said. "I saw a lot of similarities between him and my own father: the passion for the game, the passion to teach. I sensed it right away.

"Both of them came from backgrounds where they didn't have much growing up, where they had to fight and claw for everything. My dad is from Benton, Illinois, a town of about 6,000 near Carbondale. Coach K grew up in Chicago.

"They're both really blue-collar guys. Deep down, my dad wanted me at Duke because he loved Coach K and what he'd made, being an extension of what my family did in raising me."

Collins didn't know it at the time; but four years later, he would help save Duke basketball. The six-foot-three guard helped the Blue Devils regain their identity with a late-season flurry of big games after they were on the brink of falling out of the NCAA picture.

And Collins's father was there to see it all.

"He was with TNT, doing the NBA. At the time, he purposefully did not take a job. A lot of NBA teams contacted him. For seven years, he stayed in TV through my career; then he went to Detroit when I finished up. For my last three years of high school and four years at Duke, he did TV so he could come and watch."

Duke has always had its share of celebrity parents. Collins played with Grant Hill, whose father, Calvin, was a huge star with the Dallas Cowboys.

"That shows the trust they had in Coach K," Collins said. "They were both outstanding athletes. Never once did either of them intervene. We never felt like they were trying to be our coaches. They were our dads. They allowed Coach K to be our mentor, our coach—all that.

"A lot of times, in families, you get a lot of strife. Not only do fathers want to be dads, but they also want to be coaches. For the most part, here, that never happens, because Coach K has been so good with relationship-building, trust.

"I don't think that was ever an issue with me. When I went there, my dad told me, 'Look, Coach K is going to be your coach; I'm not going to be your coach. I'm going to be there to support you, to root you on. You listen to him. Just trust that he's always going to have your best interest at heart.'

"The one thing that strikes you about Coach K is that it doesn't take long to see his sincerity. You see right away he's not feeding you a bunch of B.S. It's not a sales pitch. He makes you want to believe in him, the emotions he shows, the vision he has for you.

"The vision he had for me was to make me a tremendous leader. He wanted me to come into the program and not be afraid to shoot threes.

"I'm so fortunate. I always say there are two guys in my life I've always been able to learn basketball from: my father, who's done it all in the game, and Coach K, who is the greatest coach. I'm lucky to have two guys like that who are great role models."

Collins experienced both the highs and lows of Duke basketball.

As a sophomore in 1994, he played on a team that was propelled by the brilliance of Grant Hill to the NCAA Tournament finals against Arkansas.

"It was a fun group. Every time I see the highlight tapes put to music, I remember. The theme song for that team was 'That's What Friends Are For' We had an unbelievably close group. We played like seven. Of course, we had Grant. He and Glenn Robinson of Purdue were the two best players in the country. We had a bunch of guys who were good players who loved playing together, being together and hung out all the time off the court. We just rode that all the way, with a superstar, to the finals.

"One of the things we've been fortunate with at Duke is that we've been able to attract not only just great players, but high-quality guys. You get to play with a guy like Grant Hill, who is one of the best who's ever played, talent-wise. This guy was so unselfish, he wanted to be just one of the guys. He didn't want to stand out. If there was a pass to be made, he made it. Part of that comes from Coach K; part of it comes from his upbringing."

Hill was great throughout the tournament, and Collins played courageously during a 76-72 loss to Arkansas in the championship game, making four three-pointers to lift the Blue Devils to a 10-point lead midway through the second half—much to the dismay of President Bill Clinton, a huge Razorbacks fan, who was in attendance at the Charlotte Coliseum. After Arkansas guard Scottie Thuman nailed a three-pointer to break a 70-70 tie that was almost blocked by

Antonio Lang in the final minute of play, Collins launched a three at the other end. The shot was halfway down, and then spun out.

It was a heartbreaking sequence for the Devils, and Arkansas held on to win.

"We always go into every year wanting to have the kind of unit where, at the end of the year—whether we win the national championship or we lose, or whatever—everybody's crying," Collins said. "That means you had a special team.

"That means you had guys who cared about one another. It was one of those locker rooms where everybody was balling. Not only did we want to win the championship, but that was the last time that group was going to play together."

Unbeknownst to Collins, that summer, Krzyzewski was starting to break down physically. "It takes a lot of energy to go to a Final Four seven of nine years and then go to the Olympics," Collins admitted. "I think it caught up to him emotionally."

Without Krzyzewski for most of the season, Duke completely slipped off the radar screen in the 1995 season, falling to the bottom of the ACC with a 2-14 record.

"It was the hardest year of my life but looking back on it, also the most growing year of my life," Collins recalled. "For me, I was very fortunate to be able to grow up in the NBA. My dad played in the NBA, coached Michael—a lot of good stuff.

"I never had to face serious adversity.

"Now, the first day of practice, I broke my foot. So I was out a month, two months. That set me back. I missed the first three games. I tried to rush back for our game against Illinois at the Chicago United Center. But it was a tough year for me."

Collins, who had averaged 10 points as a sophomore, averaged just 3.9 points and shot only 29.8 percent as a junior.

Then, Krzyzewski—the leader—went down with a back injury.

"We knew he was run down," Collins said. "His coloring was not good. He didn't have the same kind of energy. I'll never forget the meeting before we were getting ready to go to Georgia Tech when he stepped down. And it was almost like he was green.

"You could have heard a pin drop. He said, 'I'm not going to be able to go.' And everybody was looking around like, 'What's wrong with Superman?'

"This is a guy: we'd seen his emotion, but we'd never seen weakness. That was really the first time we saw him as a human. He was always the pillar of strength for everyone. If someone was hurt, if someone was struggling, when guys were going well, if we were in a tight game in a huddle, he was the man.

"That year, we really struggled. But if you looked at the scores, almost every game we were in, it was either tied or one possession with four minutes to go. It was excruciating, because of the way we were losing games.

"He wasn't allowed to keep in touch personally. We were told that he needed a clean break. So to see us struggle, I'm sure it just broke him up inside."

Krzyzewski came back with a renewed focus in 1996 when Duke began to reinvent itself.

"That year for me, personally, was the most special year," Collins said. "The program was at a crossroads. It was either, 'We're going to get this thing going and Coach K is going to get it back, or that might have been his phase-out time.' Maybe it was time for him to step down, or do something else, or go to the pros. Who knows? It was that fragile."

One of the first things Krzyzewski did was shake up the staff: bringing in some younger guys like Tim O'Toole and Quin Snyder to create a new energy.

Then he got down to work.

Collins was one of the few bright spots early on. But he had a signature moment January 18 when Duke visited N.C. State. Duke had opened 0-4 in the ACC and was on the verge of losing that game to go 0-5. Down 70-68 with seconds left and the shot clock running down, Collins threw up a prayer as he was falling out of bounds, right in front of the Duke bench. The ball hit the back of the rim, bounced eight to 10 feet in the air, and dropped in for the game-winning three-pointer.

A few years later, Duke was holding its annual alumni all-star game and they tried to recreate the three biggest shots in Duke basketball history— Laettner's two game-winners against UConn and Kentucky and Collins's three at N.C. State.

"Some of the moments I spent with him that year will forever stay with me, Collins said. "For instance, we were 4-7 in the ACC. We're fighting. We're playing walk-ons. And he brings me in before we have our last six regular-season games.

"We're getting ready to play Virginia at home. He started showing me some tape. We were watching one or two tapes, and he says to me, 'Look, I feel bad. It's your senior year; basically, this is your team.' I said, 'I just want you to know we're only going to go as far as your heart can lead us.'

"And he said, 'I want you to go out the rest of this year, and any time you want to shoot, I want you to shoot. Whatever you want to do. I want you to feel like there's nothing you can't do. You can't fail, because I've got your back. The team will follow you. Just do what you can. We'll make the best of this situation.

"'But I believe in you. Believe in your heart.'"

Duke had limited depth that year and was struggling at 13-10 and 4-7 in the ACC when Collins, the lone senior starter on that team, went off, averaging 25.5 points as the Devils went on a five-game winning streak.

He scored 23 points against Virginia, 12 against N.C. State, 27 against Florida State, 27 against UCLA, 27 against Maryland. He looked like he was ready to go off again against North Carolina, scoring 18 points in 25 minutes, but then he hurt his foot again and Duke lost 84-78.

The Blue Devils finished 18-12 after the ACC Tournament. They were 8-8 in the ACC. But that was enough to get them an NCAA bid, even though they lost to Maryland in the first round of the conference tournament with Collins in street clothes. Collins played in the NCAA Tournament, but he was ineffective, and Duke lost to Eastern Michigan in the first-round—the only first-round loss of Krzyzewski's career.

But they had discovered how to win again.

"Those last six games, I played on a level that I never even thought was possible. I was doing things: hitting shots, making plays. We finished up 8-8 in the ACC and went to the tournament.

"That made me feel good, because it was a bridge to getting this back. Seeing it now, you look back on that year. The other thing is, when I was a player in this program, I never had any delusions I was going to be Bobby Hurley or Grant Hill, but I wanted to leave my mark on the program.

"I got taken out of the game against Eastern Michigan with about 20 seconds left, and I remember Coach K hugging me and saying, 'It's been my honor to coach you.'

"For me, that left a lasting impression."

Collins played pro ball in Finland for a season, leading the league in scoring. He got into coaching in 1997 as an assistant with the WNBA Detroit Shock. He then spent two years as an assistant at Seton Hall, working for Tommy Amaker, before returning to Duke as an assistant in 2001, the year the Blue Devils won a third national title under Krzyzewski.

"I'm working the summer camp and I'm yelling at some knucklehead from Jersey who was being the class clown and, all of a sudden, the secretary calls and says, 'You've got a phone call.' It's eight at night, middle of July, and I'm like, 'I can't deal with this now.' And she says, 'No, no. It's Coach K; you'd better take it.'

"And he says to me, 'David Henderson just agreed to become the new coach at Delaware, and it's time for you to come home.'

"It was one of the greatest feelings. For him to trust me to impart any wisdom I'd learned from being in the program was the ultimate compliment."

Collins, who primarily works with the guards, paid Krzyzewski back that season when he convinced Mike Dunleavy Jr., who was coming off a dreadful game against Maryland in the semis, to be aggressive against Arizona in the championship game.

"I told him, 'If you miss a shot, so what?'"

Dunleavy responded, scoring 21 points, including a historic spurt of three-straight three-pointers in the space of 45 seconds, to put Duke ahead by 10 points en route to an 82-72 victory.

"To see him go out and play with that courage and take those shots, just take over the game, was such a gratifying moment for me," Collins recalled.

It must have brought back some fond memories for Collins of when Krzyzewski was the teacher and he was the pupil.

"I pinch myself every day because I'm able to go to a staff meeting and listen to him, and to watch how he runs the program," said Collins, who is married to wife, Kim, and has a one-year-old son, Ryan.

"When you have a program like this, it's far more than just coaching basketball. It's people skills, recruiting, management, fund-raising. He's the master of it all. When you play with him, you don't get a full appreciation of what he does as a coach. You don't get the feeling for the 20 different directions he's torn in and how he has to manage his time, how he has to find the energy to do all this.

"He gives me energy. I'm 30 years old. There are times I come in and I'm worn out—and I see the gleam in his eyes. This guy is 58. What a jerk I am if I can't get it going."

20

THE MIRROR IMAGE

STEVE WOJCIECHOWSKI

Duke Class of 1998

One of the most poignant photographic memories of Duke basketball shows Steve Wojciechowski running over to Mike Krzyzewski and embracing him in a huge bear hug after the Blue Devils had rallied from 17 points down in the second half to knock off top-ranked North Carolina 78-75 in the final regular-season game of the 1998 season.

It was their way of showing that Duke basketball—which had dropped to the bottom of the ACC with a thud in 1995 when Krzyzewski suffered a complete physical breakdown—was truly back.

The Blue Devils finished 32-4 that season, were ranked No. 1, and reached the NCAA Southeast Region finals before losing to Kentucky in St. Petersburg, Florida.

Wojciechowski, the gritty blond point guard and the emotional leader of that team, was one of the most unlikely impact players ever to play for Krzyzewski. He emerged from the background to become a two-year starter who was named college basketball's best defensive player as a senior.

Interestingly, Wojciechowski and teammate Ricky Price were the only players Krzyzewski recruited who have stayed in school four years and never got to experience a Final Four as a player.

But Wojciechowski will always have a special bond with his coach. "It's like player-coach, father-son, friend-friend," he said.

Krzyzewski felt so strongly about Wojciechowski, he actually cried after Wojo collapsed in the showers with a 101-degree fever after playing in the ACC Tournament finals against the Tar Heels his senior year.

Duke Photography

"I've had a couple of friends tell me, 'The only person I would worry about Mike leaving you for is Wojo,'" Krzyzewski's wife, Mickie, once said.

Krzyzewski grew up in a Polish family on the North Side of Chicago. His father was an elevator operator. His mother washed floors at the Chicago Athletic Club. And he fought his way out of poverty: signing with Army and playing for Bob Knight, and developing the tenacity to become a hard-nosed starting point guard who became best known for his competitive nature and his maddening man-to-man defense.

Wojciechowski came from Severna Park, Maryland, near Baltimore, from much the same background. His father was a longshoreman and his mother was a housewife in a blue-collar town. "I came from a blue-collar family, rooted in traditional American values: work hard, be good to people, love your family, take care of your family, and try your best."

Wojciechowski, a 28-year-old assistant on the Duke staff, was a good player at Cardinal Gibbons High School with an Ivy League profile.

"I really thought I would wind up in the Ivies," Wojciechowski recalled. "I had taken an unofficial visit to Penn, and I watched the Penn-Princeton game at the Palestra. What an unbelievable environment.

"Some of the more influential people in my life—my high school coach, Ray Mullis, and Howard Garfinkel from the Five-Star camp—had an eye out for me. They knew academics were very important to me and my family and thought either one of those schools would be a good level for me."

But Wojciechowski changed his destiny the summer before his senior year in high school. He was invited to the Converse ABCD camp, run by Sonny Vacarro, at Eastern Michigan University in Ypsilanti, on the outskirts of Detroit.

"I was a late addition to the camp, and my name was probably the very last name called," he recalled. "I went to meet my team—and my team was full of Russian kids. It was me, a bunch of Russians and a kid named Brian Hanley, who was from Indiana.

"A guy by the name of Bob Wagner was our coach; and none of the Russians spoke English. It actually worked out best for me, because it was team basketball. I didn't have to depend on going one on one. If I would have had to do it in that environment, I wouldn't have done as well. I played on a team that shared the ball, that ran offense. And I ended up having a really good week— and I was able to communicate with guys who didn't speak English.

"If you would have painted a picture for me of those circumstances, I would have said, 'There's no way.' But having gone through it—and having gone through it with guys who played the right way, who allowed me to lead them—

I found it was an environment where I was allowed to play to my strengths and go away from my weaknesses.

"It was an environment where if anyone thought there was good in my game, he would see it there. It was a chance for anyone who valued those things I did to see me. And Coach was one of the people who valued them."

Wojciechowski spoke Krzyzewski's language.

"That was where they first saw me,"Wojciechowski said. "I know Ray Mullis called [Duke assistant] coach [Mike] Brey, told him to keep an eye out. I got the obligatory, 'We've heard good things.' But after camp, they started recruiting me. I looked at a lot of other schools, but Duke was the program I most identified with.

"I grew up an ACC fan, watched ACC basketball. Some of my fondest memories were lying on my family room floor, watching ACC basketball on TV—Chris Corchiani of N.C. State, Bobby Hurley, Carolina, Walt Williams of Maryland, and on down the line. I would watch the games, then go outside and try to imitate the things I saw.

"When I met Coach, I understood it was an honor to meet somebody who was going to go down as one of the greatest coaches in the history of the game. I knew right away he was different. I knew he was different. There are a lot of really good college coaches, a lot of people I admire, a lot of programs where I liked the way their teams played.

"But his program was different: just the way he interacted with the guys; the way he carried himself; the way his team played; and for me, the way his team came together. The way Duke guys carried themselves; the way they competed; the way they played hard, smart, together—his fingerprints were on all those things.

"And the things Bobby Hurley, Christian Laettner, Grant Hill were doing— his fingerprints were all over them. Certainly those guys had extraordinary talent, but you could tell this was a result of teamwork with him."

Krzyzewski was intrigued, but he wasn't sure Wojciechowski was athletic enough or quick enough to play for Duke. Fortunately for Wojciechowski, he had an advocate in Brey. He recalled, "Coach K always tells the story about Coach Brey saying to him, 'What are we doing here? If he can lead a bunch of Russians, he certainly can lead the Duke team.'"

When Duke offered Wojciechowski a scholarship, it was a dream come true. But that dream threatened to turn to ashes his freshman year when the coach he wanted to play for collapsed and missed most of a 13-18 season.

The Blue Devils were just coming off Grant Hill's senior year and a third trip to the NCAA finals in four years. They were a fingernail away from winning another national championship.

"That was kind of the end of a streak of Final Fours, Olympic gold medals, and also increased responsibilities for Coach," Wojciechowski said. "And I got here and it was enough's enough. He finally hit the wall."

Krzyzewski began experiencing back pains after playing tennis and racquetball the summer of 1992. The doctors told him it was a degenerative disc and required surgery. Krzyzewski put the operation off, but when the pain persisted, he finally got the operation just before the start of practice.

He returned to work 10 days later, even though doctors suggested he wait six weeks.

Krzyzewski had lost two key starters, Hill and Antonio Lang, and Chris Collins was hurt the first day of practice. He figured his team needed him. The pain returned in December, and he tried to fight through it. Duke won two of three games it played in the Rainbow Classic in Honolulu, but Krzyzewski was upset because he felt the team played poorly. So he and his staff pulled some all-nighters, trying to solve the problem.

The pain had become excruciating by the time Duke's plane arrived back in Raleigh. He coached the conference opener against Clemson, but then told his staff he didn't know if he'd make it through the season.

Two days later, after Krzyzewski's wife, Mickie, actually threatened to leave him if he didn't see a doctor, he checked into a hospital, totally exhausted.

Krzyzewski missed the team's next game at Georgia Tech, spent another week at home in bed, and then realized he was too weak to come back for the rest of the year.

"It was hard for me personally," Wojciechowski said. "It was tremendously difficult. Your freshman year is difficult regardless. I was part of a program that had such high expectations—and then you're being compared to Hurley even though your game is nothing like his. But you're small and you're white.

"Throw on top of that the guy you just craved to learn from was not at his best, and it made it really hard. Ultimately, he was the example I needed to follow to be really good as a player. And not to have him there, there was a void."

Wojciechowski had other things on his mind when he went to Hawaii. His father had cancer and had had his kidney removed a few months earlier. Mullis was also critically ill with cancer.

"We were in Hawaii when he passed away," Wojciechowski said. "He was a legend in Baltimore, a great guy. I was very close to him. He was almost like a grandfather figure to me.

"That September, they were having a fundraiser for him. Coach went up there and spoke, and I wrote a letter that was read to the group.

"Coach K brought me into his room. We went 2-1 in the Rainbow Classic, but we had just lost to Iowa. He brought me into his room and said, 'I just wanted you to know, Coach Mullis passed away.'

"I remember crying. In the space of three months, I'd had three major crises."

When Krzyzewski made the decision that he wasn't going to coach the rest of the season, he decided it would be best to make a clean break. He turned the team over to assistant Pete Gaudet. Gaudet tried to hold the team together, but the season turned into a disaster. Duke finished ninth in the ACC with a 2-14 record, finishing up the season with a 17-point loss to Wake Forest in the quarterfinals of the conference tournament.

"At the end of the year, Coach K came back for one practice, and I remember he ran the practice," Wojciechowski said. "It wasn't like a three-hour monster. It was one hour just before the tournament. But it was at the speed and level of intensity he would have demanded or desired. We were, to a man, exhausted. It showed us, it showed me, the standard we were at and the standard he wanted."

When Krzyzewski returned the next year, he was more focused than ever.

"He was energized. He felt better than he had in a while. You could see it; you could feel it. First of all, he built the program to a place where it had never been before. The year he was out was the year for a lot of people to take shots at us, rubbing our noses in the dirt on the floor. It was time to go at Duke— and that sparked his competitive fire.

"I just remember going into different arenas and how happy people were that we weren't Duke. There was a joy, just elation, that we weren't Duke. That's always stuck with me. It was more than the average fan reaction.

"The experiences Trajan Langdon and I went through allowed us to be better leaders as upperclassmen," he said.

Two years later, nobody was messing with Duke.

Or Wojciechowski.

Wojciechowski had started 10 of 12 games for Duke when Krzyzewski left the team. But as soon as Pete Gaudet took over, his playing time declined. He did start the next five games before being relegated to the bench. Wojciechowski rarely got in during the last nine games of the regular season.

He played just 21 minutes total in those games—averaging barely two minutes a game. He was booed on his home court.

When Krzyzewski came back just before the ACC Tournament, Wojciechowski played 17 minutes in a play-in victory over N.C. State, then disappeared again in a loss to Wake Forest. That was one of the things that may have created a riff between Krzyzewski and Gaudet when Krzyzewski made staff changes for the next season. Wojciechowski began playing more often once Krzyzewski returned full time in 1996.

"It all clicked for me, the end of sophomore year. That's when I was able to take a step back and say this is what I have to do to be very good and help this team," he said. "That summer, I made the commitment to get in the best shape of my life. I worked out down there, played pick up every day. A handful of guys had stuck around, but I would play with professors—whoever was willing to play. That summer was huge.

"I said, 'Hey, I'm going to give this a try, lay it on the line, and see what happens.'"

Wojciechowski barged into the starting lineup at the beginning of his junior year and refused to leave. He was never a huge star statistically. He averaged just 6.9 points, but he made second-team all league as a junior and third team as a senior, largely because of his leadership and defensive skills. The Cameron Crazies used to bark when he would attach himself to an opposing player.

"Coach has the mentality of a defensive player," he said. "Part of being really good defensively is having some intangible qualities that allow you to compete on that side of the ball. And Coach has that mentality. A really good defensive player: it's not a matter of size or quickness, but the attitude that 'I'm not going to let you score.' That's his mentality. His players see that.

"I always had the desire to play defense. That helped me. Even from a young age, I understood that it was a huge part of the game where I could make an impact when I played. I understood that if the guy I was playing against was thinking about me instead of his team, it would help us."

The Blue Devils won 15 games in the ACC Wojciechowski's senior year. His fondest memory will always be their comeback win over powerful Carolina. "It was my Senior Day," he recalled. "That's traditionally a huge thing, because your family is down here, your friends—and it's the last time to play in Cameron, which is an electrifying place.

"We were playing North Carolina for the ACC championship. If we win, we win the league outright. If we lose, we tie. They had Vince Carter, Antawn Jamison, Shammond Williams. It was like pro, pro, pro. The first 30 minutes of the game, we're down like 17. They were just killing us every which way."

Duke stiffened defensively in the last 12:23, limiting the Tar Heels to just three field goals. Wojciechowski scored just one point, but had 11 assists, many of them to freshman center Elton Brand who, playing just his second game since coming back from a broken foot, scored 13 of his 16 points in the second half. Wojciechowski also had three steals and only one turnover, limiting Carolina point guard Ed Cota to just one field goal.

"The clip that's played a lot is of Coach when I run to him," Wojciechowski said. "He didn't have to say anything. I could feel it."

Duke went on to play Kentucky for the right to go to the Final Four. The Devils built a 17-point lead, only to see it slip away in the final eight minutes. But it was obvious the Devils were ready to become a national force again.

"I went through it from my freshman year—this feeling that we weren't very good—to my senior year when it was, 'Oh no. They're back.'

"What the 1986 Duke team had was unique. They laid the foundation; not enough can be said for that. The experience I was able to have was unique as well.

"Here part of the program separated itself. One of the best was going through tough times. We had a chance to build the program back up. It was almost like the house needed updates, and we were the ones that got to help put the pieces back together—hopefully, to make the house stronger than ever."

Wojciechowski, who played overseas in Poland for a year after graduation, signed up to help with more home improvement in 2000.

Duke won the national championship his second year on staff. "I played a number of sports growing up. And in each sport, I was fortunate enough to have good head coaches on every level," he recalled. "I recognized the impact they had on my life, and I always thought if I could do that for other people when I'm old enough, I would love to do that."

He is just following in Krzyzewski's footsteps again.

21

THE PRODIGY

ELTON BRAND

Duke 1998-1999

Whorn Peekskill High School won the New York Class C Federation Championship in 1996, Elton Brand and his teammates celebrated by visiting the gubernatorial mansion in Albany.

Governor George Pataki, a Peekskill native whose daughter had appeared with Brand in the Christmas pageant, even went one on one against the six-foot-eight, 270-pound man child. The results of this first-to-11-wins game were predictable. The six-foot-five Pataki tried to make a move inside, and the next day, the local paper printed a photo of Brand appearing to swat away one of Pataki's shots.

Brand, who was only in 11th grade at the time, downplayed the picture, suggesting it must have been a bad camera angle. Brand was a well-liked A student at Peekskill who was a role model and local celebrity in his hometown and didn't want to offend anyone, even back then.

Who knew he'd be contacting the governor three years later when he was considering declaring for the NBA draft after being selected National Player of the Year at Duke?

"Do what's best for your family," Pataki told him.

Brand became the first Blue Devils player ever to leave early for the NBA. He went with Mike Krzyzewski's blessing and became the first pick in the draft, selected by the Chicago Bulls.

For Brand, it was the successful culmination of a trip out of the Dunbar Heights Projects, where he and his older brother, Artie, were raised by his single mother, Daisy.

Duke Photography

Daisy Brand kept her youngest son off the streets by getting him to join the Boy Scouts and enroll in tae kwan do classes, which taught him how to gain balance and control over his massive body at a young age.

As for basketball, he picked that up on his own on the three blacktop halfcourts with metal nets located in the project. Brand used to play one on one against his brother, who was nine years older. Artie played for Peekskill High and Hartford Community College before taking a job in an engineering consulting company in West Chester County.

Brand finally beat Artie when he was 13, shoving him into the bleachers at game point.

But Artie still controlled the TV remote at home. "He always kept turning it to the Big East games," Brand recalled. "He was a huge St. John's fan, so I had no sense of how big the ACC tradition was: the rivalries, the traditions.

"When I played for the Riverside Hawks in the summer, four guys from my AAU team—Erick Barkley, Willie Shaw, Ron Artest, and Omar Cook—all went to St. John's."

Brand, a McDonald's All-American, thought about the Big East, too. He barged his way into the starting lineup as a ninth grader—after spending one game on the JV—averaged 26.1 points, 16.8 rebounds, and 7.2 blocked shots. He scored over 2,000 points, grabbed over 1,000 rebounds, and finished his career just 20 points shy of the state scoring record.

Brand heard all the sales pitches.

Then he met Krzyzewski.

"Other coaches were promising me a lot of things," he said. "Playing time. You can start. He actually said, 'I don't know what's going to happen. If you deserve to play, you're going to play.'

"I was a McDonald's All-American, top 10 in the country; hearing that, you've got to respect that. He was honest. He and the Duke tradition were the difference. I felt it was the right fit. I figured if I didn't make it in pro basketball, I would still have a great degree and would be able to write my own ticket in the work force. Playing for Coach K was the bonus."

Brand chose Duke over Kentucky, Villanova, and Virginia. His press conference was covered by 150 members of the media. He never considered making the leap to the NBA out of high school, although both Lamar Odom and Tracy McGrady from his class did and were drafted top 10.

Brand was part of possibly the best recruiting class in the history of Duke basketball. Krzyzewski signed six-foot-eight forward Shane Battier from Detroit Country Day School; six-foot-10 center Chris Burgess of Woodbridge

High in Irvine, California; and guard Will Avery from Oak Hill Academy that year.

All three were rated the No. 1 player in their class by at least one recruiting service. Burgess was the consensus No. 1 in the summer before their senior year and received the most hype but didn't play that well as a senior, and after the spring all-star games—and the Hoop Summit—Brand was clearly regarded as Duke's No. 1 incoming prospect.

But he didn't see it that way.

"It was a blockbuster class," he recalled. "Burgess was a powerful inside player. Battier played the same position. And they were both ranked higher than me coming out of high school. They were top three, top five in the class.

"I wasn't sure where I fit in. There haven't been a lot of NBA players coming out of Peekskill. The best player I had heard of was Todd Scott, who went to Davidson. I was nervous coming in, thinking these guys were top-notch Division I players, in the upper echelon."

A lot of the tension evaporated when Brand began playing pick-up games against former and current Duke stars in the offseason in Cameron. "That gave me confidence," he said.

Brand also had some concerns about attending school below the Mason-Dixon line.

"Being an athlete, I didn't see racism that might affect the average African American going down to the South," he said. "Being a Duke player transcends all color. I got nothing but love."

Brand still didn't know how much playing time he would get when Duke opened the season that year against Army at West Point, not far from Brand's hometown. "Coming from a small school, my high school coach figured they'd put me in at the end of the game," Brand said. "I started right off the bat."

Brand was an immediate force, scoring 12 points on five-of-six shooting, grabbing three rebounds and contributing three assists in a team-high 24 minutes against Army. He had given the Blue Devils the low-post threat they had lacked in the two previous seasons.

He was leading the team in scoring and rebounding when he broke a bone in his foot December 27, the first practice after Christmas, and was pronounced out for the season.

Krzyzewski juggled his lineup, starting Burgess in the middle and bringing Taymon Domzalski off the bench. And he compensated for Brand's loss by continuing to rely on three pointers.

The strategy worked. Duke won 10-straight games and climbed all the way to No. 1 with a 20-1 record before their weakness was exposed against North

Carolina. Carolina's All-America forward Antawn Jamison ripped apart the guts of Duke's interior defense, and the Tar Heels went on a 24-4 run to defeat the Devils 97-73 at the Dean Dome.

The rematch would be different.

Brand had missed 15 games. After undergoing a series of ultrasound treatments, he made an unexpected return to the lineup in late February, wearing an orthotic in his shoe. He came off the bench his first game back and went off for 14 points and seven rebounds in a 120-84 pounding of UCLA, and then moved into the starting lineup. By the time he came back, Roshown McLeod, a six-foot-eight transfer from St. John's who seemed to be fading out of the lineup by Christmas, stepped up, offering Duke another viable frontcourt option.

Brand saved the best for the Tar Heels, scoring 13 of his 16 points—including five of the first six possessions midway through the second half—as the Blue Devils rallied from a 17-point deficit to defeat Carolina 77-75, despite 23 points from Jamison, on Senior Day to clinch the ACC regular-season championship. Brand fouled out Makhtar Ndiaye in the process.

Despite the fact that the Devils reached the NCAA Southeast Regional final that year, Brand still wasn't 100 percent. But he kept working, starting for a U.S. team that won a gold medal in the Goodwill Games.

The next year, he was the dominant force in college basketball. "Basketball-wise, it wasn't as tough as I thought," he said. "The hardest part was Coach K's practices."

Brand's explosion didn't happen without a push. After two lackadaisical performances during a loss to Cincinnati and a narrow escape against Michigan State, Krzyzewski benched his star.

"I had my ups and downs," Brand admitted. "I came off the bench in three games: North Carolina A&T, Michigan, and Kentucky at the Meadowlands. Two of them were big-time games, too—national TV games. It made an impression. Coach K told me during a game that he didn't want me to get too full of myself. Those weren't his exact words, but basically he said, 'Sit at the end of the bench and take a photo.' He just wanted the best out of me."

Brand did play 36 minutes against the Wildcats and finished with 22 points and eight rebounds. After that, he became committed to getting in better shape, then playing with the intensity Krzyzewski demanded. He returned to the starting lineup for a pre-Christmas Jimmy V. matchup against Kentucky, tearing up the Wildcats with 22 points. Brand finished with 19 double doubles that year as Duke, which was being called the best team in the post-Wooden era, ran off 32 straight victories—including 19-0 in the ACC—before losing to Connecticut 77-74 in the NCAA championship game.

"I did not have a killer instinct," he recalled. "I used to let up once we got the advantage."

Duke assistant Johnny Dawkins taught him not to let up. "He told me it's not your fault if nobody can cover you," Brand said.

The pro scouts began to notice. So did Krzyzewski.

"We actually talked about it," Brand said. "When people started talking about it during the year, he actually had a meeting with me to talk about it a little more. He told me to stay focused. He told me if the time is right, he wouldn't hold me back. He was proud. He told me if I wanted to do it, to be the first, to make sure I represented Duke to my best and make him proud."

Brand was a huge favorite of the Cameron Crazies, who made up "Tickle me Elton" signs for home games.

Brand left Duke without the one thing he wanted—a national championship ring. He had 15 points and 13 rebounds against UConn, but he was bothered by the Huskies' double teams and didn't touch the ball for the final 8.02 of the game.

"I couldn't get to sleep that night," he said. "I must have run 1,000 plays through my head, trying to think of what we could have done. When I did get to sleep, I dreamt about winning the title."

After the season, Brand mulled over the idea of leaving early with his mother. The NBA scouts were talking about him going top three.

The two visited Krzyzewski at Duke Hospital, where he had just undergone hip replacement surgery. "I didn't want to do anything that might offend Duke," Brand said. "But Coach K was great about it. He said, 'Just make me proud.' I think that let guys know they can come to Duke and leave early."

Some pro scouts questioned Brand's size when he went to be measured at the Chicago pre-draft camp, whispering he might be only six foot five, which is interesting since he had a seven-foot-one wingspan. But when he took off his sneakers, he still measured six foot eight, 270, and became a lock for the first pick in the draft, ahead of Steve Francis of Maryland.

Krzyzewski was hit by two other unexpected departures that spring when Avery and freshman forward Corey Maggette left. He was against both decisions, feeling Avery needed another year to polish his game and Maggette—a great, but sometimes inconsistent talent who sat the entire second half of the UConn game—could use another year to mature.

Maggette went No. 13 to Seattle and was traded on draft night to the Orlando. He played there and was eventually dealt to the Clippers, where he is now a teammate of Brand.

Avery went No. 14 to the Minnesota Timberwolves, where he sat on the bench for two years and was out of the league before his three-year contract was over. And senior guard Trajan Langdon was drafted eighth by Cleveland, giving Duke an historic four first-round picks that year, and forcing Krzyzewski—who also lost Burgess as a transfer to Utah—to rebuild again with a young team once he got back on his feet.

"It was definitely hard for him," Brand said. "He might not have been for it at all, but he understood they had to make the decisions for themselves and their families. But it drove him more to prove he could still get it done after losing guys.

"I think it was a big adjustment for him to make, but it wasn't an adjustment he couldn't make. That's why he's still one of the greatest coaches of all times. He adapts to any situation. He recruits great kids, allows them to grow and leave early.

"He's not stuck in the Ice Age."

Two years later, Krzyzewski won his third national championship, defeating Arizona 82-72 in the NCAA finals.

Brand was there to see it.

"It was a sense of pride," he said. "I'm not a jealous person. I knew it wasn't my ring, but I was proud of the fact that some of guys I was there with reached the level to win that game.

"All the Duke guys were there. We had the best seats. We were sitting together. They all embraced me, and I went back to the hotel afterward to be part of the party. My agent, David Falk, is a big Duke fan. He took care of me. It was funny: seeing guys I played with still in college, watching them play in the Final Four, then get on a private plane to leave, go back to the NBA—wherever I had to go."

22

THE FUTURE PRESIDENT
SHANE BATTIER
Duke Class of 2001

S hane Battier has always dreamed seemingly impossible dreams.
On New Year's Eve, when he was 14, he wrote on an index card the 10 goals he wanted to accomplish the next year. He pinned the card to the wall of his bedroom. That list was the first thing he'd see in the morning and the last thing he would see at night.

His goals ranged from building a giant city of Legos to saving a human life. He also wanted to start as a ninth-grader for Detroit Country Day, an exclusive private school with a strong basketball program.

Battier hasn't changed.

Before the start of his senior season at Duke in 2001, the Blue Devils' gifted six-foot-eight forward listed the following goals: making first-team All-American and academic All-American, winning a national championship, and becoming the National Player of the Year.

Battier was all that and more, winning his third consecutive NABC Defensive Player of the Year award and scoring 18 points in his last game and then riding off into the sunset after the Blue Devils defeated Arizona 82-72 to win the school's third national championship.

When he graduated, he'd led Duke to an NCAA-record 133 victories and had his uniform retired. No one at Duke seemed that surprised.

Battier comes from a mixed-race family. He grew up in suburban Birmingham, Michigan. His father, Ed, the manager of a small trucking company, is black. His mother, Sandee, a corporate secretary, is white.

They produced a prodigy in a colorblind sport.

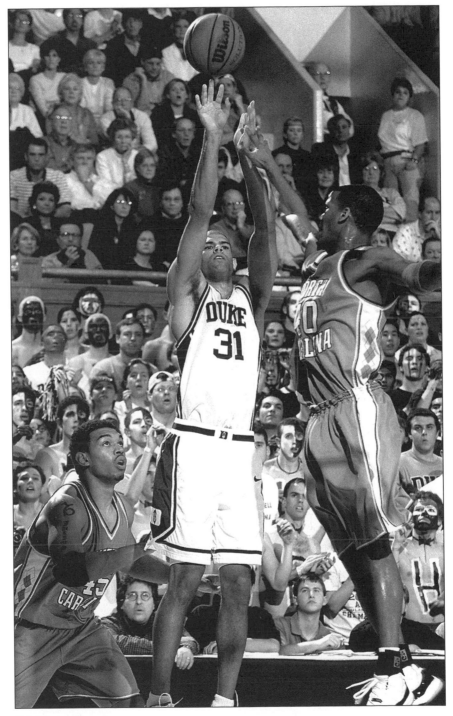

Duke Photography

At age three, Battier asked his mother, 'Do you think I would be a good president?' At five, he was reading encyclopedias for fun. At eight, he learned to type. At 12, he was first chair of 106 trumpets in Birmingham's annual youth orchestra concert.

There were other things that set him apart, too.

He was almost a straight-A student at Country Day, with the exception of that B in American History. In 11th grade, he delivered a commencement speech to the graduating seniors at another area high school.

The summer before his senior year, Battier went to a Memorial Day Tournament in Paris with the Boo Williams. David Teel, a local writer who accompanied the team, said one day he was working in his hotel room when Battier knocked on the door—he was looking for somebody to go on a tour of the Louvre. All his teammates were interested in finding a local McDonald's.

Of course, Battier was a McDonald's All-American, a top five prospect nationally, who led Country Day to three Class B state titles. Battier's final five schools were Michigan, Michigan State, Kansas, North Carolina, and Duke.

"I knew that I would have a great time and a great career and education at any of those five schools, but what set Duke apart was the time I spent on campus," Battier recalled. "I just knew I was a Duke guy. I don't know what it was. It was the place where I could see myself thriving the best.

"A lot of that had to do with Coach. He talked with me and had a vision for me as a person and a player. He never promised me anything. He said, 'If you work your tail off, you can have a very good career.' And my college career was beyond my wildest dreams. It was the ability to believe what Coach was telling me as a high school senior that helped make that all come true.

"He told me he never promises players anything: starting spots, playing time. He promised me he'd give me an opportunity to earn my minutes. He said, 'I promise you I'll make you a man and I'll let you make mistakes, but I will also try to teach you from those mistakes.'"

Krzyzewski first heard about Battier when he was in ninth grade. Krzyzewski was at Country Day, trying to recruit Chris Webber—who eventually signed with Michigan—when Kyle Keener, the coach there, told him about a young player who might be good enough to play for Duke some day.

Battier made an immediate impact long before he enrolled. He conducted part of the interview with Duke's admissions director, Christopher Guttenburg, in German.

No wonder associate A.D. in charge of academics Chris Kennedy told his wife after his first meeting with Battier, "I think I've just met the next President of the United States."

Krzyzewski took it one step further, suggesting he wanted to be the head of Duke Senior Citizens for Battier when he runs for president in 2016.

If elected, Battier said, he would appoint Krzyzewski ambassador to Tahiti.

Battier has always had an interest in politics. He became intrigued with Senator Bill Bradley, who had been an All-American at Princeton and a Rhodes Scholar, before playing for the Knicks. Battier went to a couple of fundraising events when Bradley ran for president in 2000.

But he had too much unfinished business to campaign full time for the senator from New Jersey.

Battier came to Duke with one of the most celebrated recruiting classes in ACC history. He, center Elton Brand, center Chris Burgess, and point guard Will Avery had talked about winning four national championships.

Four years later, he was the only one left. Brand and Avery left after their sophomore year for the NBA. Burgess transferred to Utah.

"When I graduated from high school, it was the very start of kids leaving for the pros after high school," Battier recalled. "Lamar Odom and Tracy McGrady came out after my class. Larry Hughes left after his first year. Then Elton, of course, and Baron Davis. My class was a transitional class in terms of the mindset of kids and the NBA. It's funny looking back at the McDonald's game; no one talked about going pro. It really wasn't a discussion. It was, 'Where are you going to school?'

"You expected to be in school a couple of years—maybe leave after sophomore year. I knew with our recruiting class, and with just how good those guys were, there was a pretty good chance I wouldn't finish with the same class I came in with.

"But I didn't know I was going to be the last one standing. It's funny how things work out. But I wasn't surprised.

"I had my own plan, my own idea of who I was as a person and as a player —and that covered four years of college. I needed every minute of it to max out my potential. Anyone who's gone to college—and I haven't met an exception yet—wishes he or she could go back and spend a week more in college. It really is one of the best times of your life. You're carefree, and I loved the experience. I loved going to class, loved hanging out with my friends, loved playing college basketball.

"I knew the NBA wasn't going anywhere, and I'd have the rest of my life to earn money, work, pay bills, pay taxes, do all that stuff. But you have only that short window to experience college, and I didn't want to give that up."

Battier became college basketball's most complete player.

And most complete student-athlete in the sport.

"When you're an 18-, 19-year-old freshman, you think you know a lot. You just graduated from high school. And I was a High School All-American, but looking back at it, I didn't know anything.

"A college coach for a college athlete really becomes a father figure away from home. I was very lucky to play for a coach who taught me what it meant to be a man and helped me grow as a person.

"You don't realize it at the time. You graduate and go into the real world and you've got to work for pay and you're facing real-life dilemmas, but you realize the things that your coach talked about in a basketball setting are applicable to life."

Battier had a rich college experience.

He spent his first summer in college interning with D. Morgan Stanley, an investment firm. He spent his second summer interning with Golin-Harris in Chicago, the advertising firm that handles the McDonald's account. He traveled throughout Europe in the student hostel program with his girlfriend, now wife, Heidi. And he was the president of the NABC student basketball council that advocated recruiting reform.

He wasn't always perfect. He got hooked on infomercials and got sucked into buying a Juice Man and a George Foreman Grill. And, oh yes, he nearly burned down his apartment with a mail-order bread maker.

But he is a perfectionist.

Battier also spread his academic wings in college. Like Bradley, Battier could have been on a fast track to a Rhodes scholarship. He was actually a candidate, but after undergoing a few preliminary interviews, he withdrew— deciding it would be too time-consuming to pursue as a senior while pursuing a national championship. Battier was considering majoring in history, public policy, or economics, but then decided to major in religion after taking a course in the New Testament and falling in love with it. At Duke, he taught classes in Daily Vacation Bible school and gave a sermon at his local church.

Battier always had faith in himself, but his faith in his game temporarily wavered when he was a freshman on Duke's 1998 regional finalist team. Battier was eager to please. He became notorious for taking charges on defense, but he constantly deferred to the upperclassmen Trajan Langdon and Steve Wojciechowski on offense, averaging fewer than five shots a game.

"I remember the first time I got yelled at," he recalled. "We lost to Carolina by 24 during my freshman year. I played horrible. I scored just two points and had four rebounds in 21 minutes. I played scared, and Brendan Haywood (Carolina's huge seven-foot-one center) had more of an impact on the outcome than our entire freshman class.

"We were in the Hall of Fame room, and Coach was going through the players and he got to me.

"'Battier,' he said in a sarcastic voice. 'I'm Shane Battier. I'm Mr. All-American. Everybody loves me. But Brendan Haywood kicks my butt when I play him.' He said it a little more colorfully than that.

"I'd never been yelled at my entire career.

"My dad was my coach when I was younger. I was always the best player, always played hard. My high school coach never yelled at me. I was my own worst critic. My parents never yelled at me like that. I was a pretty good kid.

"That was probably the worst tongue-lashing I ever got in my whole life. But you know what, I played pretty hard after that.

"Luckily, I didn't get yelled at like that the rest of my career."

Battier finally came out of his offensive shell for good midway through his sophomore year. But it took a heart-to-heart talk with assistant coach Quin Snyder, who called him into the office and told him not to be a coward.

"We recruited you to be a star," Snyder told him. "We need you to be a star. Now start acting like one."

Then Snyder had Battier—who would get so pumped up he would throw up before games—do some deep-breathing exercises and meditation.

Battier had his breakthrough game February 9, 1999, during a 98-87 victory over Maryland in Cameron. Battier scored a career-high 27 points and was a perfect four for four from three-point range. He credited his performance to watching a Discovery channel program about the Shaolin Monks in China and their ability to focus on inner strength, or Chi.

Interestingly, two years later, after Snyder left to become the head coach at Missouri, Duke played the Tigers in the second round of the NCAA Tournament. After the Blue Devils dispatched Missouri, Battier made a point of walking over to offer his condolences. "You made me the monster I am today," he told Snyder.

That 1999 Duke team had a look of dominance. The Blue Devils won 37 games—32 in a row at one point—cruising to the NCAA championship game before losing to Connecticut 77-74 in St. Petersburg, Florida.

"It was difficult because we all knew we were knocking on the Pantheon of all-time greatness," Battier said. "We were at the doorstep. All we had to do was win one game against a really good UConn team that I still think never got the credit they deserved.

"But the run we had—from the loss to Cincinnati in Alaska to the final game—was unbelievable. We won probably 75 to 80 percent of our games in layup drills. It was amazing. We would come out for layup lines, and the other team would look at us and they knew, in their hearts, that they weren't going to win. If they kept it close—12, 15 points—it was a moral victory.

"We had so much confidence. We'd jump on a team early—in the first five, six minutes—and the game would be over. I'm sure I'll never be part of something like that again. We were just a big blue machine. We kept rolling and rolling.

"When we lost to UConn, it was a blow. It had been so long since we'd tasted defeat, and it tasted pretty bitter. I was back at the hotel with my girlfriend—who's now my wife—and all I could do was throw a bag of pretzels against the wall. I didn't know what to make of the whole scenario."

The summer before Battier's junior year, Krzyzewski—who had been plagued by defections—called Battier and asked him to look in the mirror and visualize himself as the best player in the ACC.

He must have liked his reflection.

That year, Battier led the conference in three-point percentage, was third in scoring and free-throw percentage and fifth in field-goal percentage, blocks, and steals.

He made second-team All-American. And he lived up to his billing when Duke played Kansas in the second round of the 2000 tournament. Battier scored 21 points, had eight rebounds, and blocked eight shots as the Devils rallied from a 64-63 deficit with 1:18 left to defeat the Jayhawks 69-64 and advance to the Sweet 16—where they lost to Florida.

"When I was a freshman, one of the best things Coach K did was tell me, 'Don't get caught up in positions. Don't get caught up in being a power forward or a guard. Just make plays.'

"Looking back, I was essentially a center my freshman year after Elton Brand went down. Roshown McLeod played power forward, and I was a center in the ACC. I had to guard guys a lot bigger than me, so Coach said, 'Don't make excuses that you're undersized or whatever. Just make plays. I recruited you because of your ability to make plays.'

"Every year, I tried to add something to my game.

"When I first came in, I was a decent shooter. But I shot only four for 24 from three-point land my freshman year. So I said, 'I really need to work on this.' I changed some things mechanically my sophomore year. But it didn't click until that Maryland game at home.

"The next year, with Elton, Corey Maggette, and Will Avery leaving, the cupboard was pretty bare. We had some pretty good freshmen, and Cris Carrawell, Nate James, and me. But it was time to step it up and leave my stamp on the program.

"Coach said again, 'Don't get caught up in being a power forward or a shooting guard. Just make plays and do it all.' That's what I tried to do every game. My mindset was not to judge my game based on how many points I scored. I tried to judge success by how many rebounds I got or how many steals. Did I take care of the ball? Was I efficient? Those were the things that were emphasized most by Coach.

Battier's career will always be linked with Maryland.

"Carolina is always Duke's rival, but Maryland—I think it started with Steve Francis my freshman year—had some pretty good teams. There was a healthy mistrust. I don't like hatred; that's a strong word. But we had a healthy disdain for each other.

"Whenever we got together to play, there was a lot of passion in those games. I had pretty good success against them in my first two years. They got me a couple of times in my junior and senior years. Those were some of the fun games. I never lost in Cole Field House, which I loved, because I don't think there was a place in America where I was more hated than Cole Field House."

That venom poured out when the Devils played Maryland in that famous January 27, 2001, game at Cole during Battier's senior year.

The Maryland students were waiting. Many of them had on T-shirts that said, "F*ck Duke" on them. And some spent time throwing ice and aluminum foil from hot dog wrappers at the Duke bench.

"We were getting our lunch served to us the whole game," Battier said.

"They played great. Juan Dixon played great. Lonnie Baxter played great. And we didn't have an answer. But then Jason Williams had that great stretch when he hit a three, then went off for eight-straight points in 14 seconds in the last minute of regulation. And we forced overtime.

"The reason our team was so successful my senior year is that we were the more aggressive team in almost every game we played. That's a lot of Mike.

"If you look at the numbers, we shot more free throws than opposing teams. That's just from Coach: 'Be aggressive. Be aggressive offensively. Be aggressive defensively. Take control of the game.'

"After Jason went off, we could feel Maryland being very unsure about how to win this game. And you could really feel it, 'We're here. Let's go out and win it.'

"Once it got to overtime, we said, 'There's no way we're going to lose this game. No way.' And you could just see it in Maryland's eyes. They didn't believe they could win. It was great.

"After the buzzer sounded, we just walked out of there. We got pelted with batteries and ice. But when you win like that, you can take it."

Battier took the game over in overtime, making a three to give Duke a 95-92 lead, scoring the Devils' last six points, and locking up a 98-86 win when he blocked a shot by Dixon.

"Growing up, I was a big Pistons fan. I hated the Lakers, Celtics, and Bulls. I despised Michael Jordan, Magic Johnson, and Larry Bird.

"It was funny to be in those same shoes, to go into an arena where people who don't know me will be holding up 'I hate Shane Battier' signs—one of those little things that warm your heart," he told one Detroit writer.

"Reggie Miller says there's nothing better than going into an arena with 20,000 people hoping you break an ankle or air ball a shot, then playing well and winning and walking off with a smile and giving them a wink."

During Battier's four years at Duke, his teams were an incredible 30-2 on the road against in the ACC and 38-3 overall. Battier lost at Michigan and North Carolina as a freshman and at Virginia as a senior.

The lessons learned from that game at Cole helped Duke when it met Maryland for a fourth time that season in the national semifinals. This time the Blue Devils had to rally from 22 points down with 6:55 to play in the first half.

Battier scored 25 points for Duke, which outscored the Terps 78-45 the rest of the way in the second half to win 95-84.

"That was the epitome of Duke character," Battier said. "It wouldn't have been possible if we hadn't come back and beaten Maryland in Cole Field House. It was almost the same situation. We were down 20 at one point, and Coach told me, 'Hey, it can't get any worse. Just relax.'

"Down 20 in the national semifinals—in front of all our friends and family—and he said it can't get any worse. 'What are you going to do, lose by 40? Just go out and play.'

"I remember Nate James hit a big three in the corner to start the run and—almost the way it was in Cole Field House—we could see the confidence draining from Maryland's eyes.

"And Coach was telling us, 'Attack, attack, attack, attack. Be aggressive. We can get this.'

"We played our game. We were the aggressors in the second half and wound up winning going away. It was an improbable comeback."

And it set the stage for Krzyzewski to win his third national championship when Duke defeated Arizona 82-72 in Minneapolis.

Battier, who had 18 in the final, was voted Most Outstanding Player of the tournament. But he knew what this meant to Krzyzewski, who was inducted into the Naismith Hall of Fame later that year.

"I think to Coach, it gave him validation, post-1991-1992," Battier said.

"He went to so many Final Fours before 1991-1992 and had so much success. Then he got hurt, and Duke was a pretty good team, but not a contender. This pretty much brought him full circle to the top of college basketball again.

"There are a lot of coaches who can't make that turn. Sometimes you take for granted winning it and being at the top of the polls and being a contender every year. But for Coach to sort of reinvent himself and get back to the top nine, 10 years later, that's special and shows what kind of special coach he is.

"He's successful because he really does put his heart and soul into the team. I know every coach thinks about his team. But for him, it's almost constantly. There have been times, I'm sure, when he's put his family on the back burner.

"He really throws himself into the team. There may have been a day when I wasn't feeling good or had something on my mind, and he would notice it because he's so in tune with his team. That sets him apart. He spends so much time thinking about those things, trying to maximize every ounce of talent and potential from his players. Not every coach can do that. That's his strong suit."

Battier's legacy will always be his will to win. Duke was 133-15 in his four years.

"I don't know how we did it," he said. "We had unbelievable consistency, and I think that was Coach. His big thing was, 'Next play. Next play.' If you're playing a game and get a fast break, dunk. You dunk and the crowd's going crazy, what do you do? Do you pose for the cameras, or do you march your way back and play defense?

"Of course, you do the latter. You go on and play the next play. Same thing: you have a horrible turnover. You jump in the air, try to thread the needle on a pass and it gets picked off and they go down and get a three, what do you do? Do you sulk and put your head down? You go on to the next play.

"It's always about: 'What are you going to do next?'

"He would say that almost every time we had a big win. We'd beat Carolina and he'd say, 'All right, that's great. What are you going to do against Clemson next week? Let's move on.'

"We really listened. We really believed. And that was the basis of the consistency that allowed us to win an obscene amount of games."

Battier was drafted by the Memphis Grizzlies with the sixth pick in the 2001 draft and lives on the river with his wife, Heidi, and their two dogs, Bruin and Gertie.

"I am flabbergasted at the career I had," he admitted. "You can't dream that stuff up."

23

THE GRADUATE
JASON WILLIAMS
Duke Class of 2002

J ason Williams made his biggest impact on Duke basketball by winning two National Player of the Year awards during his sophomore and junior years, in 2001 and 2002. But the six-foot-two All-American guard also changed the way Mike Krzyzewski dealt with the changing landscape of college basketball.

After Williams averaged 25.7 points in the 2001 NCAA Tournament and helped lead the Blue Devils to the national championship, he was considered the hottest property in the NBA draft.

Williams had vowed he would return in February of his junior year. He did the same thing after Duke defeated Arizona 82-72 in the NCAA championship game. But then he began having second thoughts after word started to spread that he might be the No. 1 pick in the draft.

"I was seriously thinking about leaving school," Williams said. "Michael Jordan was calling me, 'Come play in D.C. We'd love to have you play here. If I ever come back, you and I could play in the backcourt.' I was like, 'Damn, this is my chance to play with Michael Jordan.'"

Another unexpected defection might have been devastating to Krzyzewski. He had been hammered at the end of the 1999 season when sophomore Elton Brand, the National Player of the Year, left, as expected. But then sophomore guard Will Avery and freshman forward Corey Maggette—who had told him they were coming back—left, too.

So Krzyzewski met with Williams's parents—David, a development manager for Global Crossing Fiber Optics, and Althea, a guidance counselor

Duke Photography

and vice principal at South Plainfield, New Jersey—and talked about a plan whereby Williams would spend his junior year in college and earn enough credits to graduate in three years.

"We were at the John Wooden Award, and Coach K and I were talking," Williams said. "He was trying to get me to come back to school. He said, 'You know the thing I've always liked about you is you.'

"Funny, how people say these one-liners just to make you think.

"'What, Coach?' I asked.

"He said, 'You've always had the ability to be different from everybody else. You never follow the norm. Right now, the norm is everybody who gets a chance to be the No. 1 pick in the draft will leave school—any kid. But you know, I don't know if you want to be like everybody else.'

"And he was right. That's why I came to Duke: I wanted to be the best. I just didn't want to be the king of the guys in Jersey. I wanted to be the best. That was incentive for me to stay."

Then Krzyzewski offered Williams—and eventually six-foot-nine sophomore teammate Carlos Boozer—the best of all possible worlds.

"The great thing about it was Coach K and my family, without me even knowing it, devised this plan. He felt I was ready to go after one more year. He wanted me to have my own team. The year before it was Shane Battier's team. And he felt the thing that would make me great was being the leader of a team.

"As soon I told him I was going to stay, he said, 'All right, you're going to go to summer school.' I took four courses that summer, and I overloaded my junior year with five courses each semester. I took one final course the next summer and I graduated. I got the best of all worlds. I got my Duke degree in sociology, which a lot of people said couldn't be done in three years, won the Wooden Award, and was the second pick in the draft.

"It was a storybook ending."

Williams has carefully choreographed his success story from the time he was a kid growing up in South Plainfield, New Jersey. He learned the game from watching videotapes of former Pistons great Isiah Thomas.

"I didn't start playing basketball until fourth grade," he recalled. "It's really funny because I played with my friends that summer. We lived in a not-so-good area, and I came home yelling to my mom, 'Mom, there's a shootout. There's a shootout.'

"She kind of grabbed me, pulled me down, and said, 'Are you okay? Are you okay? Did anybody hurt you?' She was thinking gun shootout. 'No,' I said, 'a basketball shootout. It's a chance for me to play on a team. The coaches picked me.'

"I was really good at it. My parents were really astonished, because I had never played before and I picked up on it so easily."

Williams was good at everything he'd tried at St. Joseph's High in nearby Metuchen, New Jersey. He won a poetry contest when he wrote a poem about Christmas. He was a member of the National Spanish Honor Society. He captained the chess team. He was a two-time all-state soccer player and an all-state volleyball player. He had a 3.7 GPA.

And, oh yes, he was also the McDonald's National High School Player of the Year and was invited to the White House to meet President Clinton.

His only disappointment in high school occurred after his 10th grade year when most of the players on his AAU team were invited to the elite sneaker company invitational summer camps, and he was bypassed.

"I finally got invited to the Nike All-American camp the summer before my senior year," he recalled. "I was known for scoring. I could score points all the time, but I was like, 'Now is there some way I can show these guys I'm a really good basketball player? Can I dominate games without scoring, because everybody who goes to Nike tries to score?' So I averaged 16 to 17 assists a game for the week."

The recruiting letters piled up.

Williams was particularly fond of North Carolina.

"I was a big Dean Smith fan," he said. "I loved North Carolina. I had North Carolina shorts, the jersey, everything. I had a picture of Michael Jordan on the wall in my bedroom.

"But there was no real interest from North Carolina. I went there on an unofficial visit and met Bill Guthridge, met all the players—Ed Cota, Joe Forte, everybody. I was excited. Then Bill Guthridge told me, 'We think you're a really good player, but we don't think you can fit into the North Carolina system.'

Guthridge told Williams Carolina already had their future point guard Ron Curry, and they didn't think he could score well enough to play the two guard position.

Williams, who lived less than 10 miles from Rutgers, thought hard about attending the state university and playing with one of his best friends, Dahntay Jones, who eventually transferred to Duke.

"I got caught up with all the hype," he said. "Being from Jersey, I used to hang out there all the time. I met Governor Christie Whitman and she was telling me I was going to be on television and I was the Second Coming. I got it into my head that I was going to Rutgers, and the only school that could take me away from that was North Carolina.

"In the meantime, my parents had scheduled all these unofficial visits for me, and I told my mom I didn't want to go. I told my mom literally—it was right before I was supposed to visit Duke—'I don't want to go.'

"I told her, 'I don't want to be that far away from home. I want to be close to home. I want to go to Rutgers. I want to be the savior. My mom and I got into this huge argument. We were yelling back and forth. We ended up arguing for two days. She has a strong personality, so basically, I had to give in.

"We all drove down to Durham, and I didn't talk to my mom the whole trip. I said barely 10 words."

That all changed after Williams arrived on campus. "I loved it," he recalled. "But I was still really excited about Rutgers. But my dad said something I'll never forget. He knows me. He said, 'Do you want to be the king among paupers or the king among kings?'

"After he said that, I said, 'You know what, I want to play against the best so I can say I was the best of the best.' And that's what made me go to Duke: that one comment."

The day Williams arrived, he began keeping a journal in a black spiral notebook. It included a daily to-do list and chronicled the ups and downs of his career. Williams reviewed the passages to gain some perspective, a technique also used by teammate Shane Battier. His mother also made her thoughts available during his career, posting them on the Duke chat board under the name "Blue Devil Momma."

Williams kept the notebook a secret his first two years.

"I still have it," he said. "I write in it to this day. I remember writing a passage for church and I had to go back to my journal and actually read my first entry—about my first game against Stanford in the preseason NIT at the Garden and how nervous I was. I was 17.

"You're such a wimp when you're 17. It's funny to go back and see how you've grown up."

Williams's first game was nothing to write home about. He scored 13 points, grabbed 10 rebounds and had three assists, but he also shot three for 15 and had six turnovers, including one in the final 30 seconds that allowed Stanford to tie the game, force overtime and beat Duke.

Williams grew up quickly. He was a starter on a Sweet 16 team as a freshman and a star by the time he was a sophomore—once he'd ironed out the mechanical flaws in his shot and built his upper-body strength.

And he was Maryland's worst nightmare. The Terps—who were a year away from winning their national championship—had emerged as Duke's chief rival in the ACC when North Carolina was going through an uncharacteristic, brief down cycle.

The night of January 27, 2001, will always ring bells with the Maryland fans.

That was the night Williams awakened from what had looked like a comatose state to score eight points in just 14 seconds as the Blue Devils staged a miracle rally, coming back from a 90-80 deficit in the final 54 seconds to force overtime, and then stun the Terps 98-96 in overtime.

It happened so fast.

Williams had not made a three-pointer and had committed 10 turnovers against Steve Blake's nagging man-to-man defense. Then he went off. Williams made a layup, and then stole the inbound pass and made a three. Then, eight seconds later, he made another three, pulling the Blue Devils within two and setting the stage for Nate James to force overtime with two free throws. Williams's explosion came after Blake fouled out.

Battier took the game over in overtime, making a three to give Duke a 95-92 lead, then blocking a potential game-tying shot by Juan Dixon at the end.

"I was thinking that was one of the worst games I'd ever played," Williams recalled. "It was one of those games where my head was up my butt. Whatever the coaches were trying to say to me, I was just in one of those funks, and I couldn't get out of it.

"My teammates were trying to push me, but everything that could go wrong did go wrong. Every time I made a move, somebody would cut me off; or every time I took a shot, it would be awkward. Nothing was going my way. We were in the huddle and we were down.

"It's funny. You play basketball in front of thousands and thousands of people and never, ever hear what the fans say. You're so focused on the game you don't pay attention to that. This is how unfocused I was: I was listening to what the fans were saying. My head wasn't into the game. Some fan was like, 'Williams, you guys suck and your team is overrated.' In the midst of 20,000 fans, I heard this one guy say this to me.

"We're in the huddle, and all of a sudden, everybody kind of looks at one another. And I just got this burning passion; I don't know where it came from. It was almost like, 'I want to play. I want to win this game.' That's what sparked it, and everything else was fate—for me to get two steals and knock down two threes.

"It's funny: after the game, it was like I was in a trance. I look back on that moment and I always wonder, 'How did you do it?'

"When Coach K asked me about it afterward, I had only one answer.

"I told him, 'I hate that overrated cheer.'"

Immediately after the game, angry Maryland fans pelted the small contingent of Duke fans with water bottles, hitting Boozer's father and Chris Duhon's mother.

The next time Duke played Maryland that season in Cameron, it was Senior Night. Only this time there were no miracles, only a sense of tragedy when Carlos Boozer—who had scored 16 points against the Terps in the first half—broke a bone his right foot early in the second half. Maryland won 91-80.

And Duke's chances in the NCAA Tournament slipped from good to questionable.

"We pretty much had an all-star game that year, but Carlos was our only center, our only big guy," Williams said. "We came into the locker room and everybody was so down. We were thinking, 'There's no chance.' I remember looking at Shane Battier—who's always Mr. Optimistic—and his face was so glum.

"We had a meeting before practice the next day. Coach came in, sat down, and said—I'll never forget this—'If you guys believe in me, if you guys have the same kind of passion and fire I have in my eyes right now, we're going to win the national championship.' He said that, and everybody kind of bought into the team concept.

"And with two guys who didn't play that much—Casey Sanders and Reggie Love—we won the national championship."

Boozer actually came back for the East Regional, but played just 22 minutes against both UCLA and Southern California, combining for just three points and 10 rebounds in those two games. But he was a huge factor in the Final Four.

Everyone had to step up against Maryland in the national semifinals. Duke had to stage another huge comeback to beat the Terps 82-72 at Minneapolis. The Blue Devils had to come back from a 22-point first-half deficit in this one.

"Coach K got us out of our funk that game," Williams said. "He came into the locker room at halftime and said, 'You know what's funny about this rivalry, the team that's down at halftime always wins the game.' When we were in the middle of our comeback, Maryland fans were just going crazy."

Williams had a huge tournament. He scored 34 points during a victory over UCLA in the Sweet 16—including 19 straight in the second half—and led the tournament in scoring with 154 points and in assists with 31. Both he and Battier made first-team All-America that year and won the NABC National Player of the Year award.

But it wasn't always easy.

Midway through February that dream season, Duke played at Virginia—a team they had beaten 103-61 at Cameron—and lost 91-89. When the game ended, Williams—who had shot just five for 21 and had played in a daze—saw freshman point guard Chris Duhon crying in the locker room and went over to console him.

"Chris was like a little brother to me," Williams said. "I told him that I felt sorry, it was my fault, I was out of it. When it came time to make critical plays, I had held back.

"Coach K looked at me and said, 'Get your hand off him. You don't deserve to cry with him. You didn't do anything to help him win this game. He wanted it more than you did.'

"He was just going at me.

"That was the first time we actually argued. I said to him, 'You didn't help me out.' After that game, we had a little falling out. Our relationship wasn't the same for about a month. He was down on me for yelling at him. I felt very bad. I was like, 'Wow, I got screamed at.'

"That's what I came back to school for, that's what I had to learn. It was my team. And no matter if I was getting touches or not, that was my responsibility. I learned so much from that. He's always teaching. A lot of times he doesn't even know it."

Krzyzewski could be tough on his players when he felt it was necessary.

The Blue Devils were ranked No. 1 for 14 of 18 weeks during Williams's junior year. But there was the time in December when Duke played Kentucky in the Jimmy V Classic at the Meadowlands and Krzyzewski, down 10, benched the starters at the beginning of the second half to kick-start the team during a 95-92 victory in overtime.

Then there was the 77-76 loss to Florida State that culminated with the team arriving at the locker room for practice the next day and finding that their name plates, chairs, and individual pictures were gone.

"So many people say about coaches: this is a guy who can teach you things or this is a guy who is a great strategist," Williams said. "He does all that, but he coaches you in more than basketball. He coaches you in life. He coaches you to be a man."

Williams won all the Player of the Year awards in 2002, and Boozer and Mike Dunleavy Jr. were also NBA first-round picks. But Duke's season ended prematurely when the Blue Devils blew a 19-point lead and lost to Indiana, 74-73 in a Sweet 16 game when Williams drained a three in the closing seconds and was fouled on the play but then missed a game-tying free throw, and Boozer, who grabbed the rebound, missed the game-winner at the buzzer.

Williams was drafted by the Chicago Bulls. He had a solid rookie season, but he never got a chance to take his game to the next level.

On June 19, 2003, he got on his new motorcycle and took off for dinner. When he went to put the bike into second gear, it got away from him and slammed into a utility pole. Williams suffered a fractured pelvis, a broken leg, and severe ligament damage to his left knee. It took him close to a year to walk again.

"Coach K was there for me the night I got hurt," he recalled. "He was in Vegas the day I got hurt, and when I woke up, he was by my side. My mother; father; and fiancée; my agent, Kevin Bradbury; and he were all there. I was so shocked to see that. We had been close. He had been to a couple of my games that year—trying to talk to GM Jerry Krause about the way they were playing, because they were trying to run that stupid triangle.

"That's the first time in my life I'd ever seen Coach K almost cry. When we won the national championship, he was teary-eyed, but that was a feeling of happiness. When I was in that bed, strung up, couldn't move, he had tears in his eyes. As soon as I saw that, he sucked it up.

"He gave me a pendant—Our Lady of Mt. Carmel. It's around my neck right now. He patted me on the back and said, 'You're going to play again one day.'

"That says a lot about him.

"It's funny: when people are on top, so many people try to break them down. I've heard so many negative things people say about Coach K. Another thing that's funny: fans are fans, so I'm sure some people don't like Duke. But what it really comes down to is that he's one of the best people I ever met. He cares about people. He's got such a big heart. You can hate him as much as you want because he coaches Duke, but he's a great guy."

Williams has started planning for the future. He has worked as an analyst for ESPN, brought a printing plant and a small farm, and taken his Cirrus test so he can get into financial equities.

But he still wants to give the NBA one more shot. When Krzyzewski learned Williams was attempting to make a comeback last spring, he put in a phone call, offering his encouragement.

"'Hey, Jay,' he said in that Coach K voice," Williams recalled. "Then he said, 'I've been hearing so much how much you want it. I want to see it for myself. I want to see the passion you have in your eyes. I miss you and I love you.'"

24

THE SHOOTIST

J.J. REDICK

Duke Class of 2006

The legend of Jonathan Clay Redick, also known as J.J., began in Cave Springs, Virginia, on a quiet, out-of-the-way mountain top in a southwest suburb of Roanoke, Virginia.

Duke's six-foot-four All-America guard grew up there, working on his shooting touch by practicing on a backyard hoop on an unpaved road made of dirt and gravel. "I taught myself how to shoot in my backyard," Redick said. "I would stay out there for hours when I was a kid. And even when I was 13, 14, I would shoot all the time."

The work habits he developed in his personal laboratory have produced one of the most dangerous shooters in the history of college basketball.

Redick led the ACC in scoring. He averaged 21.8 points, made 121 three-point field goals, and shot a near-perfect 93.8 percent from the free throw line as a junior in 2005, playing for a third-ranked, 27-6 Duke team that won the ACC Tournament for the sixth time in seven years and reached the NCAA Sweet 16 for the eighth-straight season. He was a first-team All-American who will be remembered as the best pure shooter to play for Mike Krzyzewski since All-America guard Johnny Dawkins.

He has a 93.8 career free throw percentage headed into his senior year, which currently makes him the top free throw shooter in NCAA history. He also has 318 career three-pointers, which means he is on pace to break the NCAA career record of 411 set by Virginia's Curtis Staples.

Redick became a Duke fan when he was just seven years old.

Duke Photography

"The first game I remember watching was the Duke-Michigan NCAA championship game in 1992," he said.

"We taped it. I probably watched it 15, 20 times. I just fell in love with Duke. When I would work out in the backyard, shooting, I would always pretend I played for Duke. And I'd go against other ACC teams. I'd always be on Duke's team.

"I was undefeated in my backyard."

Redick came from good bloodlines. His father, Ken, had played two years at Ohio Wesleyan. Twin sisters, Alyssa and Catie, both played for Campbell. Younger brother J.J. looked like he might not grow to be big enough to play big-time basketball. He was just five feet, six inches tall when he was in seventh grade.

"That's when I hit my growth spurt and started developing some skills and a little bit of a shooting touch. And I started developing a little bit of a swagger," he said. "By the middle of eighth grade, I had sprouted up to six foot three. I tacked on another inch in ninth grade."

Redick was pretty much unbeatable in AAU and high school, playing for the Hampton Roads, Virginia, Boo Williams All-Stars, which won two national championships. He then led an otherwise average high school team to a 70-62 victory over George Wythe, scoring a career-high 43 points in that game despite playing with a bad right leg. Redick was also selected MVP in the McDonald's All-America when he shot 10 for 15, made five threes, and scored 26 points.

None of Redick's accomplishments were lost on Duke, which had had Redick on its radar screen since the end of his ninth grade year when he attended the Nike Junior All-American camp in San Diego.

"Bobby Hussey used to be the coach at Virginia Tech and spent a couple of years as an assistant at Clemson. In between, he worked for Nike. I met him in San Diego. We built a relationship.

"In my sophomore year, he told Coach K and assistant Steve Wojciechowski about me. Wojo called my high school coach and said, 'If J.J. wants to come to a game, have him choose one.' I decided to come to the UNC game on Chris Carrawell's Senior Day. That was the first time I met Coach K. The first time he saw me play was at the Nike camp the summer before my junior year.

"I listened to other schools. I really wanted to stay close to home. I was close to my family. I wanted my family to see all my games so schools in the West Coast and the Midwest were pretty much out. I entertained Virginia and Florida. And I was interested in N.C. State, because I really liked their coaching staff. But all along it was, 'If Duke offers, if they want me to commit, I'll commit.'"

Redick actually committed to Duke in the fall of 2001, before his junior year. He was the first member of Duke's Super Six to commit. The others were center Shelden Williams from Midwest City, Oklahoma; forwards Shavlik Randolph from Raleigh, Michael Thompson from Chicago, and Lee Melchionni from Ft. Washington, Pennsylvania; and point guard Sean Dockery from Chicago.

Redick has been a three-year starter, playing as a sophomore for a 2004 team that pushed Connecticut to the limit before losing in the NCAA semifinals.

But 2005 was his breakout year.

It could not have come at a better time. Krzyzewski was hit with another round of defections. Six-foot-eight forward Luol Deng—who finished second to Chris Paul of Wake Forest for ACC Rookie of the Year—declared for the NBA draft and valuable six-foot-seven point guard Shawn Livingston, a McDonald's All-American from Peoria, opted for the pros when he discovered he would be a lottery pick. Livingston went fourth to the Los Angeles Clippers. Deng was taken seventh by the Chicago Bulls.

Redick, six-foot-eight Shelden Williams, and senior guard Daniel Ewing were left to pick up the pieces and supply a thin team with a three-pronged offense.

"We had reached a crossroads," Redick said. "We could stay as one of the elite programs or kind of fade away."

There was a point when Redick didn't know if Krzyzewski would even be there to lead the way. During the last week of June 2004, word leaked out that Krzyzewski had met with Mitch Kupchak, the GM of the Lakers, about replacing Phil Jackson as the head coach there.

The numbers—$40 million over eight years—were staggering.

"I don't know how crazy it was around campus, because I wasn't there," Redick said. "I was taking a little vacation. My aunt lives in Iowa, and we went out there—my mother, my sister, my brother, and me—for the Fourth of July.

"I actually heard about it when we were flying out. They called me and told me. And we had to deal with it all weekend. I tried calling Coach, but he wasn't answering any messages.

"I was definitely worried about it. At the same time, I was pretty confident that he was going to come back. He's a man of principle, and he loves his team. That's what college is all about.

"There was definitely an uneasiness. I talked to some of my teammates, and we weren't sure what was going on. I remember, I was watching ESPN and I saw kids holding rallies for him to stay.

"It was definitely a relief when he decided he was coming back."

One of the first things Krzyzewski did after he decided to stay at Duke was to make sure that Redick was in the best shape of his career. Redick had developed a bad habit of making late-night trips to Bojangles, a fast-food chicken place in Durham.

"I lived about three miles from campus. I wasn't eating breakfast, because I didn't want to be late for class, so I started eating late at night. I loved their biscuits and gravy."

Redick began to realize it was becoming problem when he saw himself in his sister Alyssa's wedding pictures that May. "My face was puffy," he said. "That's when I realized I needed to drop some weight."

"During my first two years, I had never committed myself to being in good shape. It really wore on me mentally, physically, and emotionally. I couldn't be at my best all the time, and it was really frustrating. I sat down with Coach K in May, and he said to me, 'Just get in the best shape of your life.'

"At that time, I was about 215.

"I worked out all summer, living a different lifestyle, bulking myself up, working my butt off. By the time preseason started, I was down to 192. And my playing weight all season was about 188."

Being in shape helped Redick survive Krzyzewski's preseason boot camp and set the stage for him to explode onto the national stage.

"Preseason was as hard as ever," Redick said. "Coach K pushed us because he knew it had to be that way for us to win. He knew this year was kind of a turning point in our program. Coach K had so much pride in Duke that he pushed us to reach our maximum level and potential. And I think we did that.

"It was definitely one of his best coaching jobs and definitely his best coaching job since I've been here. There was never a day when he didn't demand our best from us. In the past, we could get away with maybe having a mediocre practice here and there. But I'll tell you what, that year, there were no easy practices."

Redick was a marked man from the start of the season. And he stepped up big in Duke's biggest games—like the 102-92 victory over Wake Forest February 20, 2005, at Cameron.

The Blue Devils were coming off an uncharacteristic two losses in a row— at Maryland and at Virginia Tech. And Wake, which had already defeated Duke 92-85 in Winston-Salem two weeks earlier, was playing like a Final Four team.

"The two practices leading up to that game were just men's practices," Redick said. "Everything was physical, and there were a lot of contact drills. It was a rough two days."

None of the players ever knew who was starting before tip-off. Krzyzewski had made a decision to shake up the lineup in an attempt to create a more physical, competitive look. He opened with Redick, Sheldon Williams, and three walk-ons—six-foot-six ex-football player Reggie Love, six-foot-10 Patrick Johnson, and guard Patrick Davidson, a soccer player.

After Wake got the opening tap, Davidson, a six-foot sophomore from Mellborne, Arkansas, jostled Wake Forest All-America point guard Chris Paul all the way up the floor. The whistle blew. Krzyzewski jumped up, yelling at officials to call an offensive charge. The infraction went against Davidson. But the tone was set.

When Davidson left the game two minutes later, he received a standing ovation. Krzyzewski and his teammates rushed out to give him a bear hug.

"It was great," Redick said. "Patrick was my roommate. When he came off the court and Coach gave him a hug, I was like, 'All right, we're going to win this game.'

"That, and winning the ACC Tournament were my two favorite moments of the season,' Redick said.

"There are a couple of reasons why it was special," Redick said. "The previous year I'd played terrible and we lost to Maryland in the championship game. I hit rock bottom in my confidence. A little bit of confidence is what I have to play with to be successful. I was really frustrated. I had a chance to win the ACC championship and missed a three. I was really down about that.

"The other reason it was special for me was that all year everyone was telling us we weren't going to do anything, that we weren't that good. All that stuff was going around down here. For us to win the ACC Tournament and earn a No. 1 seed, that's just special. That showed us that the hard work paid off."

Redick took a while to get going in the 2005 tournament, which was played at the MCI Center in Washington, D.C. Redick normally warms up for an hour before games. When the Blue Devils played Virginia in the quarterfinals, he had only 20 minutes.

It showed. Redick couldn't get into his rhythm. He missed 11 of his first 12 shots during a victory over the Cavs.

But the next night, he began to heat up, going off for a Duke ACC Tournament—record 35 points against N.C. State—a team that had limited him to just one field goal during their only meeting in regular season—as Duke advanced to the finals. Then Redick scored 26 more as the Blue Devils held off Georgia Tech in the Sunday afternoon championship game.

Krzyzewski squeezed the most out of that team. Redick was a consensus first-team All-American. Williams, the National Defensive Player of the Year, made second-team All-American. Ewing played his way into the draft. And role players such as Melchionni, Dockery, and freshman DeMarcus Nelson filled their jobs.

Not everybody was happy about Redick's—or Duke's—success.

Redick had been labeled Public Enemy No. 1 throughout the last two seasons. He was so disliked by Maryland fans, they began chanting "***** you J.J." when Duke played at College Park. The sound got so loud, it was impossible not to hear the obscenity on ESPN.

"It's tough," Redick said. "I think if you sat down and got to know me, I wouldn't have to deal with it. But I'll be honest with you, I'm a jerk on the court. Mike Schrage, our director of basketball operations, made everybody a little highlight tape during the season. I was watching it the other day and I said, 'Man, I am really a jerk.'

"But you know what it is, I have to play with cockiness. I have to play with a little bit of swagger. It's what gives me my edge. My attitude on the court is totally different from that off the court. I'm just a really low-key guy off the court. I can't be that way on the court. I think that was just survival skills picked up along the line. In AAU, I was the only white kid on the team. And that was my way of dealing with it—showing people I wasn't going to back down."

There is a softer side to Redick, who is majoring in history with a minor in cultural anthropology. He writes poetry.

"The first poem I ever remember writing was in ninth grade," he said. "My grandmother had died, and it was really hard on my mom. She was really close to her mother. It was kind of hard to see my mom in that state of mind, so I wrote a poem about it and read it to my class. After that, I just started writing poetry to help me release stress and kind of escape things."

There are times when Redick would like to escape the physical pounding he takes from opposing teams.

"I think teams were physical with me all year," he said. "There's never a game where I get total freedom to move around. It's a war every game. It's a battle. The game is officiated differently in the NCAA Tournament. I understand that. It's not like the referees did a bad job, but guys get away with more stuff in the tournament.

"Our game with Michigan State in the Sweet 16 was really physical. I know my jersey kept coming out. Somebody had ahold of it. I don't know if I was pulling it out."

Redick helped Duke defeat Iowa State 63-55 in Charlotte to reach that point. That day, Krzyzewski broke Dean Smith's record for NCAA Tournament victories with 66.

"I was aware of it," Redick said. "Everyone on the team was. We were huddling up, getting ready to take the court, and I just mentioned it to the team. I was like, 'Look, guys, he's taken care of us all year. Let's take care of him today.'

"I don't even know how important it is for Coach K. I know he's a competitive guy, but it's something he never talks about when he's reaching these milestones.

"It's never really mentioned."

The clock struck midnight for Duke against Michigan State in Austin. Redick had no legs left. He shot four for 14 during a 78-68 loss.

A week later, Redick was at the Final Four in St. Louis to accept the Adolph Rupp award as the National Player of the Year. "It was tough to accept that award with a happy mood, because I was in St. Louis and I really felt we had a chance to be there," he said.

"I don't necessarily think I'm the best player in the country. It's a very subjective thing. I had a great season. But I can't win an award unless our team has a great season, so it was more of a testament to what we did."

25

THE FINAL WORD

DICK VITALE

ESPN and ABC Sports

Dick Vitale has no problem with his nickname. "People get on my case all the time about my being 'Dukie Vitale' and scream at me, 'You love Duke,'" the ESPN college basketball analyst said.

He pleads guilty as charged.

"Yeah, I love great college basketball, man. I love winning programs. And Duke has given me nothing to sit and rip and rip and rip. What is there to rip about Duke? I love good basketball, and Duke is about good basketball, about good coaching, and good kids.

"I'm not going to make any excuses. Now if I praise them and they don't deserve it, that's something else."

So far, that hasn't happened.

Vitale's respect for the Blue Devils goes way back—which could explain his reaction when Mike Krzyzewski was named head coach. "I was shocked and surprised. Duke had been one of the great programs for years, prior to Krzyzewski. Vic Bubas did an amazing job there.

"I was a fan, years ago, of Dick Groat. They had Art Heyman, Bobby Verga, Jeff Mullins—guys like that. Then you had the 1978 team going to the Final Four the year Kentucky cut down the nets. I was a close friend of Bill Foster, who I'd known quite well since I'd been an assistant at Rutgers and worked with one of his favorite people, Dick Lloyd.

"When the job opened, I thought immediately that it would go to a mega mega star. Tom Butters had stacks and stacks of resumés on his desk—from

Duke Photography

guys with big-time successful programs, guys who would have crawled to be the coach of Duke.

"In a sense, I was totally shocked when Mike was named coach.

"But Mike's a winner. He's won six of the last seven ACC Tournaments, been to 10 Final Fours, won three national titles.

"I've known him for years. My first contact with him was through my doing ESPN games. But because I've always been a basketball fan, I was aware of his situation at West Point."

Vitale recalled Krzyzewski's early, lean years:

"Things were tough at first. He lost recruiting battles for guys like Chris Mullin. But he battled, never wavered in his philosophy. I remember telling my wife, Lorraine, 'They got a winner, man. They got a winner.'

"Then he backed it all up."

But it didn't happen overnight.

And Krzyzewski was lucky: he had the luxury of time.

Vitale said, "If things were then as they are today in the climate and landscape of college basketball, I don't know if we'd have the Hall of Famer Mike Krzyzewski, because his first three years were mediocrity, mediocrity, mediocrity.

"In today's climate, if you don't make the tournament, it can become a big negative. Numerous guys are fired quickly, because everyone wants instant gratification; everyone wants instant success.

"Today, I'm not sure Mike could have survived with those first three years he had. Just look at Ty Willingham and football at Notre Dame. But when Mike started at Duke, there wasn't the media situation there is today—coaches being scrutinized 24/7 on *SportsCenter*, Fox Sports, talk radio.

"Mike was lucky he had Tom Butters."

But a guardian angel can do only so much.

Vitale also credits Krzyzewski with being the architect of his success.

"He had that great recruiting class, with Dawkins, Alarie, Bilas, and Henderson. And the beat went on—starting with Danny Ferry.

"It's been one player after another.

"It's just been the place where top notch-students wanted to go. They wanted to be part of it. It was a bonanza certainly with Bob Hurley, Christian Laettner, and Grant Hill. Then the beat has gone on this year. Duke probably has the best recruiting class it's had in over a decade. And that's saying a lot when you're talking about the Brand, Battier class."

And when you're talking about the competition between Duke and Carolina.

"I'm happy to see Carolina back," Vitale said.

"To me, there's no rivalry like the one between Duke and Carolina. It has everything you want in a rivalry. The schools are in the same league—only eight miles apart. Both programs are usually nationally ranked, year in and year out. Each inspires intense loyalty from its passionate fans. Best of all, for me, they have a history of good coaches, good players."

For a basketball fan, there's a little bit of heaven on Tobacco Road.

And Vitale was in paradise when he covered the Duke-Carolina game on February 2, 1995, at Cameron.

"It was an incredible feeling to be part of that game," Vitale recalled. "Man, that was special. My partner, Mike Patrick, and I had so much fun, even though we were broadcasting from way up in the rafters, sitting on a cement block, because we didn't have courtside access.

"Duke was the underdog team, 0-7 in ACC games, playing without Krzyzewski. They were a David playing a Goliath. Carolina was a giant at the time with Jerry Stackhouse and Rasheed Wallace.

"Carolina played so perfectly in the beginning, jumping out to a 26-9 lead, I thought I'd need filler material, man. No way did I believe Duke would come back, play them to the buzzer in double overtime."

Nor could he believe in all the great plays he saw—until one had an up-close and personal effect on him.

"When Jerry Stackhouse made a reverse one-handed jam," he admitted, "I was going so bananas that I stood up and hit my head on the concrete ceiling. Blood was pouring out of me. Mike Patrick tells me to this day, 'You played hard. You just kept going. No blood or anything was going to stop you.'"

Vitale wasn't the only one unstoppable that night.

As he recalled, "Wallace would dunk. Then Duke would come back with jumpers from Cherokee Parks. Jeff Capel made a 40-footer at the buzzer to send it into double overtime.

"And the crowd at Cameron was rocking—all 9,000 of them—willing their team to a W."

Carolina finally got control of the game back when Jeff McInnis scored on a layup and then scored off a steal of the inbound pass. But Duke still had a chance to send it into triple overtime when Steve Wojciechowski put up a 10-footer before the buzzer. The shot bounced off the rim.

Carolina won 102-100.

Vitale remembers other games:

"I'll never forget the 1992 game at Carolina," he said. "Duke was undefeated, with Laettner, Hurley. They came into Chapel Hill with 17-straight Ws.

"It was a physical game. I still remember North Carolina center Eric Montross bleeding. And Bobby Hurley: he was in pain, man. He broke his foot midway through the first half—and still played the entire second half.

"Carolina won 75-73, and their fans, who never show they're excited, emptied out on the floor after that game and cut down the nets."

Fast forward to February 9, 2005: the Duke-Carolina game at Cameron went right down to the wire.

"The Tar Heels were down by a point with 18 seconds to play and they gave the ball to their Thomas Edison point guard, 'Everybody Loves' Raymond Felton, to make a play. But Felton had nowhere to go. Daniel Ewing went for a steal and missed, leaving Felton open an instant where he could have improvised and driven the lane for either a dump off or a short jumper. Instead, he hesitated, trying to run the play that Roy Williams had called in the huddle. But J.J. Redick anticipated the play and denied a pass to Rashad McCants. When Felton saw he was in trouble, he tried to dump the ball off David Noel, who got a hand on it but couldn't control the ball.

"These games always bring out the best in players. Sean May had 23 points and eight rebounds for the Tar Heels. But the star of stars in this game was

DeMarcus Nelson, a diaper dandy from California. Nelson had set all kinds of scoring records in that state. He committed to Duke as a sophomore.

"But until this game, he had been pretty much invisible.

"Then Nelson went off for 16 points in his first Duke-Carolina game. Unbelievable."

Duke won 71-70.

That was Duke's 15th win in the last 17 meetings with Carolina.

But on March 6, 2005, they met again—at the Dean Dome.

Carolina won 75-73.

And the Tar Heels won it all a month later in St. Louis, winning the 2005 national championship—as Vitale had predicted earlier in the season.

"This year, I was a big Carolina fan because I felt in my heart that Carolina was going to be the team. I'd had a similar feeling about the Huskies the year Connecticut won.

"But that shouldn't take anything away from the coaching job Mike did with that team, which had three stars—J.J. Redick, Sheldon Williams, and Daniel Ewing—and a bunch of role players and limited depth," Vitale said.

"Mike won 27 games, won the ACC Tournament, and advanced to the Sweet 16. All that—despite losing Luol Deng after his freshman year to the NBA and never getting to coach Shawn Livingston, a six-foot-seven point guard from Peoria, Illinois, who was supposed to be the next great one there.

"Sure, Duke had five players who played in the McDonald's All-America game on its roster, if you include Shavlik Randolph and DeMarcus Nelson. But just because a kid is a McDonald's All-American doesn't always mean he's a legit player.

"I thought Mike did everything he could do with what he had.

"In fact, I wrote him a note: 'Mike, the definition of coaching is very simple. It's the ability of a leader to get the most out of his people. Any way you cut it, this year you got the most out of that team. Have a nice summer.'

"I got a note back from Mike: 'Thanks, Dick. That really means a lot. Thank you for your thoughts.'"

Vitale recalled that his thoughts had been with Krzyzewski at an earlier time—when the Duke coach missed most of the 1995 season with back problems:

"I was very concerned. He's such a perfectionist. And people like that are their own worst critics.

"He was worried about this team from the start. He didn't have Grant Hill. And Trajan Langdon and Cherokee Parks hadn't blossomed into first-round picks, yet. It was a fragile group.

"When he felt he wasn't getting the most from his players, he tore himself apart. That, combined with the back injury, was just too much. Mike took a leave of absence in January. Anyone who knew him had to be concerned."

Without Krzyzewski, Duke struggled. Pete Gaudet tried to hold the pieces together, but the team finished the season 4-15.

Krzyzewski returned the next season and began putting the program back on track. Two years later, Duke was in the regional finals against Kentucky. The next year, he was in the national championship game. Duke won it all in 2001.

"After he came back to the team, he had a better feeling about what he'd achieved," Vitale said. "I think he feels phenomenal now. He should know that no matter what the record may be, he is one of the elite. He's no dummy."

Krzyzewski is appreciative of his good health.

He had watched in sadness while Jim Valvano—who had become a close friend—battled cancer and died on April 28, 1993.

A dozen years later, Krzyzewski has not forgotten Valvano.

Both Vitale and Krzyzewski are on the board of directors of The V Foundation for Cancer Research—an organization that raises money to fund cancer research.

"There aren't many guys who can pick up the phone and ask me for money. But Mike can," Vitale said.

"Last year, I was getting ready to go to the U.S. Open to address a group of youngsters on Arthur Ashe Day—the day before the start of the tournament.

"I was getting in a taxi and my phone rings.

"'Dickie, Mike Krzyzewski. Hey man, I need a favor.'

"'What is it, Mike?'

"'I need $50,000.'"

The reason?

"'Because you, [ESPN commentator] John Saunders, and I are going to start the President's Club of The Jimmy V Foundation. We're going to go out and raise some serious money. We're kicking it off because we've been fortunate in our lives and we can afford to give that amount. And because of our involvement, others will join in.'

"Well, in a matter of two or three months, we put together a group to make some calls," Vitale said. "Guys such as Rick Pitino, John Calipari, Mike Brey: they all responded. We got 20 people—and raised a million dollars very quickly."

Vitale has nothing but respect for Krzyzewski's contributions to The V Foundation:

"I watched with admiration his incredible efforts in raising millions for The V Foundation. He's done an amazing job. His involvement, his leadership skills, and the discipline he learned at West Point playing for Bobby Knight make him very special.

"He's just a good person."

And Vitale thinks Krzyzewski and Duke are great for ESPN.

"I've done so many Duke games over the years," Vitale said. "Fortunately for me, my bosses—bless them—think enough of me to assign me to teams of that caliber.

"I just met with some ESPN executives. Part of the discussion was what a plus it is in the ratings when Duke is on the air. People want to watch Duke. People want to see them—whether they root for them or not. They're like Notre Dame in football, the Yankees in baseball: people either love them or hate them."

And why do some people hate them?

"Because of what they've achieved. They are very popular on ESPN."

It is even easy to make a case for the Blue Devils as America's team, based on cable ratings. Duke holds the top two spots on ESPN's most-viewed regular-season college games—January 17, 2002, against Maryland and December 22, 1998, against Kentucky—and six of ESPN's top-10 spots.

The Blue Devils hold the top three spots on ESPN2: February 5, 1998, February 1, 2001, February 2, 2004—all against North Carolina.

"Mike's been great to me," Vitale said. "Because of my doing so many of Duke's games, we've built a good relationship. We don't go out socially on a regular basis, but it's more than just a relationship between an analyst and a coach. If I call upon Mike Krzyzewski for a favor, he's going to respond positively.

"We do have one big thing in common: we overachieved in marriage. Both Mickie and Lorraine function well in our environment; they are able to put up with guys who are very visible.

"For both of us, everything starts with family, so there's always been a mutual respect. And it kicked into a higher gear because of our involvement with The V Foundation.

"It's not all about basketball, basketball, basketball."

But some of it is.

When the Lakers made their run at Krzyzewski in 2004, Vitale made a phone call to him and left a message:

"'Mike, forget about me being with ESPN. I'm calling you as a friend. How many times have you sat with me and told me how much you love Duke? How you fit into the puzzle of what Duke is all about? How you fit into what college athletics and college basketball are all about?

"'I hope in making the decision, those thoughts come into your head. Whatever you do, I'm going to respect you and I'm going to be your friend. That won't change.

"'But, Mike, you belong in college, man. You are everything the college game needs and what the college game is all about.

"'You're a teacher, a motivator, a guy who is really, really important to college basketball.

"'I am very confident, Mike, that there is no dollar amount that could lure you to the NBA. I hope and pray I'm right.'

"That was it.

"The day he announced he was staying, I'm having breakfast at the Broken Egg. My phone rings. It's Mike.

"'I want you to know I was really touched by your message. You were right. There was never any thought of my going.

"'I was flattered. But hey, man, I can't leave Duke.'"

So he stayed and solidified his position as the face of college basketball.

Krzyzewski's become so big he has his own American Express commercial—just like Robert DeNiro.

This comes as no surprise to Vitale, who said, "Mike is at the top of his profession, but he also has to hear criticism from other coaches who are envious of his success. You got people moaning and groaning about his American Express commercials.

"I have one simple question for these coaches: how many of them would have turned down that opportunity for 1) monetary gain or 2) visibility? Obviously, Mike's going to take some hits behind the scenes because there's that jealousy factor, just like in baseball—with Alex Rodriguez of the Yankees. When guys get up that ladder of success, people want to knock them down.

"But Mike is a winner."

AFTERWORD

I n the classic film *Citizen Kane*, a team of reporters scour the country, interviewing friends and associates of a famous man, trying to learn the secret of his character. What they find instead is a kaleidoscope of varying perceptions. Each interviewee sees Kane through the prism of his or her own experience.

The result is a fascinating portrait of a complex and interesting man.

It seems to me that what Dick Weiss has done in this book is much the same thing. He's illuminated Duke coach Mike Krzyzewski by piecing together dozens of individual observations of another very complex and interesting man.

My first view of Duke's accomplished basketball coach came on the night of May 4, 1980, when the young Army coach with the unpronounceable last name was introduced to the North Carolina media as the successor to Bill Foster.

I think it's interesting that the press conference was not held in Cameron Indoor Stadium—where almost every other athletic press conference over the last 40 years has been held—but in the university's Public Affairs Building on the corner of Duke University Road and Chapel Drive, a few yards from the main gate to Duke's West Campus.

The unusual location is probably not significant in itself, but it does seem to me symbolic. Krzyzewski would become more than a mere basketball coach at Duke. He would become a university vice president, a lecturer in the Fuqua School of Business, the founder of the Michael Krzyzewski Human Performance Lab, a major fundraiser for the Duke Medical Center … in short, he would become the public face of Duke University.

None of that was evident on the night he was introduced as Duke's head basketball coach. Frankly, those of us in attendance were shocked to see the dark-haired young coach standings at the podium alongside Duke athletic director Tom Butters. None of us—not the writers, TV reporters, or radio guys—had suspected his candidacy until the very last minute.

I got a tip from an old friend that afternoon, about three hours before the press conference, warning me that I ought to take a close look at "Mike Ker … Mike Krez … Mike Kar … oh, hell … the coach at Army."

It's interesting to read Tom Butters's version of events in Chapter 1 and learn of Bob Knight's reason for turning down the job. I don't think I'm one of the reporters he would have been throwing out of second-story windows—I was just too young and insignificant in 1980 to matter to a coach such as Knight. However, when Butters tells Krzyzewski four years later: "We've got a public who doesn't know how good you are. We've got press who are too stupid to tell them how good you are," well, I'm pretty sure I was a part of the press that Butters was talking about.

I've covered Krzyzewski for more than a quarter of a century now, and I have to admit that it took me a long time to realize how good a coach he really is. In my 30-plus years covering ACC basketball, I've been lucky enough to cover some fascinating and brilliant men—Jim Valvano, Lefty Driesell, Stormin' Norman Sloan, Bill Foster, and Roy Williams were all great characters as well as successful coaches. Dave Odom, Terry Holland, Bill Guthridge, and even less successful ACC coaches such as Les Robinson, Bucky Waters, and Pete Gillen were all admirable and interesting men.

But the one figure that every other ACC coach had to be measured against was, of course, Dean Smith at North Carolina.

I always considered myself blessed that I had a chance to cover one of the two or three greatest coaches in basketball history. It never occurred to me—certainly not on that May night in 1980—that I would get to chronicle the career of an equally successful coach.

The day after Krzyzewski's introductory press conference, I called an acquaintance who was at that time an assistant coach at an Ivy League team and asked him about the young Army coach. He was full of praise for Krzyzewski, suggesting that he was a great motivator, a first-rate teacher, and an excellent on-court tactician.

"Al, my only concern," he told me, "is recruiting. Except for his one year at Indiana—and I don't know how involved in recruiting he was that year—he's never had to recruit the kind of big-time prospect that he'll need to recruit to win at Duke."

Of course, in hindsight, we know that Coach K has become perhaps the most successful recruiter in history. But that first year, as he missed on player after player, my source's concern seemed justified. It was only during the 1981-1982 season, when Krzyzewski corralled the Dawkins-Alarie-Henderson-Bilas class that would carry him to his first Final Four, that the thought began to penetrate my thick skull that this guy might know what he's doing.

I like to think that by the time Butters gave Krzyzewski that long-term contract in January 1984, I had come to the conclusion that Coach K was a good coach. I first saw the potential of his young players during a loss to

Louisville in 1983 when for a brief five- or six-minute spurt, Dawkins, Alarie, and company matched one the nation's most talented teams (the one that would engage Houston in the Final Four dunkathon later that season) high-flying play for high-flying play. Certainly when his 1983-1984 team got off to such a good start, it was clear that Coach K was on the right track.

But Butters was still right—even in late 1984, I was too stupid to know just how good Krzyzewski really was.

Even when Duke reached the title game in Dallas in 1986, I only had the feeling that he had proven himself a good, solid coach—nothing more. He had built a single great team. Well, Norm Sloan built a great team around David Thompson and Tommy Burleson. Bill Foster built a great team around Mike Gminski and Gene Banks. Terry Holland built a great team around Ralph Sampson.

Building a great team is one thing ... but only UNC's Smith had been able to sustain that success through team after team after team.

Over the next seven years, Krzyzewski did just that. I'm not sure when I realized that he was on the same exalted plane as his rival in Chapel Hill. Certainly by the time he won back-to-back national titles in 1991 and 1992, it was obvious. Even before that—during the Final Four run that started in 1988—it became clear that Coach K was not the architect of one great team, but of a great program.

When you look at the nation's elite basketball schools, they are all the product of a great coach. Phog Allen made Kansas a giant in the sport. Adolph Rupp is at the heart of the Kentucky dynasty. John Wooden lifted UCLA out of obscurity on the West Coast, and Dean Smith made North Carolina more than a Southern power.

Duke had a fine program before Krzyzewski. I'm too young to remember Eddie Cameron's success, but I grew up during Vic Bubas's glory years and Bill Foster had a brief run of excellence. Still, in May 1980, no one would have included Duke in a list of the nation's top programs. Krzyzewski has done that, just as Rupp did at Kentucky, Wooden did at UCLA, and Smith did at UNC.

Best of all, he's still in business, adding to his legacy.

And while we might not ever find the key to his greatness—as the reporters in Orson Welles's movie never discovered the meaning of "Rosebud"—the dozens of snapshots provided in this book give us a compelling portrait of *Citizen K*.

—AL FEATHERSTON

APPENDIX

MIKE KRZYZEWSKI'S CAREER RECORD AT DUKE

Year	Overall	ACC	Postseason
1981	17-13	6-8	NIT
1982	10-17	4-10	—
1983	11-17	3-11	—
1984	24-10	7-7	NCAA Tournament
1985	23-8	8-6	NCAA Tournament
1986	37-3	12-2	NCAA Final Four Finalist
1987	24-9	9-5	NCAA Tournament
1988	28-7	9-5	NCAA Final Four Semifinalist
1989	28-8	9-5	NCAA Final Four Semifinalist
1990	29-9	9-5	NCAA Final Four Finalist
1991	**32-7**	**11-3**	**NCAA CHAMPION**
1992	**34-2**	**14-2**	**NCAA CHAMPION**
1993	24-8	10-6	NCAA Tournament
1994	28-6	12-4	NCAA Final Four Finalist
1995	9-3	0-1	out after back surgery
1996	18-13	8-8	NCAA Tournament
1997	24-9	12-4	NCAA Tournament
1998	32-4	15-1	NCAA Tournament
1999	37-2	16-0	NCAA Final Four Finalist
2000	29-5	15-1	NCAA Tournament
2001	**35-4**	**13-3**	**NCAA CHAMPION**
2002	31-4	13-3	NCAA Tournament
2003	26-7	11-5	NCAA Tournament
2004	31-6	13-3	NCAA Final Four Semifinalist

Duke Career Record (24 years)　621-181 (.774)
NCAA Tournament Record　　　64-17 (.790)

HIGHLIGHTS FROM MIKE KRZYZEWSKI'S CAREER AT DUKE

621   TOTAL VICTORIES
239   ACC VICTORIES
202   WEEKS RANKED IN TOP 10
78   WEEKS RANKED NUMBER ONE
35   NBA DRAFT PICKS

     1981   Gene Banks, Kenny Dennard
     1982   Vince Taylor
     1983   Tom Emma
     1985   Dan Meagher
     1986   Johnny Dawkins, Mark Alarie,
             David Henderson, Jay Bilas
     1987   Tommy Amaker, Martin Nessley
     1989   Danny Ferry
     1990   Alaa Abdelnaby, Phil Henderson
     1992   Christian Laettner, Brian Davis
     1993   Bobby Hurley, Thomas Hill
     1994   Grant Hill, Antonio Lang
     1995   Cherokee Parks, Erik Meek
     1998   Roshown McLeod
     1999   Elton Brand, Trajan Langdon,
             Corey Maggette, William Avery
     2000   Chris Carrawell
     2001   Shane Battier
     2002   Jason Williams, Mike Dunleavy, Carlos Boozer
     2003   Dahntay Jones
     2004   Luol Deng, Chris Duhon

29   ALL-AMERICA SELECTIONS

Gene Banks (1981)
Johnny Dawkins (1985, 1986)
Mark Alarie (1986)
Tommy Amaker (1987)
Danny Ferry (1988, 1989)
Christian Laettner (1990, 1991, 1992)
Bobby Hurley (1992, 1993)

Grant Hill (1992, 1993, 1994)
Roshown McLeod (1998)
Trajan Langdon (1998, 1999)
Elton Brand (1999)
Chris Carrawell (2000)
Shane Battier (2000, 2001)
Jason Williams (2001, 2002)
Carlos Boozer (2002)
Mike Dunleavy (2002)
Chris Duhon (2004)
J.J. Redick (2004)
Shelden Williams (2004)

10 NCAA FINAL FOURS

10 REGULAR-SEASON ACC CHAMPIONSHIPS
1986, 1991, 1992, 1994, 1997, 1998, 1999, 2000, 2001, 2004

8 ACC TOURNAMENT CHAMPIONSHIPS
1986, 1988, 1992, 1999, 2000, 2001, 2002, 2003

8 NATIONAL COACH OF THE YEAR HONORS
1986, 1989, 1991, 1992, 1997, 1999, 2000, 2001

7 NATIONAL DEFENSIVE PLAYERS OF THE YEAR
Tommy Amaker (1987)
Billy King (1988)
Grant Hill (1993)
Steve Wojciechowski (1998)
Shane Battier (1999, 2000, 2001)

7 NATIONAL PLAYERS OF THE YEAR
Johnny Dawkins (1986)
Danny Ferry (1989)
Christian Laettner (1992)
Elton Brand (1999)
Shane Battier (2001)
Jason Williams (2001, 2002)

5 ACC COACH OF THE YEAR HONORS
1984, 1986, 1997, 1999, 2000

1 NAISMITH MEMORIAL BASKETBALL HALL OF FAME INDUCTION IN 2001